THE WAINSCOT BOOK
The Houses of Winchester Cathedral Close and their Interior Decoration, 1660–1800

D1356863

Hampshire Record Series   *Volume VI*

THE WAINSCOT BOOK

The Houses of Winchester Cathedral
Close and their Interior Decoration,
1660–1800

Edited by John Crook

HAMPSHIRE RECORD OFFICE for
HAMPSHIRE COUNTY COUNCIL, 1984

ISBN 0 906680 03 4

Printed in England by
Hobbs the Printers of Southampton

Contents

*Now known as No. 11, The Close.

Illustrations

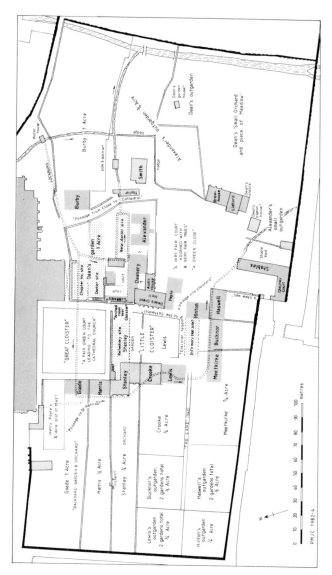

Fig. 1. Conjectural plan of Winchester Cathedral Close in the first half of the 17th century, based on the 'Parliamentary Survey' of 1649. Cross-hatching indicates monastic buildings known to have been demolished by that date. Base map, OS sheet Hampshire XLI 13, 2nd edition, 1897.

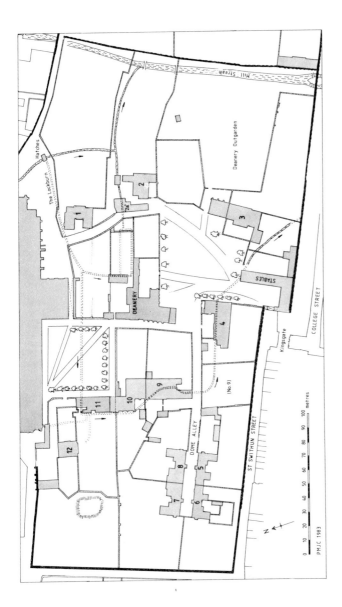

Fig. 2. Winchester Cathedral Close in the mid 18th century. Source: Godson's map of Winchester, 1750, but incorporating other evidence. Base map, OS sheet Hampshire XLI 13, 2nd edition, 1897.

Preface

This study of one of the lesser-known Winchester Cathedral documents is not intended as a complete history of the houses of Winchester Cathedral Close. The Wainscot Book provides a starting point for the study of two aspects of these houses: their interior decoration and their occupants, over a period of about 150 years, from the Restoration of 1660 to the beginning of the nineteenth century. It so happens that this was a time of rapidly-evolving fashions in interior decoration; and the fact that so many of the items recorded in the Wainscot Book have survived lends an exciting reality to what is at first sight a rather repetitive administrative document.

I owe a huge debt of gratitude to a large number of people without whose co-operation and help this study would not have been possible: the Dean and Chapter of Winchester, for their kind permission to publish this edition of a manuscript in their possession; the Canon Librarian and his staff, for allowing me access to material in the Cathedral Archives; the Administrator to the Dean and Chapter of Winchester, Mr John Lamplugh, for facilitating my researches in the Close; the Architect to the Dean and Chapter, Mrs Corinne Bennett, for kindly providing plans used in the preparation of a number of the drawings in this book; the General Editor of the Hampshire Record Series, Miss Margaret Cash, for encouraging me to prepare the text for publication. Others have helped on points of detail: the Fellows' Librarian of Winchester College, Mr Paul Yeats-Edwards, generously followed up a daunting list of enquiries and produced a large number of references; the College Archivist, Dr Roger Custance, kindly allowed me access to the material in the Winchester College archives; Dr Beatrice Clayre of the Winchester Research Unit provided numerous cross-references relating to the workmen employed both in the Close and the City; and Mrs Barbara Carpenter Turner has, over the years, kindly shared her unrivalled knowledge of Winchester matters.

Thanks are due also to the County Archivist, Miss Rosemary Dunhill, and her staff at the Hampshire Record Office; to the Curator, Winchester City Museums, Miss Elizabeth Lewis, and her assistants; and to the librarians of other cathedral libraries or equivalent institutions whom I have consulted in an admittedly largely fruitless search for parallels to the Wainscot Book; in particular Mrs Grace Holmes, Honorary Archivist of St George's Chapel, Windsor, where I was able to consult a surviving parallel text. I also acknowledge the help of Messrs Peter Thornton and Simon Jervis of the Department of Furniture and Woodwork at the Victoria and Albert Museum, and Mrs Victoria Gabbitas, Keeper of the Museum of Leathercraft, Northampton, for kind assistance on points of detail.

Last, but by no means least, I should like to thank the occupants of the Close Houses, and in particular their wives, for being so tolerant of my frequent invasions of their homes.

It will quickly be seen that much of my interpretation of the text must inevitably remain conjectural. I believe this to be the first major published study of the domestic buildings of Winchester Cathedral Close; which encourages me to beg the reader's indulgence for any errors that may be detected.

P. M. J. Crook
The Close, Winchester, 1984

Introduction

In contrast with the carefully-preserved muniments of William of Wykeham's neighbouring collegiate foundation, the archives of the Dean and Chapter of Winchester show an uneven and rather disappointing rate of survival. There are good reasons for the shortage of pre-Commonwealth documents: the Cathedral muniment room was twice ransacked by Puritan soldiery during the Civil Wars, as the then Chapter Clerk, John Chase, ruefully recorded. But, lacking statutory guidelines like those laid down for Winchester College, successive Chapter officials did not until the present century feel it necessary to preserve those minor documents, relating to the day-to-day running of the Cathedral, which are now of such value to the historian; and such *miscellanea* as have survived were preserved more by fortunate accident than design. Amongst these are the fascinatingly vivid 'Diary of John Young' (Dean of Winchester, 1616-54), extracts from which have been published;[1] the 'Account Book' of the seventeenth-century Clerk of Works, William Fletcher, dealing mainly with the rebuilding of the Close Houses in 1661-2;[2] and the corpus of miscellaneous material, still only partially sorted, and not yet fully indexed, some of which is said to have been discovered in an oak chest in the South Transept of the Cathedral at the beginning of the present century.

Inevitably, the documents which have most fully survived are those official volumes and records whose preservation was important as an account of the day-to-day business of the Chapter: the 'Ledger Books', dating from the early fifteenth century (the first volume of which has been published in *précis* form);[3] the Chapter Minute Books, dating from 1553, of which the volume spanning the years 1600-1622 has alone disappeared; the Treasurers' Computus Rolls

1. F. Goodman, ed., *The Diary of John Young*, London, 1928.
2. MS, WCL.
3. J. Greatrex, ed., *The Register of the Common Seal*, London, 1978 (Hampshire Record Series).

(poorly preserved from before the Commonwealth, more completely surviving from 1660–1690, and complete from 1690); Receivers' Books, Woodwards' accounts, and so on.

The 'Wainscot Book' is one of those miscellaneous Chapter documents which was preserved by good fortune after it had become obsolete. As its title implies, it is a register firstly of wooden panelling, or 'wainscot' and secondly, by extension, of many other kinds of decorative and functional fixtures in the Canons' houses of Winchester Cathedral Close. Its great interest lies in the fact that many of the items recorded in it have survived; and so the precise date and cost of these items are known. The Wainscot Book is consequently an important document in the study of the history of the interior planning and decoration of 'middling houses'[4]; for while building records of 'Great Houses' have often been carefully preserved, those of more modest town houses, of which the canonry residences of Winchester Close may be taken as typical, have less frequently survived. The Wainscot Book therefore has its place in the study of changing fashions in the interior fittings of such houses over a period of approximately 150 years, from shortly after the Restoration to the beginning of the nineteenth century; a period of particular interest in the history of interior decoration.

It seems that the installation of wainscot in the Prebendaries' houses at Winchester was from earliest times regarded as the concern of the particular occupant. No doubt this was a survival of the medieval practice whereby textile hangings, as well as what we now call 'furniture', *mobilia*, were moved from one residence to another as an important personage travelled in progress about the country. There is however no evidence in the Chapter records that fitted oak panelling was ever removed by a retiring Canon, or by his executors after his death, and a more usual arrangement may have been for the new occupant of a house to come to a financial agreement with his predecessor, just as nowadays one might negotiate a price for fitted carpets when buying a house. Other Canons may have followed the generous example of Christopher Perin, who died in 1612, leaving 'to my successors in my Prebend in Winton all my Wainscott in the Great Parlour of my Prebend House'.[5]

At the Restoration of 1660, however, the procedure for the succession of wainscot and other fixtures was regularised by the Chapter. The Dean and Chapter were then involved in an extensive

---

4. The convenient term of Horace Walpole, quoted in M. Jourdain, *English Interiors in Smaller Houses, 1660–1830*, London, 1923, p.5.
5. P.R.O. P.C.C. wills. Prob. 11/121 f.12 (proved 1613).

rebuilding programme to replace those houses which had been pulled down during the Parliamentary occupation of the Close in the years of the Commonwealth. According to a *Narrative*[6] of 1675, of the Deanery and twelve prebendal houses only three survived completely unscathed, and two 'in part', while the remainder were demolished for the value of their building materials, which had been valued in a *Parliamentary Survey*[7] taken in 1649. While some authorities have suggested that the depredations of the Commonwealth were exaggerated in the Chapter's account of the matter,[8] there can be no doubting the expense of the rebuilding programme, which is well documented. As a result, the Cathedral Close of Winchester contains a high proportion of precisely dated houses of the mid to late seventeenth century, and these houses and their surviving fittings are worthy of study.

By an Act of Chapter dated 1 December 1662 the Dean and Chapter provided for wainscot to be installed in each of the newly-built houses at the expense of the individual occupant. This Act was annulled (and rendered almost illegible in the Chapter Minute Book) the following year, but the paragraph relating to wainscot was retained in the superseding Act of 22 September 1663. The relevant clause in the deleted Act reads: 'That all manner of waynscott of the severall howses of Mr Deane & . . . the Prebendaries shalbe made & finished at their owne proper charges respectively by the perticuler owner of every such howse, They or their executors to be repayd for the same of their Successors abating one fowerth parte of the charge thereof.'

By this last clause the Dean and Chapter ensured that the expenditure for 'wainscot' of each successive occupant was repaid to him or his heirs by the next Canon, after a deduction of 25% had been made for 'wear and tear'. The Chapter Clerk was responsible for keeping a record of such transactions, and a book was procured for that purpose. Into this 'Wainscot Book' were also entered details of any further 'wainscot work' paid for by each occupant of the Close houses. Such expenses had first to be approved in Chapter, and, for this reason, many entries date from the two main Chapter meetings of the year, at the end of June and November, although some bear the actual date when the bills for 'wainscot work' were submitted.

6. Printed in *Winch. Cath. Docs. II*, pp.158-70.
7. Printed in *ibid.*, pp.75-93.
8. e.g. W.R.W. Stephens and F.T. Madge in *ibid.*, p.xxviii-xxix.

At first, the scope of the Wainscot Book was restricted to wooden panelling made of oak or deal, including accessories such as wooden cornices and architrave mouldings round doors, and also wooden chimney-pieces and their surrounding mouldings. Doors were eligible for the Wainscot Book, it seems, but not their furniture: an entry relating to hinges, locks and bolts used at the Deanery in the early 1670s was subsequently disallowed by the Chapter.[9] On that occasion the Chapter also disallowed the Dean's expenditure on painting wainscot; though this seems to have been an anomaly, as the occupant of No. 12, The Close, Dr Darell, was allowed the cost of all painter's work at around the same date.[10] As deal wainscot, which replaced oak panelling at the end of the seventeenth century, was invariably painted, it was felt appropriate to include the cost of painting it as one of the items allowed in the Wainscot Book; though this was to be the subject of controversy in the eighteenth century when the question of whether repainting should be eligible was argued at some length in Chapter. In November 1739 the Canons ruled that 'no painting of Old Work in the inside of the houses be allowed to be charged on the Wainscott book Except only for the first time by each of the respective Occupiers'.[11] A year later, an apparently contradictory Order was passed 'that after this present Chapter no Painting either on the Inside or Outside shall be allowed to be charged to the Wainscott book or the book of repairs'.[12] In fact, this second Order seems to have been ignored; and from 1739 Wainscot Book entries involving painting all relate either to new panelling or to the first redecoration by a new occupant. The terms 'new painting' or 'first painting' are often included to make this clear.

In spite of these restrictions, the scope of the Wainscot Book was gradually enlarged. Window shutters, for example, although occasionally listed with the 'standards' or fixtures of each house, were entered in the Book as late as 1788,[13] by which date the shutters referred to must surely have been completely permanent, built into the reveals of the windows. Shelves, too, which could presumably be more easily removed from houses if required, were listed sometimes as a 'standard' and sometimes as a 'wainscot'

---

9. See pp. 11–12 and Notes to Text, 38.
10. See p.123.
11. CA 26 Nov 1739.
12. CA 25 Nov 1740. The 'book of repairs' was called *Liber de Reparatione in usum Thesaurarii*. The two books have survived (MSS, WCL). Vol. I covers 1735–1801; Vol. II, 1802–84.
13. See p.73.

item, as were certain fitted cupboards, such as a 'closet' at No. 2 in 1744,[14] and a 'corner cupboard' at No. 7 in 1751.[15]

As already mentioned, wooden mouldings round fireplaces were always deemed eligible to be entered in the Wainscot Book. In the eighteenth century, however, many of the Canons invested in marble chimney-pieces and the term 'wainscot' was eventually enlarged to include these. At first, though, it seems to have been the practice for such chimney-pieces to be removed on the departure of a Canon, and by a Chapter Act of 1731 it was ordered that any Canon thus removing such a chimney-piece should pay his successor 'the summe of Thirty Shillings in respect of each Chimney peice soe taken away to be applyed towards putting up a stone chimney peice in the place thereof or otherways making good the same'.[16] But by a further Act of November 1747 it was agreed 'that in case the Dean or any Prebendary be not willing to take away any Marble Slab or Marble Chimney peice with the carved or plain Mantle-tree, Mouldings and other appurtenances . . . he may cause the same (together with the Sum which it cost him) to be enter'd in the Wainscot book, subject to the same deduction as the Wainscot is'.[17]

A careful distinction was made, during the period covered by the Wainscot Book, between 'wainscot' items, which had been paid for by the incoming Canon, and which were therefore his property (though there are no records of a Canon disposing of wainscot other than by selling it to his successor according to the rules of the Wainscot Book), and 'standards', which were the fixtures installed in the houses, and therefore Dean and Chapter property like the fabric of the houses themselves. Occasionally these 'standards' included wainscoting, when this had been installed before a house was first brought into the Wainscot Book system. Thus the pages of the Wainscot Book contain a number of inventories listing such fixtures: kitchen utensils, shelves and dressers; brewing equipment found in the brewhouses which were attached to each house; trestles for supporting barrels in the cellars; spit-racks and the 'iron bar in the Chimney' on which pots were hung; certain tables and benches; and various other items of furniture. Sometimes a Canon would declare that he had given particular items to the house as 'standards': these might include textile hangings or even the keys and

14. See p.35.
15. See p.84.
16. CO 11 Dec 1731.
17. CA 25 Nov 1747.

locks in the house, which do not always appear to have been regarded as fixtures. The inventories in which these items are listed are of particular interest, even though few of the fittings which they describe have survived.

The most interesting entries in the Wainscot Book are generally the earliest ones relating to each house, while those of the second half of the eighteenth century give little more than a list of occupants of each dwelling; though this is in itself an important aspect of the text. The decline of the Wainscot Book was, no doubt, hastened by changing fashions in internal decoration, whereby wooden panelling was gradually replaced by plasterwork and paper hangings. The Book was finally made redundant by a Chapter Act of 23 June 1798, when new rules relating to the repair of the Close houses were formulated. Henceforth the Dean and Chapter would bear the cost of materials used in repairs, but the occupant would pay for workmanship out of the money allocated to him yearly from the building fund known as the *Cista Aedium*. After this date, no further items were entered in the Wainscot Book, although its pages show that diminishing payments of 'wainscot money' continued to be made by new occupants to their predecessors until the sums involved had dwindled to negligible amounts.

THE WAINSCOT BOOK AND OCCUPANCY

As well as being a record of internal fittings installed in the houses of Winchester Cathedral Close from the late seventeenth century until the beginning of the nineteenth, the Wainscot Book also provides the names of all the prebendal occupants of those houses, during a period when the arrangements for allotting the houses to the Canons were more complex than they had been before the Commonwealth, and during which the names of successive occupants of the houses are not clearly set out in any other Cathedral document.

The question of occupancy was simple enough before the Commonwealth: each house was considered as belonging to one of the twelve Prebends, and each Canon inherited the house occupied[18] by his predecessor in the Prebend. This procedure had been laid down in the original Statutes of the Dean and Chapter of

18. It should be emphasised, however, that many Prebendaries, whose main homes may have been elsewhere, and who lived in the Close only during their statutory periods of Residence, installed tenants in their Winchester houses. Documented examples are given in the Notes to the Text.

Winchester, dating from 1544, and the particular Statute, *De Officio Thesaurarii*, was not altered when the Statutes were revised under Charles I. The relevant clause reads: *Ut Canonicorum aedes melius diligentiusque imposterum reparentur, STATUIMUS ut Canonicus de novo electus et admissus, in demortui aut resignantis aut quovismodo cedentis aedes succedat, easque cum orto et stabulo et aliis commoditatibus ad dictas aedes pertinentibus sibi habeat et possideat.* There is no doubt that this rule was carefully observed: this is proved by those early documentary references to identifiable houses, some of which are mentioned in the separate Introductions to the several houses which form the subject of the present book.

With the return of the Canons to a devastated Cathedral Close in 1660, it was hard for the Dean and Chapter to comply with the strict letter of Statute. The new houses that they began building no longer occupied their old sites; and the opportunity was taken of redistributing the many outgardens and stables, which had formerly been situated in a somewhat arbitrary fashion about the Close, so that they now lay nearer to the houses to which they belonged. At the November Chapter of 1662 it was resolved that 'Whereas there may . . . arise many differences by the claymes of the successors of the said Dean & Chapter to their old respective scites, It is therefore ordered for prevention thereof and for the fixing of their respective titles to procure the Kings Majesty's and the Lord Bishop of Winchester's confirmation of these alterations as soone as it may conveniently be obteyned'.[19] Although this Chapter Act was annulled the following year, as already explained, the above clause was incorporated unaltered in the superseding Act of 22 September 1663,[20] and the Dean and Chapter's Petition to the King was drafted shortly afterwards and transcribed into the Chapter Minute Book at the following November Chapter.[21] In their petition the Dean and Chapter summarised the situation, pointing out that the new houses they were building, as well as their outbuildings and gardens, lay on new sites; not only did they ask for these new sites to be confirmed, but they also requested that the clause in the Statutes relating to the succession of houses should be repealed.

It seems, however, that this petition was not immediately presented to the King, for on 4 May 1670 a new Chapter Act was made, again ordering that the petition should be presented. The text of the new petition of 1670 is more lengthy than the version of

---

19. CA 1 Dec 1662.
20. Printed in *Winch. Cath. Docs. II*, pp. 135–7.
21. CA *c.*7 Dec 1663.

seven years earlier and includes an additional argument that, though perhaps implied, was not explicitly set out in the earlier text: 'That there now happens to be great inequality betweene the howses of the Prebendaries in regard our new erections doe much exceed the old in beauty and convenience. That in the nynteenth Chapter of our Statutes there are certaine clauses requiring that the new Prebendarie upon every vacancie shall succeede in the same howse with th'appurtenances which his predecessor enjoyed, and shall stand charged to keepe the same in good repayre. Whereby it often comes to passe that the senior Prebendarie hath the worst howse, and the junior (who commonly resides least upon the place) hath the best in our close . . . contrary to equity and good order.'[22]

The Dean and Chapter were therefore seeking royal permission for a scheme whereby, upon a house falling vacant, the remaining Prebendaries could, in order of seniority, elect to move into it. They also applied for leave to formulate their own rules for the repair of canonry houses out of a fund known as the 'Common Stock', rather than at the expense of the particular occupant, as enjoined by the earlier Statute.

The petition was granted on 13 June 1670, one of the royal requirements being that the text of the Instrument should be copied into the Chapter Minute Book and subscribed by the Dean and Canons and all their successors. Thus the Chapter Book in question includes a list of all Deans' and Canons' signatures from 1670 until the twentieth century, although in recent years the practice has been discontinued, following the revision of the Cathedral Statutes in 1942.

It will readily be observed that the death or resignation of a Canon could bring about a chain of house-moving in the Close. This indeed happened on a number of occasions, as is made clear in the pages of the Wainscot Book. Various Acts of Chapter were passed during the eighteenth century in order to try to hasten the process by which Canons, in order of seniority, chose or refused houses that had fallen vacant, the problem being that the most junior Prebendary was 'frequently disabled from performing his Statutory Residence . . . by Unnecessary Delays in not proceeding to make such choice of Vacant Houses'.[23] Were it not for the invaluable record provided by the Wainscot Book it would be

---

22. CA 4 May 1670. This Petition and the Reply of the King are printed in *Winch. Cath. Docs II*, pp.142–8.
23. CA 1 July 1740.

difficult, if not impossible, to establish the succession of occupants of the several houses of the Close during the period 1660–1800.

PARALLELS

The Wainscot Book is virtually, though not completely, *sui generis*. There is of course no particular reason why the system established by the Winchester Canons for the succession of 'movables', such as wainscot, should have been found elsewhere, and a variety of practices seem to have been followed at other Cathedrals and collegiate institutions.[24] However, the system adopted at St George's Chapel, Windsor appears remarkably similar to that of Winchester. In the archives there a volume is preserved, reference No. Aerary XIII.B.8, whose full title is 'A Register of the severall Incombs due to the Deane and Canons upon their respective houses by those that shall succeed in their said houses after their death or remove. And likewise of the heirloams or Stenders belonginge to every one of the said houses.' Entries in this volume span the period 1678–1759 and show many similarities to those of the Wainscot Book, though the Windsor volume contains an enviable amount of detail. This 'Income Book'[25] was established by an Order of Chapter dated 12 June 1607, by which if any Canon moved out of one of the Windsor houses 'haveinge bestowed any Charges for Waynscot in the same house or any part thereof, then whosoever shall come into the same house shall satisfie the Charge thereof to him or his executors as it coste, abating only iiijs. in the pounde'. The system for the succession of wainscot was, therefore, similar to that which later was to operate at Winchester, though with a slightly smaller discount for wear and tear. The list of items eligible as 'income' appears to have been somewhat wider at Windsor, however, and by an Order of 29 November 1737 was enlarged still further to include 'all Kitchin grates with Crane, Fireshovell, Tongs, Fender & Iron stoves & Coppers for washing'; items which hitherto had occasionally been noted as 'standards'.[26]

---

24. Inquiries at over twenty Cathedral and Collegiate foundations have suggested that the 'Wainscot Book' system was peculiar to Winchester and Windsor.
25. The useful term 'Income' is used in three Winchester Chapter Acts to refer to items eligible for the Wainscot Book. See Notes to Text, 43, 47 and 165.
26. The arrangements at Windsor may be studied more fully in the relevant Chapter Acts, printed in S.M. Bond, ed., *Chapter Acts of the Dean and Canons of Windsor*, 1966 (Historical Monographs relating to St George's Chapel, Windsor Castle, Vol. 13).

Brief History of English Panelling

The use of timber as a wall-covering providing a measure of insulation from chill, stone walls appears from documentary evidence to have been normal practice in great houses from the thirteenth century or earlier. The documented examples are mostly from royal works; for instance, in 1252 Henry III gave orders to his bailiff 'to buy in our town of Southampton, for our use, two hundred Norway boards of fir and deliver them without delay to our sheriff of Southampton to wainscote therewith the chamber of our beloved son Edward, in our castle at Winchester'.[1] Such deal boards were probably affixed vertically to the wall, rather in the manner of 'clapboarding', and seem usually to have been painted. Green was a favourite colour, often ornamented with gold stars: the Queen's wardrobe at Winchester was ordered to be decorated with 'green paint and golden stars' in 1252.[2] The green paint often formed a background for roundels depicting biblical or historical scenes, known as 'histories'. An idea of the appearance of such wainscoting, though not of its decoration, may perhaps be obtained from the surviving vertical oak boarding forming part of the infill of one of the trusses of the late thirteenth-century 'Pilgrims' Hall', in the Close at Winchester.[3]

We are concerned here, however, with framed panelling, whereby a framework of horizontals ('rails') and uprights ('stiles') is jointed so as to enclose rectangular panels. The earliest examples were tall and narrow, but the proportions of the panels were gradually changed during the sixteenth century until the height of each panel was only slightly greater than its width: this is the type of panelling referred to by the somewhat inaccurate term 'small-square panelling', and it was almost universally formed of oak. The very term

1. Liberate Roll, 37 Henry III. Quoted in M. Wood, *The English Mediaeval House*, London, 1965, pp.395–6.
2. *Ibid*. p.396.
3. See J. Crook, 'The Pilgrims' Hall, Winchester', *Proceedings*, 38 (1982), pp.94–5.

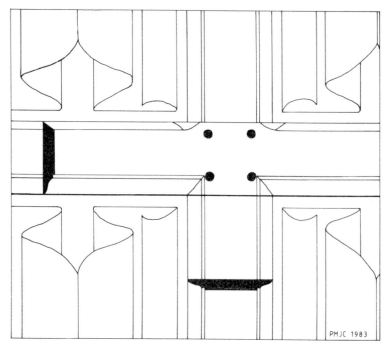

Fig. 3. 'Linenfold' panelling, circa 1520, in South Transept of Winchester Cathedral. Detail, showing joint between stiles and rail, with 'mason's mitre'.

'wainscot' seems to have made its appearance as a term denoting a particular quality of oak suitable for this purpose.

The stiles and rails were moulded, and in earlier examples the panels themselves were decorated in a variety of *motifs*, the most common of which were the linenfold pattern, or a pattern derived from a stylised vine-shoot, or carved Renaissance medallions showing classical or portrait heads in profile. Linenfold panelling owes it name to a resemblance, consciously exploited in later examples, to pleated drapery, though it may have developed from a simple abstract pattern of vertical ribbing. The linenfold motif appears to date from the mid fifteenth century. Although no examples of such panelling survive in Winchester Close in a domestic context, the canopied seats at the end of the South Transept of the Cathedral have tall panels of this type (Fig. 3), apparently dating from *c.*1520, when the woodwork here was first installed by Prior Silkstede;

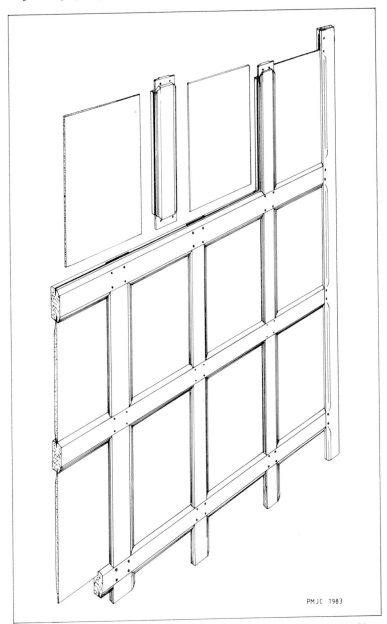

PMJC 1983

Fig. 4. Small-square oak panelling, dated 1661–2, from No. 7, The Close, Winchester ('Little Parlour'), showing method of assembly.

though it was altered and extended by Dean Rennell in 1816, the date which appears above the south door.[4]

The characteristic wainscoting of the late sixteenth and early seventeenth century consisted, however, of plain oak panels in a moulded framework (Fig. 4). Such panelling frequently covered entire walls from floor to ceiling: it was installed in sections and was generally unrelated to the architectural scheme of the room it adorned. A more 'architectural' treatment was achieved in grander houses by installing classical pilasters at intervals, thereby dividing the wall-surface into widths related to the general proportions of the room. An excellent example of this is found in the first-floor 'Oak Room' of No. 10, The Close, where Italian Ionic pilasters directly support a dentilated cornice of the same Order (the architrave and frieze having been omitted, probably because of the low ceiling height). The pilasters rest on typical Jacobean pedestals with a round-headed arch motif. Such round arches were sometimes used as a decorative device for the actual panelling of a room, and further examples may be seen re-used as the panels of a door leading from the South Transept of the Cathedral into the 'Dark Cloister'.[5]

The detail of the assembly methods used in framing such panelling is worthy of study, and well illustrated by extant examples in the houses of Winchester Cathedral Close. In the case of linenfold and other early types of framed panelling, the joint between the rails and the stiles was at first achieved by means of the so-called 'mason's mitre' (Fig. 3): a joint borrowed from stone-working technique where it was used, for example, at the joint between the sill and the mullion of Tudor windows. A different procedure was followed in the case of Jacobean small-square panelling. Here, the upper surface of the rail was chamfered at an angle of 45° to the horizontal, and so the joint between this surface and the moulded stiles presented no problem; the joint between the moulded underside of the rail and the similarly moulded stiles was more difficult to achieve. One solution was to avoid the difficulty by using the type of moulding known as 'scratch-moulding', in which the moulding of the rail dies out before the junction with the stile (Fig. 5). This is somewhat unsatisfactory visually, however, and by the end of the sixteenth century a more sophisticated joint had been devised, in which the mouldings of the stiles intersect those of the underside of

4. See S. Jervis, *Woodwork of Winchester Cathedral*, Winchester, 1976 (Friends of Winchester Cathedral), pp.9–10.
5. *Ibid.* p.12: 'a 19th century deal framework containing early 17th century panels'.

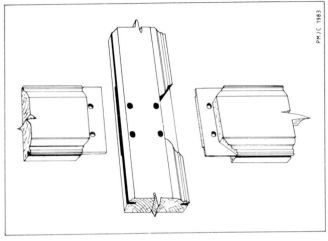

PMJC 1983

Fig. 5. *Small-square oak panelling, dated 1661–2, from No. 8, The Close, Winchester ('Entrance Hall), showing scratch-beaded rail.*

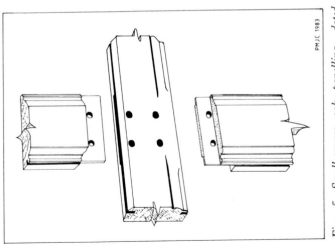

PMJC 1983

Fig. 6. *Small-square oak panelling, dated 1661–2, from No. 7, The Close, Winchester ('Little Parlour'), with true mitred joint.*

the rail at 90°, forming a true mitred joint (Fig. 6). Both varieties are found in the Dome Alley houses.

It is interesting that small-square panelling was apparently being made and installed in the Close houses in the 1660s, at a time when it was undoubtedly being superseded by newer fashions. Some, albeit re-used, small-square panelling was installed at No. 1, The Close, as late as 1727, but only in minor bedrooms and a study. But the best example of the combination of old and new is at the Deanery, where, as the Wainscot Book shows, small-square panelling was built and installed by local joiners in the 'new Deanery' in the early 1660s, while within a decade 'London joiners' were brought down from the Capital in order to instal the latest type of large deal panelling in the 'Great Dining-Room' in the Prior's Hall.

The use of large panels, increasingly of painted deal, dates from the second quarter of the seventeenth century, and if not initiated was at least favoured by the pupils of Inigo Jones, among them John Webb, and by later architects such as Roger Pratt. Such treatment, with large, rectangular panels above a substantial middle rail with projecting 'chair rail', and horizontal 'lying panels' below, together with classical architrave, frieze and cornice, lent itself well to the 'architectural' approach to interior decoration associated with Jones and his followers.

The large panels were formed by glueing a number of planks together edge to edge, and subsequently planing the face. Deal panelling, which eventually completely superseded oak and other hardwoods, was usually painted; and Roger Pratt, in his instructions relating to joinery at Kingston House in 1665, insisted that the panels be 'well glued, and clean wrought on the foreside so that no sign of the planes appear, as I have often seen even after painting'.[6] The wainscoting of the end wall of the 'Great Dining-Room' formed in the 'Prior's Hall' of Winchester Deanery is a good example of deal panelling of the years immediately following the Restoration.

Other architects, such as John Webb, showed a preference for hardwoods left in their natural state. At a later date, this attitude was shared by Christopher Wren; and examples of Wren panelling are found in the King's Dressing Room at Hampton Court, in Trinity College Chapel, Oxford; and perhaps include the panelling once in Winchester College Chapel and now in New Hall, and that installed *c.*1687 in No. 3, The Close (Fig. 14), which the Wainscot

---

6. Quoted in R.T. Gunther, ed., *The Architecture of Sir Roger Pratt*, Oxford, 1928, p.274.

Book proves to have been the work of Valentine Housman, one of Wren's leading craftsmen.

Panelling of the Wren 'school' is distinguished by its heavy bolection moulding, the way in which the panels stand well forward from their frame, and the fact that the panels are 'fielded', by bevelling the edges so that a raised rectangle is left.

By the end of the seventeenth century, such panelling had been superseded by deal panelling which it resembled as regards the general disposition of frame and panels. At first, deal panels were

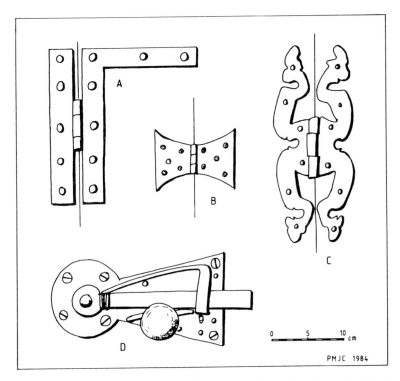

Fig. 7. Examples of 17th-century door furniture from Winchester Cathedral Close.

A) *Upper door-hinge ('Joint'), No. 5, The Close. Dated 1661–2.*

B) *Wing-hinge ('Gimmer'), No. 5, The Close. Dated 1661–2 (See Note to Text, 121).*

C) *Ornate H-type of hinge from redundant shutter in Deanery (west wall of 'Chamber over the Hall'). Dated 1661–5. (See Note to Text, 16).*

D) *Spring-latch, front door of No. 7, The Close. Dated 1661–2.*

often fielded in the Wren style, but early eighteenth-century panell-ing shows a return to a simpler pattern, with plain deal panels in an ovolo moulded frame. This development may be traced in Winchester Cathedral Close, in the deal wainscoting installed in 1727 at No. 1, The Close (Fig. 13) and, probably of rather later date, the eighteenth-century panelling of several rooms in No. 7.

Description of the Manuscript

The Wainscot Book is a narrow volume measuring 407mm by 155mm. It is bound in board and vellum, formerly closed by means of two clasps which have now disappeared. The cover bears the words **Wainscott Book** in ink, to which the dates '1660–1812' have more recently been added in pencil. The spine is simply marked:

Wai

nsco

tt

Book

The book now consists of eight gatherings of five or six double sheets, comprising the following number of leaves in each gathering:

9* . 10 . 13† . 12 . 12 . 10 . 12 . 12

*leaf cut out between pp. 6 and 7.
†leaf added.

The first three folii are blank, with the exception of fo. 1v, which carries the index, and the MS is paginated from fo. 4r onwards, which is numbered 1. These numbers are written over an earlier, erased system of pagination, which is now partially illegible, but which suggests that two complete gatherings were removed from the front of the volume before it was re-used for its present purpose.

A number of pages are blank. This is because John Harfell (Chapter Clerk 1660–80) clearly intended that in the first instance two pages should be set aside for each house: inevitably, though, some houses demanded more space in the book than others. Thomas Cranley (1680–1720) was less methodical, and merely started a new page further on in the book as the need arose. His successor, Charles Barton, reverted to Harfell's scheme. From page 64 onwards the entries show no consistent pattern, and many pages left blank by Barton were never filled.

Editorial Procedure

It would be hard to justify the Wainscot Book as a work of outstanding literary or linguistic interest, and the value of the document lies in its content rather than its form. The aim of this edition has been to provide a printed, working version of the document, and readability has been a prime aim. At the same time, it is hoped that the present edition preserves something of the feel of the original. The following procedure has been adopted:

ALL ENTRIES have been re-arranged in chronological order for each house. The houses are listed according to their present conventional order: the Deanery, then Nos. 1–12. The original PAGINATION is indicated by figures in bold type. The SPELLING of the MS has been retained. CAPITALS and a minimum amount of PUNCTUATION have been introduced in accordance with modern conventions. ABBREVIATIONS have been extended, with the exception of those in common use today (e.g. Mr, Dr, Revd). This treatment includes abbreviated versions of first names: e.g. Wm and Chas are written in full as William and Charles. INITIALS of first names have been retained, however. LATIN entries are italicised, but Latin proper names are written in their English form. ROMAN NUMERALS are printed as used. The signs £ and li are rendered by £ without distinction. SUMS OF MONEY are shown in columns on the right hand side of the page, as is generally the case in the MS, but the signs £, s and d are then omitted. The variant forms used for expressing DATES e.g. 23, 23rd, 23°, etc have been regularised in accordance with modern practice. MONTHS are written in full. The original order has been retained; e.g. 23rd January or January 23rd. SUPPLIED MATERIAL is contained within square brackets. INTERPOLATIONS or INTERLINEAR additions are rendered thus: e.g. [example]^{i}. DELETIONS in the MS are rendered thus: e.g. [example]^{d}. ILLEGIBLE DELETIONS are shown thus: [*deletions*].

DOUBLE DATING is editorial when the last figure is given in square brackets, e.g. 1713[/4]. CATCHWORDS and indications such as 'see page 59', 'from page 33' and sums of money carried forward are usually omitted, except when these affect proper understanding. PAGE HEADINGS identifying the houses are similarly omitted, except for the first page relating to each house.

Bibliographical Notes

Occasional sources are given in the notes to each section, or in the Notes on the Text. Sources more frequently used are referred to by initials or an italicised title: details of such sources are provided here.

CA: 'Chapter Acts'. These are contained in a series of minute books, known as 'Chapter Books', dating from 1553. MSS, WCL.

CO: 'Chapter Orders'. A special 'Chapter Order Book' was kept as well as the Chapter Books from 1666–1737. MS, WCL.

HRO: Hampshire Record Office.

Insurance Memorandum: CA November Chapter 1740. The houses of the Close had been insured under seven policies taken out with the Sun Fire Office on 8 July 1740, and to clarify which houses were referred to in the insurance schedule, they were precisely described and located in this *Memorandum*.

LB: 'Ledger Books'. MSS, WCL.

Narrative: *A Narrative of the Proceedings of the Dean & Chapter of Winchester in their buildings and reparations with respect more particularly to the house which is now in the possession of Dr Thomas Gumble, for the satisfaction of the Rt. Reverend Father in God, George [Morley] Lord Bishop of Winton. 20 Feb 1674/5.* MS, WCL (Box file 89). Three versions of this are in existence: the second draft, dated 4 Feb 1674/5 was transcribed rather inaccurately in *Winch. Cath. Docs, II* (see below), pp. 158–70.

Parliamentary Survey:	*The Parliamentary Survey of the Close, 1649,* MS, WCL. The text was published, somewhat inaccurately, in *Winch. Cath. Docs. II* (see below). An earlier version exists in HRO called 'A Survey of the Estates of the Dean & Chapter of Winton, 1649': refs. HRO (D & C) 59492–3 (2 vols). The section dealing with the Close is on fos. 4–19 of Vol. I.
Proceedings:	*Proceedings of the Hampshire Field Club and Archaeological Society.* Published annually.
Record:	*Winchester Cathedral Record.* Published annually by the 'Friends of Winchester Cathedral'.
TR:	'Treasurers' Rolls'. Computus Rolls kept year by year by successive Canon Treasurers. MSS, WCL.
WB:	*Wainscot Book.* MS, WCL.
Winch. Cath. Docs. II:	W.R.W. Stephens and F.T. Madge, eds., *Winchester Cathedral Documents, AD 1636–1683,* London and Winchester, 1897 (Hampshire Record Society).
WCL:	The Library and Archives of the Dean and Chapter of Winchester.

TABLE OF CONCORDANCE BETWEEN PAGINATION OF
THE MANUSCRIPT AND THAT OF THIS EDITION

WB	present edition	WB	present edition	WB	present edition
1	9	27	82-3	55	113-4
3	74-5	28	13-14	56	114-5
4	75-6	29	26	57	15
5	86-7	30	28-9	58	16-17
6	87	31	87-8	59	88-9
7	122-3	*32a	112-3	60	89-90
8	123	33	113	61	126-7
9	9-10	35	45-6	62	127-9
10	11-12	36	46-7	63	129
11	12	37	77	65	84-5
12	80, 82	38	77-8	68	17-18
13	12-13	39	34	69	18
14	124-5	41	14-15	71	58
15	123-4	43	70-71	72	105-6
16	43	44	71-2	†73[72v]	106
17	68	45	56-7	73	79
18	68, 70	46	57	74	72-3
19	55, 70	47	96-7	75	58-9
20	43, 45	48	97-8	76	115-6
21	76	49	103-4	77	36-7
22	112	50	104-5	78	37
23	96	51	34-5	79	90-91
24	103	52	35-6	80	47
25	55-6	53	83	81	98
26	125-6	54	83-4	82	117

*Page inserted between pp. 32 (blank page) and 33.
†The WB has two p. 73s. In this edition the *verso* of p. 72 is therefore referred to as 72v.

The Wainscot Book

	[Modern No.]
The pages wherein the parrticulars relating to each house may be found.[1]	
Dean'ry 1,9,10,11,13,28,41,57,58,68,[69]	
House over against South Door[2] of Dean'ry 19,25,45,46,71,75	**4**
House next the Dean's Stable[3] [16],20,35,36,80	**3**
House North of the Dean's Garden[4] 39,51,52,SN[5],77,78	**2**
New House behind the Cloyster[6] 29,30	**1**
House over against West side of the Dean'ry 23,47,48,81	**9**

On the Mount[7]

House at North-West Corner 7,8,14,15,26,61,62,[63]	**12 (now 11)***
House at S. West Corner of *Ditto* 24,49,50,72,73 [= 72v]	**10**
Middle House on West Side of *Ditto* [22,32a],33,55,56,76,[82]	**11**

In Dome Alley[8]

First on the Right Hand 5,6,31,59,60,79	**8**
First on the Left Hand 17,18,19,43,44,74	**5**
Second on the Right Hand 12,27,53,[54],65	**7**
Second on the Left Hand 3,4,21,37,38,73,80	**6**

[Little House at W. End of the Church[9] 22]	**11**

*After house No 11 was demolished in the mid 19th century the 12th house was re-numbered 'No. 11, The Close'. In this edition I have used the original numbering scheme, which was introduced in the late 18th century. See Plan of Close, Fig. 2.

1

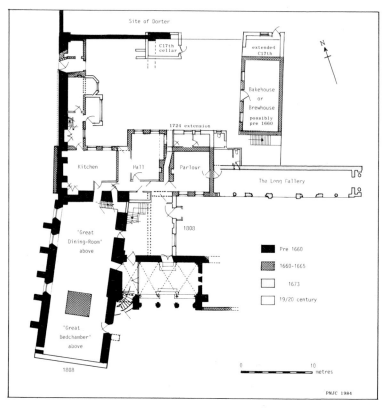

Site of Dorter

C17th
cellar

extended
C17th

N

Bakehouse
or
Brewhouse

possibly
pre 1660

1724 extension

Kitchen   Hall   Parlour

The Long Gallery

'Great
Dining-Room'
above

1808

	Pre 1660
	1660-1665
	1673
	19/20 century

'Great
Bedchamber'
above

1808

0   10
metres

PMJC 1984

Fig. 8. Ground-floor plan, The Deanery, Winchester, showing phases of construction.

The Deanery

The present Deanery, a mainly seventeenth-century building, occupies the former site of the monastic Prior's House, which was situated south of the long Dorter range (Fig. 1). The Prior's House appears to have extended eastwards for some distance, roughly on the site now represented by the 'Long Gallery' and the area of lawn to the south of it. Of the medieval Prior's House only the mid thirteenth-century porch (considerably altered in its upper storeys and re-roofed in the sixteenth century), the fifteenth-century 'Prior's Hall', parts of the west wall and fragments of the north wall have survived.

The nature of the original 'Prior's House', later used as the first Deanery, is a subject inviting further research,[1] though documentary evidence is scarce. A Probate Inventory[2] taken in 1548 of the possessions of William Kingsmill, last Prior and first Dean of Winchester, lists the rooms, but provides few clues as to their relative disposition. Rather more informative is the description of the first Deanery buildings provided by the *Parliamentary Survey*[3] of 1649, which mentions in some detail both the 'Prior's Hall' ('a very faire large Hall') and the adjoining 'Audit House' over the porch. It is not possible, however, to establish the plan of the first Deanery from either of these documents.

During the Commonwealth the Deanery was assigned by the Hampshire Parliamentary Committee to Nicholas Love, regicide, M.P. for Winchester and son of a former Warden of Winchester College (though not himself a Wykehamist). Love appears to have had most of the domestic part of the old Deanery demolished for the value of its materials (lead, timber, wainscot, glass, iron and

---

1. See J. Crook, 'Winchester Cathedral Deanery', *Proceedings* (forthcoming).
2. Inventory of William Kingsmill, B. Wills, 1548, MS, HRO. A full summary has been published by B. Carpenter Turner, '1548; The last Prior and the first Deanery', *Record*, 42 (1973), pp. 12–21.
3. Printed in *Winch. Cath. Docs. II.* pp.76–8 for Deanery.

tile), which had been dutifully itemised and evaluated by the
Parliamentary Surveyors. Instead of living in the Deanery, therefore, he had a new house built in the Churchyard[4]: this was in
turn demolished at the Restoration of 1660. Whether this vanished
building was his residence when in Winchester is not known; but
he was one of thirteen prominent residents who, in 1654, contributed
towards a fund for repairs to the Cathedral, on the grounds that it
was 'a very emenent and usefull place for preaching and hearing
God's word'.[5]

The main source for this period of the building's history is the
Narrative of the Dean & Chapter in their proceedings with Dr Gumble,
dated Jan–Feb 1674/5, which states that the Deanery was 'totally
demolished'.[6] The extent of the 'demolition' has been questioned,
but the fact remains that the fabric of the present Deanery is of
undoubted seventeenth-century character, built in brick rather than
the 'strong stone walls' mentioned in the 1649 *Survey*, and there is
nothing in the surviving records (notably in the important *Diary of
John Young*,[7] which spans the years 1616–45) to suggest a major
rebuild of the house during the first half of the century. In any
case, the 'building' of the new Deanery is well documented. In
December 1661 Richard Frampton of Kingsgate Street, Winchester
was appointed 'to oversee & order in all things in repayring &
building the said Deanes howse and other buildings necessary
thereto'.[8] The cost of Frampton's building operations is given in
the Treasurers' Account Rolls of the period, and in greater detail
in the surviving *Account Book of Wm. Fletcher*,[9] dated 1662, which
gives the cost of materials and labour used in the rebuilding. We
must therefore conclude that the Deanery was completely rebuilt
under Frampton's supervision, from 1662 onwards (as the phrase
in WB p.1 'when the house was built' suggests), and that most
remains of the earlier building, except for the Prior's Hall and the
Porch, were cleared away as part of the same operation. There
appears to have been little re-use of the earlier structure except for
part of the west wall of the 'North Gallery'.

4. See 'Answers of the Dean & Chapter to the Visitation Enquiries of Archbishop
   Juxon', MS, WCL, printed in *Winch. Cath. Docs. II*, p. 114. See also the
   Parliamentary Survey of the Estates of the Dean and Chapter of Winchester, 1649, MS,
   HRO, ref. 59492–3, Vol. II, fo.285, 'Certeyne howses of Nicho: Love Esq . . .'
5. 'Subscription List, 1654', MS, WCL, printed in *Winch. Cath. Docs. II*, p.98.
6. *Narrative*, para. 2.
7. MS, WCL. Partially printed by F. Goodman, ed., *The Diary of John Young*,
   London, 1928.
8. CA 7 Dec 1661.
9. MS, WCL.

The rebuilding of the Deanery evidently took rather longer than might have been hoped, because of the Plague and a shortage of money to finance building operations in the Close. A Chapter Act of 9 December 1667 allotted anticipated income from leases first towards the repair of the Cathedral and then 'to the building and finishing the Deanes howses [and] appurtenances'. The following year the sum of £400 was granted the Dean for 'the Finishing of the worke in the Great [Prior's] Hall'[10], and four months later the Chapter ordered a survey of the Deanery and other houses to be made so that a sum of £900, which had been earmarked for building operations, could be wisely used.[11]

The Wainscot Book shows—and in greater detail than the Chapter Minute Books—that the construction of the 'new' Deanery took place in two phases (Fig. 8). The first phase, during the decanate of Alexander Hyde (1660–5), involved completely rebuilding the northern part of the complex, in brick on a shelly limestone plinth. During the building operations, Dean Hyde lived in No. 2, to the east of the Deanery.[12] The conversion of the Prior's Hall into a 'Dining-Room' and 'Great Bedchamber' was delayed by several years, though the fact that the huge chimney towards the south end of the Prior's Hall was built soon after 1663[13] suggests that the work formed part of Frampton's plan. Two causes of the delay— the Plague and a shortage of money—have already been mentioned; a third difficulty was that part of the cellarage under the Prior's Hall and even, it seems, some of the rooms of the Deanery itself were held under lease by one Henry Foyle, Steward to the Dean and Chapter, whom it proved difficult to dislodge.

Only during the decanate of Hyde's successor, William Clarke (1666–79), was the conversion of the Prior's Hall completed. It was Clarke, too, who was responsible for the addition of the elegant 'Long Gallery' on the east side of the Deanery, traditionally said to have been built so that Charles II could be received in appropriate style during his visits to the city that he hoped to make a rival to Versailles. The *Narrative* of 1675 states that Dean Clarke paid for the Long Gallery himself,[14] hence there are no references to its cost in Chapter records; and one entry in the Wainscot Book confirms

---

10. CO 17 Aug 1668.
11. CA 9 Dec 1668.
12. *Narrative*, para. 3.
13. See the *'Protest of Henry Foyle'*, MS, WCL, printed in *Winch. Cath. Docs. II*, pp. 138–9.
14. *Narrative*, para. 6. This detail does not figure in the version printed in *Winch. Cath. Docs. II*.

that work carried out in the Long Gallery was not eligible as a 'wainscot' item.[15] At Clarke's removal from Winchester, the Long Gallery and all its fittings passed to his successor without charge.

With the completion of the Long Gallery, the Deanery attained more or less its present form. A minor extension was made in the early eighteenth century, with the creation of a passage on the north side of the Parlour. This 'Passage to the Parlour' is mentioned, and its measurements accurately given, in the *Notebook of Dean Zachary Pearce*, dating from 1739–48.[16]

Some important alterations took place in 1808. The entrance hall was enlarged, by demolishing its eastern wall and rebuilding it several feet to the east, in brick faced with stone, incorporating the original windows. At the same time, a building popularly known as 'Nell Gwyn' was taken down; evidently that referred to by Milner, writing in 1798: 'At the south end of this ancient [Prior's] hall is a brick building, said to have been added by Charles II, when he resided at the deanery, for the accommodation of Mrs Ellinor Gwynn'.[17] The south gable wall of the Prior's Hall was rebuilt in the form in which we see it today.[18]

The entries in the Wainscot Book relating to the Deanery show the same trend as those for the other Close houses: a fairly detailed analysis during the years immediately following the Restoration, and an increasingly laconic treatment during the second half of the eighteenth century, when the entries consist of little more than names of successive occupants.

15. See pp. 10–11, and Notes to Text, 33.
16. MS, WCL.
17. J. Milner, *History of Winchester,* London, 1798 (3rd edn., 1838) Vol. II, p. 138, footnote.
18. These various building operations were approved by CA 23 Mar 1807.

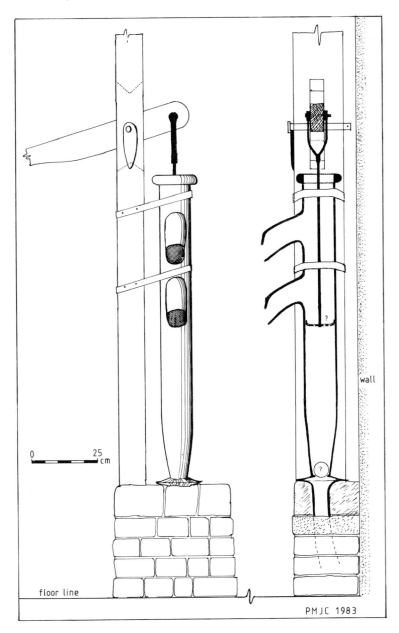

Fig. 9. Front elevation and section, lead pump in Deanery 'Old Bakehouse' (Brewhouse in 1740) (WB p.1).

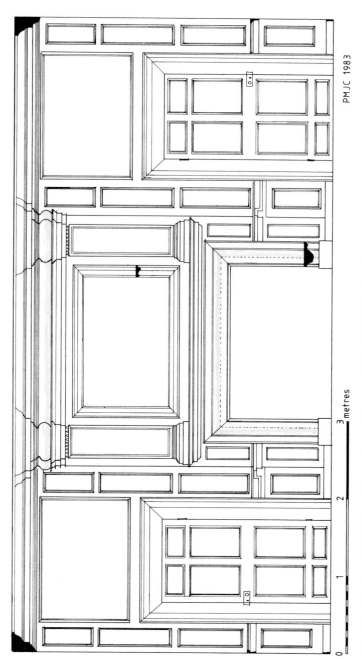

PMJC 1983

3 metres

Fig. 10. South wall of 'Great Dining-Room' (present 'Prior's Hall'), The Deanery, Winchester, showing chimney-piece and panelling dated 1666–70 (WB p.10).

THE DEANERY

1 Deanery

Ecclesia Cathedralis Sanctæ Trinitatis Winton.

AN INVENTARY[10] of such heyreloomes and utensills which
Alexander Hyde, Doctor of Lawes, Deane of the said Cathedrall
Church, *Anno Domini* 1660, left for his Successors when the house
[was][i] built [11] for the Deane there, *vizt:*

In the Hall[12]: The waynscott & benches with lock & key to the
doore.
In the parlour: The way[n]scott round.[13]
In the Pantry: Two dresserbords, seaven shelves, six tacks [for][d] of
wood (to hang up *[illegible]* shelves).
In the kitchin[14]: Two dresserbords & frames, six shelves, eighteene
yron hookes for racks, the way[n]scott behinde the long dresser,
the racks for spitts, A leaden pump with the case & yron handle,[15]
an yron grate for seacoale [with the wings & two yron gates][i].
In the chambers over the parlour, over the hall & over the kitchen:
The wainscott round those 3 chambers with shuttings[16] to the
windowes of wainscott. *[4 words deleted].*
In the roome called the old Auditt howse[17] and closett there: the
wainscott & shelves. [One box of glasse][i].
In the sellors[18]: Two shelves in the outer seller and two shelves in
the inner seller. [One side table to fold clothes on & a stoole to
whett knives on.][i]
In the Brewhowse[19]: Two furnaces with [leaden][d] grates [&] [doores][i]
of yron. One leaden pumpe,[20] One meash fat & a tunn & two
coolers, *[2 items deleted]* a tunnell, [a mashing tubb][d], a wat [vat]
to lade liquors out of the furnace, a hopp baskett, [three ?knives][d]
& an oare to stirr the malt, one stand, One stepp by the pump.
In the new larder[21]: One Dresser bord, eight shelves, one square
planck with tenderhookes the whole length of the roome fastned
at each end, to hang meat on.

9 Money Laid out by Dr William Clarke, Deane of Winton, for
wainscott in the Deanrie, to be repayd to him, his executors,
Administrators or assignes, by his Successor after the accustomed
deduction of a fourth parte is taken out of the same, *vizt:*

To the right Reverend Alexander, Lord Bishop
of Sarum,[22] for the wainscott sett up by him when
he was Deane, the 4th of the first price being
deducted, payd in money, as per his acquitance   36   19   0

And for wainscott sett up by the sayd Dr William
Clarke when the Deanry was finished[23] as
followeth:

For slitting deale for wainscott   1   13   6

For cutting stuffe for Architrives   0   3   6

For inlarging the hall wainscott in the place of
the old stayers &c[24]   0   11   4

For making the wainscott doore in the parlour
leading into the open cloyster,[25] and making up
the place with wainscott about the sayd doore
where the parlour window once stood, and for
making the wainscott doore in the hall at the
stayer foote,[26] all at Dayworke   0   19   10

For making the wainscott in the chamber next the
new gallery where the windowe formerly was[27]   0   6   0

Which two last summes were payd to the country joyners,[28] Bates
& Willis,
And which payments aforesaid are attested by John Baskervile[29]
and appeares as they were layd out in his building accomt book.

Payd to Willis for making the wast[30] wainscott in
the greate bedchamber at task worke, as per
acquittance   4   0   0

Payd to Whetstone, Lewis & Oke, three London
joyners, for making the dowble doores in the
gallary, and also the fower dowble doores in the
chambers betweene the two galleries,[31] and for
the cornish from window to window backward[32]
in the great bedchamber, at day-worke, as per
acquittance £11 6s 8d. Out of which summ
deduct for making the dowble doores in the new-
gallery 15s which is not proper for this

10 Amount though it be wainscott work,[33] and also deduct for soe much taken away of the first wainscott, when these fower double doores in the Chambers were sett up at the rate of one shilling tenn pence halfpenny per yard, which was the rate payed to Deane Hyde after a fowerth was deducted, which at 6s a doore is in all fower £1 4s 0d[34]: which summ of 15s and £1 4s 0d being deducted out of the sayd £11 6s 8d then remaines, layd out for making the wainscott

| | 9 | 7 | 8 |

Paid more to the London joyners for making the wainscott & cornish & chimney peice in the dyning-roome[35] (the quarters sett up there and in the great bedchamber to keep the hangings from the wall not accounted),[36] at Taskworke, as per acquittance

| | 25 | 6 | 0 |

Payd more to the London joyners for wainscotting the Chimneyside of the great bedchamber, with the chimney peice, at taskeworke, as per acquittance[37]

| | 12 | 7 | 0 |

Payd to the sayd joiners by contract at London, towards their charges downe & up, as per acquittance

| | 1 | 0 | 0 |

Payd for stuffe for all the sayd wainscott sett up by Dr William Clarke, Deane, computed & attested by John Baskervile out of his account-booke to be at the least

| | 18 | 0 | 0 |

For joynts, gimmers, locks & bolts for the said wainscott doores as followeth:[38]

Gimmers and joynts for the little parlor doore[39]	0	6	0
Joyntes for the wainscott doore in the hall at the stayer foote[40]	0	5	0
Joynts for the dyning roome doores	1	10	0
Seaven bolts & staples for the seaven double doores[41]	0	15	0
Eight payre of joynts for the oke-wainscott doores	0	16	0
Joynts & Longbolt for the bedchamber doores	0	12	6
Two springbolts 3s, three spring Locks 15s	0	18	0
One spring Lock	0	4	4

Three payre of H Joyntes	0	5	6
Two spring bolts	0	3	0
One payre of H joynts	0	1	0

11 Payd to Samuell Masters for laying the wainscott in the Dyning roome and great bedchamber
in white oyle colours at xijd per yard, as appeares
by John Baskerviles Account[42]   15   0   0

Octavo Die Decembris Anno Domini 1673
This Bill is approved of by the Chapter and by their Order entered
accordingly into this Wainscott Booke
per me John Harfell, *Clericum Capituli*.

13 The Charges of Dr Richard Meggott, Dean of the Cathedrall
Church of Winchester, to be repayd by his Successor, according to
the Custome of the said Church.

Payd in money to Robert Pocock, Executor of the
last will & Testament of Dr William Clarke who
was Predecessor to the said Dr Meggott (the
fourth part of the first price being abated), for his
wainscott in his dwelling house, the summ of
Eighty three pounds [tenn shillings &][d] four pence
halfe penny,[43] and for the Kings Armes in the
Dining roome thirty shillings,[44] as appeares by an
acquittance under the hand & seale of the said
Mr Pocock   lxxxiiij £   xs   iiijd *ob*.

Payd to Mr Cole, the Joyner, for wainscott in the
Roome over the parlor   ixs

And for window shutts in the parlour seventeen
shillings & six pence as appeares by bill & acquittance   xvijs   vjd

                          Summ   lxxxv £   xvjs   xd *ob*.

This bill hath been examined & approved by the Chapter, the 5th
of December 1681,
In praesentia Thomas Cranley, *Notarii Publici*.

The Charges of Dr John Wickart, Dean of the Cathedrall Church of Winchester, to be repayd by his Successor according to the Custome of the Church.

Payd in money to Mrs Timothea Meggott, widdow, relect & Executrix of Dr Meggott the late Dean, deceased, (the fourth part being abated) for his wainscot in his dwelling house, the summ of sixty four pounds eleven pence halfe penny,[45] as appears by her acquittance   lxiiij £   xjd *ob.*

February 26th 1693[/4]
Payd William Pryor, Joyner, for four yards & a quarter of Wainscot over the two Doores in the great Chamber,[46] Sixteen shillings, as appears by acquittance

		xvjs	
Sum	lxiiij £	xvjs	xjd *ob.*

27th November 1693
Examined and approved of by the Chapter
In præsentia mei Thomas Cranley, Notary Public, Chapter Clerk.

28   The Charges of Dr William Trimnell, Dean of the Cathedrall Church of Winchester, to be repaid by his Successor according to the Custome of the Church.

February 22nd 1721[/2]
Paid by Dr Trimnell, the Dean, to Mr Jacob Blaying and Mr John Gachon, Executors of Dr Wickart, the late Dean, deceased,[47] for the Wainscott in his Dwelling house (the fourth part being abated), the summe of forty eight pounds twelve shillings, as appeares by their acquittance

     xlviij £   xijs

26 Februarii 1721/2
This accompt was examined and approved by the Chapter.
Present: Thomas Rivers, Vice-Dean; William Lowth; Charles Woodroffe, Treasurer; Thomas Newey; John Cooke; John Cobbe
Ita Testor Charles Barton, *Clericus Capituli.*

Expended by Dr Trimnell, the Dean, for Wainscott & worke about the Deanary, as appears by
Workmens bill produced att November Chapter
1724, the summe of tenn pounds, to be added to
the sume abovemencioned   10   0   0

Which bills were then seen and allowd by the Chapter.[48]
Ita Testor Charles Barton, *Clericus Capituli.*

June 30th 1729
Paid by Dr Naylor, the Dean, to the Executors
of Dr Trimnell, the late Dean, for Wainscott etc
in the Deanary (the fourth part being abated),
the summe of Forty three pounds and nineteen
shillings   43   19   0

This Accompt was examined and approved by the Chapter, the
30th June 1729,
In presence of Charles Barton, Chapter Clerk.

41   The Charges of Dr Naylor, Dean of Winchester &c, to be
repaid by his Successor (the 4th parte deducted).

Paid by Dr Naylor to the Executors of Dr
Trimnell, late Dean, as in folio 28   43   19   0

Expended more, as per bills produced & approved
att November Chapter 1729   2   4   0

This Account was examined & allowed 11th December 1729,
In presence of Charles Barton, Chapter Clark.

Expended more by Dr Naylor, the present Dean,
for painting and Varnishing,[49] as by a Bill pro-
duced and allowed att November Chapter 1731   10   11   5

Examined and allowed the 11th of December 1731,
In presence of Charles Barton, Chapter Clerk.

Expended more by Dr Naylor, the present Dean,
for making & altering doores & dorecases and
for painting, as by Bills produced & allowd att
November Chapter 1732   10   0   6

Examined & allowed the 9th December 1732,
In presence of Charles Barton, Chapter Clerk.

Expended more by Dr Naylor, the present Dean,
for painting, as by bills produced and allowed at
November Chapter 1737   3   0   5

Examined and allowed the 3rd of December 1737,
In presence of William Pescod, Chapter Clerk.

57   Paid by Dr Pearce to the Administrator of
Dr Naylor, late Dean   52   6   6

Expended for Wainscott in the Staircase and passage to the three Chambers.[50] 34 yards at 3s per
yard   5   2   0

For painting the same, as per Bill   0   19   0
                                                                              58   7   6

This account was examined and allowd, 5th December 1739,
In presence of William Pescod, Chapter Clerk.

Expended for Wainscott in the Garrett over the
Greatroom[51] & painting the same   6   0   8

For Wainscott in the [great]d new room[52] [over
the Kitchen]i   5   13   5

For Wainscot in the Hall[53] & painting   2   8   5
                                                                              14   2   6

This account was examined and allowd, 29th November 1743,
In presence of William Pescod, Chapter Clerk.

Expended for Wainscott at the end of the Galary
over the Pantries[54]   3   16   8

Paid for a [Marble]i Chimney peice in the New
room [with]d Carved Moldings and Mantle tree[55]   10   3   6

A Marble Slabb and Fenders in the great Bed-
chamber   2   19   2
                                                                              16   19   4

November 26th 1747
William Pescod, Chapter Clerk.

A Marble Chimney Peice in the Parlor bought of
Dean Naylors Executors[56]   2   18   0

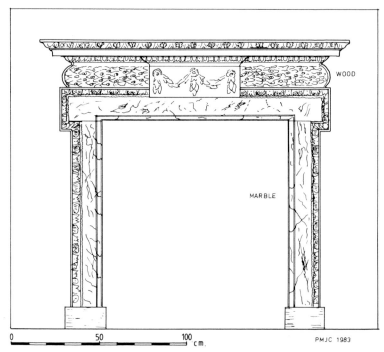

WOOD

MARBLE

0   50   100 cm.   PMJC 1983

Fig. 11. Chimney-piece in 'New room over the Kitchen' (present Dining-Room), The Deanery, Winchester, dated 1744–7 (WB p.57).

58	Brought over, paid by Dean Pearce	92	7	4
	Deduct one fourth part	23	1	10
	Remainder	69	5	6

Which summe was paid by Dr Cheyney to Dr Pearce, the late Dean.

Expended by Dr Cheyney[57]	13	1	9
	£82	7	3

December 11th 1749
Expended more by Dr Cheyney in Wainscott [&]ᵈ
Cornice & Painting, as by bills allowed   6   18   0
W. Pescod, Chapter Clerk.

December 1750
Expended more by Dr Cheyney for Wainscott   2   16   1
Witness, W. Pescod, Chapter Clerk.

December 11th 1752
Expended more by Dr Cheyney, for bills allowd   3   0   5

December 11th 1753
Expended more by Dr Cheyney, for bills allowd   5   15   6
Witness, John Dison.

December 12th 1754
Expended more by Dr Cheyney, for bills allowed   8   9   8
Witness, John Dison.

7th March 1757
Expended more by Dr Cheyney for bills allowed   3   12   1
Witness, John Dison.   112   19   0

68   Brought over, expended on the Deanry   112   19   0

October 1756
Expended more by Dean Cheyney, by bill allowd   3   5   0
Witness, William Pescod, Chapter Clerk.   0   14   3
   116   18   3
     Deduct one 4th, being   29   4   6
11th February 1760   87   13   9
This Sum to be paid to the Executors of Dr Cheyney by his
Successor.
Paid. John Dison, Chapter Clerk.

Dr Jonathan Shipley Dean:

November 1761
Expended by Mr Dean and allowd   1   12   0
Witness, John Dison, Chapter Clerk.

November 1766
Expended more by bills produced & allowed   25   4   11
John Dison, Chapter Clerk.

November Chapter 1768
Expended more by Mr Dean, by bills allowed   6   15   5
   121   6   1
     Deduct One 4th, being   30   6 $6\frac{1}{4}$
December 9th 1770   90   19 $6\frac{3}{4}$
The said Sum was paid by Dr Ogle to the Bishop of St Asaph.[58]
Witness, B. Burt, Deputy Chapter Clerk.

November Chapter 1771
By Bills allowed   0   18   9
B. Burt, Deputy Chapter Clerk.

November 1774
Expended more, by Bill produced & allowed   9   17   8
Witness, William Yalden, Chapter Clerk.

7th December 1786
Biden carpenters Bill for Work done etc, as by
Bill produced & allowed   11   14   11
Witness, J. Ridding, Chapter Clerk.
                                                 _____
                                                 113   10   10¾

69   [12th December 1759
Expended and Allowed Dr Cheyney, by bills allowd   0   14   3]^{d}

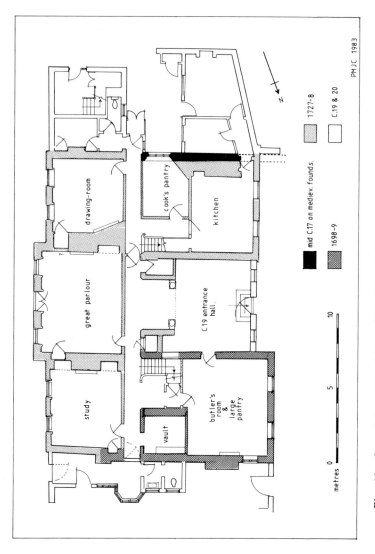

Fig. 12. Ground-floor plan, No. 1, The Close, Winchester, showing phases of construction.

No. 1, The Close

The small number of recorded occupants of this house between
1727 (when it was rebuilt) and the end of the nineteenth century
(see pp. 157-8) is a measure of the prestige it enjoyed as one of the
most attractive houses in the Cathedral Close. Though the building
in its present form dates mainly from 1727, it incorporates part of
the earlier house, a wing built in 1699, as shown by a date-
stone and documentary evidence. The date-stone misled earlier
researchers into assuming that the whole house was built in that
year. T. D. Atkinson also confused this house 'behind the Cloyster'
with No. 12 on the other side of the Close,[1] but, as shown
elsewhere,[2] the term 'the Cloister' denoted in the eighteenth century
the 'dark passage' adjoining the South Transept of the Cathedral,
and certainly not the western walk of the monastic cloister, which
had been demolished two centuries earlier!

The addition made to the original stone building in 1699 and
the reconstruction of the rest of it in brick in 1727-8 have obscured
virtually all traces of the first house, which is known only from
documentary evidence. The south wall seems to survive, however,
with its flint and ashlar checkered face, and fenestration suggesting
a date in the mid seventeenth century: the window mouldings are
similar to those of the rebuilt Deanery. The south wall is built on
medieval footings which are exactly aligned with the south wall of
the monastic Chapter House, and it may be supposed that the first
house adjoined or incorporated monastic remains which have since
disappeared, though probably not the Infirmary range as Canon
Goodman suggested,[3] for this seems to have been situated south-
west of the Deanery, near No. 4.[4]

---

1. T.D. Atkinson, 'Winchester Cathedral Close', *Proceedings,* XV (1941), p.21.
2. See Notes to Text, 6.
3. A.W. Goodman, 'Under Two Queens', *Record,* 5 (1936), pp.10-12.
4. See pp. 50-1.

Early references confirm that the house was, from the New Foundation, the residence of the 1st Prebend. The building is first mentioned in the will of Christopher Perin,[5] who died on 13 October 1612, leaving 'all my Wainscott in the Great Parlour of my Prebend House' to his successor, Nicholas Love Sr., father of the Parliamentarian M.P. who was assigned the Deanery during the Commonwealth.[6] Love was succeeded in turn by Edward Burby, whose servants gave evidence, many years later, which allowed the pre-Commonwealth garden boundaries to be accurately re-established.[7] The 1649 *Parliamentary Survey* makes particular mention of the 'one parlour well wainscotted' of Perin's will, and of the other rooms of the house, none of which has survived in the present building.[8] The house was allotted to Robert Wallop during the Commonwealth: he was a member of a notable Portsmouth family and, like Nicholas Love Jr., who had been assigned the Deanery, contributed towards the fund for repairs to the Cathedral in 1654.[9]

The house was thus constantly occupied during the Commonwealth, and as a result escaped the demolition (total or partial) that befell so many other Close houses at this time. At the return of the Church in 1660 only minor repairs were needed to make the building habitable for the new Canon of the 1st Prebend, Joseph Gulston. Details of these expenses are given in the *Account Book of Wm. Fletcher*: approximately 40 man/days' work in 1661-2.[10] Also itemised in this document are the hearth-tax payments, showing that No. 1 had eleven hearths at that date.

Gulston's successor, Robert Sharrock, does not appear to have occupied the house himself, except, presumably, during his periods of statutory residence. The house was let to John Reading, the Cathedral Organist, until he was finally ejected in 1682 for 'loude and scandalous behaviour on the night of Christ's Passion'[11]: he had in any case been replaced as Organist by this date, and was employed by Winchester College. Sharrock died two years later, leaving a number of items to his successor, including two large tables (one round and one square), a garden roller and furniture,

5. See Note 5, p. xiv.
6. See p.3.
7. 'The Testimonies of Deverenx Batt and Richard Davis, 4 Dec 1674', MS, WCL. The boundaries concerned were those between the houses of Dr Burby, Dr Duncan (who was succeeded by Dr Smith) and Dr Alexander. See Fig. 1.
8. Printed in *Winch. Cath. Docs. II*, p.79.
9. See p.4.
10. MS, WCL.
11. CO 27 April 1682.

kitchen fixtures and window shutters.[12] Because these 'standards' were handed on as a legacy, there was no reason for them to be entered in the Wainscot Book. By 1684 the house was once again in a poor state of repair, and it was ordered that 'the Decayes in the Outward Walls and covering of Dr Sharrock's Kitchin, the pump and the outward walls of the Buttery, Buttery Chamber & Parlor be forthwith repaired to prevent further ruin . . .'[13] Some of this work was carried out during the tenure of Sharrock's successor, Samuel Palmer. The next occupant, Baptista Levinz, paid for a brewhouse to be added to the outbuildings: this was converted from the northern half of a house which for many years had been let to successive generations of the Taylor family, all Minor-Canons of the Cathedral, two of whom became Precentors.[14] After some indecision, the Chapter resolved to divide the house into two brewhouses for the use of Nos. 1 and 2, the cost being borne by the two Canons concerned.[15] But the major repair work to No. 1 began during the tenure of John Warner, who succeeded Levinz: in December 1698 the Chapter ordered that the 'roof and timber-work' of his house should be repaired, and the following year he was granted just over £100 for 'new building': the extension whose date-stone bears the words 'Aug ye 22 1699'.[16] It is significant that he was Chapter Treasurer during that year and for some time afterwards: this did not mean that he was necessarily in a stronger position to order work on his own house, but the nature of his office demanded permanent residence in the Close and thus a habitable dwelling-house.

No further large-scale repair operations are recorded at No. 1 until 1727. In January of that year the new occupant, Benjamin Woodroffe, was given permission to demolish 'the prebendal house late Mr Soley's adjoining the northside of the house called the Chauntry' and build in its place 'a good convenient dwelling house of five roomes on a floor, to containe sixty foot in the front next the garden [actually 66ft (20.1m)] with a wing returned of forty foot'.[17] Much of the work was to take place at Woodroffe's own expense, but the Chapter promised to contribute £200.[18] The

---

12. 'Dr Sharrock's Legacy to his Prebend house', MS, WCL.
13. CO 25 June 1684.
14. The house is shown as No. 2a in Fig. 2.
15. CO 8 Dec 1691.
16. The relevant documents are CO 9 Dec 1698 and TR 1698–9 and 1699–1700.
17. CO 14 Jan 1726/7.
18. *ibid.* In fact, the sum of £210-0-6 appears in TR 1726–7 under 'repairs' to Woodroffe's house; and a further £25 was paid in TR 1727–8.

'Chauntry' may possibly have been part of the building formerly belonging to the line of 'Chaunters', the Taylors, most of which had, as already mentioned, been converted into two brewhouses: the only other reference to this building occurs in a slightly earlier Chapter minute (dated 1724): 'That the Chantry be pulled down'.[19]

The wing of 1699 was retained as part of the house. The new building consisted of a large L-shaped structure, incorporating the earlier wall to the south, with a grand façade on the east side. On the west side, the southern wing was constructed so as to match the northern as regards brickwork and fenestration—though not in length. In fact, it was not possible to match the brickwork exactly— the number of courses differs as a result of the slightly thicker bricks used in the southern wing—and the first-floor window openings of the southern wing, taller by comparison with the corresponding windows of the older part, reflect the changing fashions of the three decades that had elapsed between the two phases of the building. The windows on the ground floor, though of late seventeenth-century type, have evidently been reinserted, and the detail of their rubbed brick arches, identical to those of the mid nineteenth-century entrance porch, suggests that they were re-sited during improvements to the 'back' of the house.

It is important to realise that the house was originally conceived as oriented towards the east. The west side, though it included the entrance porch (originally set back between the two wings), did not command a distant prospect of the Chapter House arcade as it does today, but lay opposite the high walls of a narrow lane—the area to the west of the house was opened up only in the mid nineteenth century. The west side was the 'back' side therefore, and contained the service rooms in the two wings, while the important reception rooms lay on the east side of the house.

As one of the conditions of his building operations, Canon Woodroffe was allowed materials from the earlier, demolished building.[20] Retiling work in 1982 revealed that a considerable number of roof timbers were salvaged, and the house contains a significant amount of seventeenth-century small-square oak panelling in those more private rooms, where the dictates of fashion were of less importance. The main reception rooms, however, were panelled in the more modern style of the late 1720s.

The most important change to the house since it was 'newly-built' occurred in the mid to late nineteenth century, when the east

19. CO 30 June 1724.
20. CO 14 Jan 1726/7.

side of the house was altered so as to give the impression of a more fashionable 'front', facing the newly opened out lawns of the former Chapter House site. At the same time, the former courtyard between the two wings was roofed over to form an imposing entrance hall, later embellished with *sgraffito* work by Heywood Sumner, a leading figure of the 'Arts and Crafts' movement.[21] He was the son of two of the most celebrated inhabitants of No. 1, The Close: George Sumner, Archdeacon of Winchester from 1885 and Bishop of Guildford from 1888, who died in 1908; and his wife Mary, founder of the Mothers' Union, who continued to live in the house until her death in 1920.

Despite its many alterations, the house, like so many in the Cathedral Close, contains many good examples of original panelling, windows, shutters, doors and door furniture; all of which may be precisely dated to 1727–8. A number of items are mentioned in the Wainscot Book.

21. See R. Bassett, 'A legal training but an etcher's eye', *Country Life,* Vol. CLXIV No. 4238, 28 Sept 1978, pp. 886–7.

NO. 1, THE CLOSE

29   The New house behind the Cloyster[59]

The Charges of Mr Benjamin Woodroffe, one of the prebendaries, in his prebendall house for wainscott, to be repaid by his Successor (the fourth parte to be deducted).[60]

For Wainscotting the Study[61] &c	16	13	3
For Wainscott in the drawing room[62]	15	7	2
For Wainscott in the great parlour[63]	31	10	$1\frac{1}{2}$
For Wainscott [in] the Chamber over the drawing roome[64]	5	17	$11\frac{1}{2}$
For Wainscott in the Chamber over the Kitchen[65]	5	11	11
For rough wainscott behind the hangings[66]	2	16	6
For painting (as per bill)[67]	13	4	5
	89	1	4

Standards in the said House

In the Vault[68]: the Bins and one hanging shelf

In the Kitchen[69]: two Dressers & all the Shelves & Spitt racks over the Chimney.

In the Large pantry or Strong be[e]r Sellar[70]: all the Shelves fastened to the Walls, and one hanging Shelf.

In the Butlers roome: the Shelves fastned to the Walls (Except the cupboard for glasses).

In the Cooks pantry by the Kitchen: all the Shelves.

In the Scullery[71]: a Leaden pump (but not the Stone Cistern).

[In the laundry: one very fine large ironing table board[72]]^d

Memorandum.[73] That the Executors of the said Mr Woodroffe shall also have liberty, if they think fitt, to take down the two marble Chimney peices in the great Parlour and Drawing roome, unless they can Agree with his Successor for the same.

[December 8th 1762
Memorandum. That I disdain this article to give these Chimney Pieces to the House.   B. Woodroffe.]^i

This Account was examined and approved by the Dean and Chapter, the 12th day of December, 1728.
Charles Barton, Chapter Clerk.

Present: Mr Dean, Mr Louth, Dr Rivers, Mr Cooke, Mr Sturgis, Mr Soley, Mr Woodroffe & Dr Hayley.

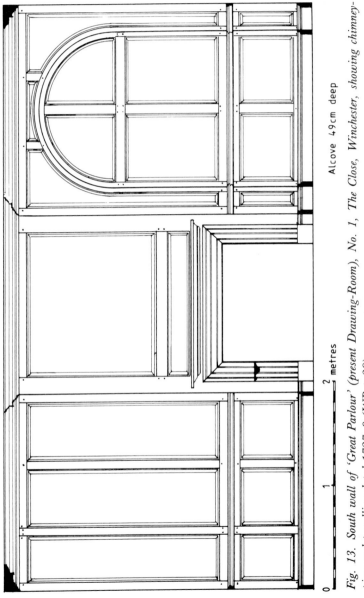

Alcove 49cm deep

0   1   2 metres

Fig. 13. South wall of 'Great Parlour' (present Drawing-Room), No. 1, The Close, Winchester, showing chimney-piece and panelling dated 1727–8 (WB p.29).

30   Brought over   89   1   11

December 11th 1749
Expended more by Mr Woodroffe for Marble
Chimney Peices, as by bills allowd   10   7   0
William Pescod, Chapter Clerk.

November 1761
Expended more by Mr Woodroffe for Wainscot   0   5   9
Witness, John Dison, Chapter Clerk.
                                                    ————————————
                                                    99   14   8

Deduct—see Mr Woodroffs Memorandum in the
foregoing Page under his own Hand   10   7   0
                                                   ————————————
                                                   89   7   8
                  a fourth Part   22   6   11
                                                   ————————————
                                                   67   0   9
Allowed by the Executor of Mr Woodroff upon
account of 42 years Possession[74]   15   0   0
                  & there remains   £52   0   0
Which sum was paid by Dr Walton
                  deduct ¼   13   0   0

December 20th 1770
Paid by Mr Lowth to Dr Waltons Executors   39   0   0

November Chapter 1771
By Bills allowd   14   19   0½
B. Burt, Deputy Chapter Clerk.

November Chapter 1772
By̌ Bill allowed   3   1   11½
B. Burt, Deputy Chapter Clerk.

November Chapter 1790
By Bill allowed   8   4   8
J. Ridding, Chapter Clerk.
                                                    ————————————
                                                   65   5   8

Midsummer Chapter 1795   16   6   5
The Sum of £48:19:3 was paid by Mr Hare to   ————————————
the Executor of Mr Lowth.   £48   19   3
J. Ridding, Chapter Clerk.

November Chapter 1795
By Mr Hayes Bill allowed at this Chapter

	2	15	1
Ridding, Chapter Clerk.	51	14	4
¼	12	18	7
	£38	15	9

5th August 1797
The Sum of £38:15:9 was paid by Dr Rennell to the Executors of Mr Hare.
J. Ridding, Chapter Clerk.

Deduct ¼	9	13	11¼
	£27	1	9¾

15th August 1798
The Sum of £27:1:9¾ was paid by Mr Woodford to Dr Rennell.
J. Ridding, Chapter Clerk.

Deduct ¼	6	15	5
	£20	6	4

January 14th 1808
The Sum of [£15:4:9]^{d} £20:6:4 was paid by Mr Poulter, for Mr Woodford[s] Executors, to Mr Ridding.
Ridding, Chapter Clerk.

Deduct ¼	[5	1	7
	£15	4	9]^{d}

No. 2, The Close

During the first half of the nineteenth century this house, though in a poor state of repair, was considered one of the most picturesque in the Close, and it was drawn by a number of local artists, of whom George Frederick Prosser and Richard Baigent are the best known.[1] The site of the house before its demolition in 1856 is shown in Fig. 2. Although it was oriented on the same lines as the monastic buildings, the house lay at some distance from them, and it seems likely that it was purpose-built as a canonry residence soon after the New Foundation of 1541. The house is first referred to in a Chapter Act of 1571,[2] and from that date the list of occupants—all Canons of the 5th Prebend until 1676—is easy to establish.

There are no descriptions of the house earlier than the Parliamentary Survey of 1649,[3] and this valuable document is supported by a probate inventory taken in September 1658 following the death of a Commonwealth occupant, Pistor Hyde Esq.[4] The house was 'built with Stone and covered with Tyle'. On the ground floor were a hall, a parlour and a study, and a service end or wing containing a kitchen and butteries. There were six 'lodging chambers' on the first floor and in the garrets. Before the Restoration, the garden attached to the house was rather small, but in compensation the occupant had the use of an outgarden to the north-east of the Cathedral, in the area known as the 'Paradise'. These gardens were rearranged in the early 1660s.[5]

1. Baigent's drawing is published in J. Vaughan, *Winchester Cathedral Close*, London, 1914 (facing p. 136). Another print is published in J. Crook, 'The Gumble Affair and the House of Thomas Ken', *Record*, 52 (1983), pp. 5–16. The version shown in E. Marshall, *Winchester Meads*, London, 1902 (facing p. 136) and reproduced in F. Bussby, *Winchester Cathedral*, Southampton, 1979, was copied from the earlier drawings 50 years after the house had been demolished.
2. CA 5 Dec 1571.
3. Printed in *Winch. Cath. Docs. II*, pp. 75–93.
4. 'Inventory, Pistor Hyde Esq. 13 Sept 1658', MS, HRO, ref. PCC 1658.
5. CA 2 Dec 1663.

No. 2 was one of those three houses which escaped total or partial demolition during the Parliamentary occupation of the Close of 1645–1660. At the 'return of the Church' the house reverted to the new 5th Prebendary, Dr Thomas Gumble, whose various duties in London (he was Chaplain to the Duke of Albemarle's troop of Guards) kept him almost totally absent from Winchester until 1672–3. The house was therefore used as a temporary residence for Dean Hyde during the reconstruction of the Deanery in the early 1660s, who 'therein kept very good hospitality'.[6] Gumble's irregular dealings with his fellow-Canons, which were tolerated at first, developed into a major row.[7] Not only did he repeatedly fail to comply with the Statute which laid down the obligatory periods of Residence which a Canon had to observe in the Close each year, but he allowed his prebend-house, formerly considered one of the best in the Close, to 'grow into a ruinous and scandalous spectacle'.[8] The building fell into a lamentable state of disrepair, for which he blamed the Chapter, even though he is recorded as having actually hindered the workmen sent by the Dean and Chapter to repair it. It appears that he considered the deteriorating state of the house a useful excuse for non-residence; it was not in his interests to have the house put in order. No. 2 was eventually completely repaired in 1672, to such an extent that even the workmen 'could not find themselves any more worke that they could say was needful'.[9] Gumble moved into his house and—rather unwisely, one might feel—was elected Chapter Treasurer for 1673–4. Abusing the powers thus invested in him, he proceeded to demolish much of the recently rebuilt house and constructed a new three-storey extension, without Chapter permission. His fellow-Canons reacted by withholding Dr Gumble's 'dividend' or share of income from Chapter leases. He appealed to the Cathedral Visitor, Bishop Morley, who delivered his judgement on 18 March 1674/5, finding in favour of the Chapter, and admonishing Dr Gumble 'to be more careful in the government of his tongue and pen and to behave himself with that modesty, justice, peace and love as becomes a member of such a society'.[10] The amount of the confiscated dividend just covered the cost of the unauthorised extension. Gumble was not granted much

---

6. *Narrative*, para. 3.
7. For a fuller account, see J. Crook, *op. cit.* in Note 1, above.
8. *Narrative*, para. 5.
9. *ibid.*, para. 8.
10. 'Final Order and Decree of Bishop Morley re. Dr Gumble, 18 March 1674/5', MS, WCL.

time to show that he could indeed live at peace with his neighbours in the Close, for he died rather suddenly in September 1676.

The next occupant was Thomas Ken, the well-known hymn-writer, later Bishop of Bath and Wells, who refused the house to Charles II's mistress, Nell Gwyn, on the grounds that 'a woman of ill-repute ought not to be endured in the house of a clergyman'. She was accommodated instead in a suite of rooms at the south end of the Prior's Hall.[11]

Ken's successor but one in the house, Charles Layfield, bore a share of the cost of converting 'No. 2a' (see Fig. 2) into two brewhouses for Nos. 1 and 2 respectively. This long building remained in use, first as a pair of brewhouses, and, later, as wash-houses, until the middle of the nineteenth century.

The entries in the Wainscot Book relating to this house begin only in 1729, which rather implies that no large-scale alterations or decorative work had taken place since Dr Gumble's occupation of the dwelling, a conjecture borne out by the absence of entries in the Treasurers' Rolls or Chapter Minute Books of the period. For the same reason, the list of occupants of No. 2 between Charles Layfield and Christopher Eyre is conjectural, inferred mainly by a process of elimination. The Wainscot Book shows, however, that a considerable amount of building work was carried out during the late eighteenth century, while Samuel Nott was living in the house (from 1771 to his death in 1793).

The last occupant of the house, Canon Edward James, died in 1854. His Prebend was suspended, in accordance with the Ecclesiastical Commission's recommendations for reducing the number of Canons at Winchester from twelve to five, and there was felt to be no need to retain a building said to be 'much delapidated and out of repair',[12] despite considerable expenditure on repairs during the early years of the century.[13] Arrangements for demolishing the house were sealed at the November Chapter of 1855.[14] It was taken down the following spring, and the site and the former garden were added to the Deanery.

11. See p.6.
12. 'Scheme for the demolition of House No. 2', MS, WCL ('Goodman Collection', Vol. III, item 11).
13. Over £600 was spent on repairing the house during the tenure of Thomas de Grey (in No. 2, 1807–17).
14. CA 25 Nov 1855.

NO. 2, THE CLOSE

39   The House on the North Side of the Dean's Garden

The Charges of Mr Christopher Eyre in his prebendall house, to be repaid by his Successor (a fourth parte to be deducted) according to the Custome of the Church.

Expended by Mr Eyre for Work & Materialls, as by the Bills produced & examined att November Chapter 1729	14	10	10

Examined and allowd by the Dean & Chapter, 11th December 1729.
In presence of Charles Barton, Chapter Clerk.

June 30th 1732 Paid by Dr Noyes to Mr Eyre [three parts in four]^{d} of the abovemencioned sume Charles Barton, Chapter Clerk.	10	18	8

15th December 1732 Paid by Mr Bourne to Dr Noyes for the Wainscott of the abovemencioned house (a 4th parte being deducted)	8	4	0

December 1733 Paid by Mr Stephens to Mr Bourne (the 4th parte deducted)	6	3	0

51   The Charge of the Reverend Mr Henry Stephens in his prebendall house, late Mr Bournes, to be repaid by his Successor according to the Custom of the Church.

Brought over from page 39	6	3	0
Expended by Mr Stephens	1	17	0
	8	0	0

Examined and allowd, 30th June 1737
In presence of William Pescod, Chapter Clerk.

June 28th 1739 Then Dr Cheyney paid, deducting one fourth parte	6	0	0
Then Mr Whishaw paid Dr Cheyney	4	10	0

February 7th 1740[/1] Then Dr Maurice paid Mr Whishaw	3	7	6
March 5th 1740/1 Then Dr Sykes paid Dr Maurice[75] Witness William Pescod, Chapter Clerk.	2	10	7½
December 10th 1744 Expended by Dr Sykes in making a Closet, as by bill allowd William Pescod, Chapter Clerk.	1	7	7
December 1747 Expended more by Dr Sykes for Wainscott & Painting, as by bills allowd	24	2	0
December 1748 Expended more by Dr Sykes, by bills allowd	8	8	0
52 December 11th 1749 Mr Eden paid Dr Sykes William Pescod, Chapter Clerk.	27	6	0

December 1750
Expended more by Mr Eden for Wainscott

3 12 0

Expended more for New Painting[76]

3 6 7

Witness, William Pescod, Chapter Clerk.

————————

34 5 5

12th December 1759 Mr Lowth paid the Executrix of Dr Eden (deduc- ting a 4th)	25	14	1
[November 1764 Expended more by Mr Lowth, as by bills pro- duced & allowed Witness J. Dison, Chapter Clerk.]ᵈ Entered by mistake.[77]	3	10	4

November 1766
Expended more by Mr Lowth, as by bills produced & allowd

4 10 4

John Dison, Chapter Clerk.

————————

30 4 5

deduct ¼   7 11 1

————————

Paid by Mr Nott to Mr Lowth   22 13 4

November 1771
By Bills Allowed   7   10 $8\frac{1}{4}$
B. Burt, Deputy Chapter Clerk.

November 1779
Expended more by Mr Nott, as by Bill produced
& allowed   1   13   9
W. Yalden, Chapter Clerk.

November 1780
Expended more by Mr Nott, as by Bills produced
& allowed   25   11   9
W. Yalden, Chapter Clerk.

February 1786
Expended more by Mr Nott, as by Bills produced
& allowed at the last November Chapter   27   12   8
J. Ridding   £85   2 $2\frac{1}{2}$

77   Brought over from Page 52   85   2 $2\frac{1}{2}$

December 3rd 1786
Expended by Mr Nott for a Marble Chimney
Piece, as by Bill produced & allowed at this
Chapter   6   6   0
Witness J. Ridding, Chapter Clerk.

January 10th 1772
Allowed to Mr Nott for work done by Mr Smith,
Carpenter, but not entered before, as by Bill
produced   4   5 $11\frac{1}{4}$

January 13th 1772
Allowed to Mr Nott for work done by Cave,
painter, by Bill then produced but not before
entered   3   4   9

These two Bills were produced to me by Mr Nott, November
Chapter 1789.[78]
J. Ridding, Notary Public, Chapter Clerk.

[November Chapter 1791
Allowed to Mr Nott for Hayes,   4:18:6
Carpenter, & Willis, Painter   1:18:0
Bills   6   16   6
Examined per J. Ridding, Chapter Clerk.][d]

This was entered wrong. It should be as under.

J. Ridding, Chapter Clerk.

Allowed to Mr Nott for Hayes the Carpenter's Bill	1	18	0
Allowed to Mr Nott for Willis the Painter's Bill	2	11	3
Allowed to Mr Nott for Widdell the Stone Mason's Bill	0	11	8
J. Ridding, Chapter Clerk.	£103	19	9¾
Deduct ¼	25	19	11¾
	£77	19	10

The above Sum of £77:19:10 was paid by Mr Garnett to Mr Nott's Executors. 1st August 1793.

J. Ridding.

78 Brought from Page 77	77	19	10
Deduct ¼	19	9	10
	£56	10	0

November Chapter 1800

The above Sum was paid by the Reverend W. Heathcote to Mr Garnett.

Witness, J. Ridding, Chapter Clerk.

Deduct ¼	14	2	6
	£42	7	6

The above Sum [of £42:7:6][i] was paid by the Reverend Mr Garnier to Mr Heathcote's Representatives by Mr Garnett.

J. Ridding, Chapter Clerk.

Deduct ¼	10	11	10
	£31	15	8

January 14th 1808

The above Sum of £31:15:8 was paid by Mr de Grey to Mr Garnier.

J. Ridding, Chapter Clerk.

Deduct ¼	7	18	11
	£23	16	9

December 15th 1817

The above Sum of £23:16:9 was paid by Mr Legge to Mr de Grey.

J. Lampard, Chapter Clerk.

No. 3, The Close

The canonry house formerly known as No. 3, The Close, which in 1931 became the original building of the Pilgrims' School, presents a fascinating challenge to the architectural historian. The house was built in several stages during the seventeenth century by adapting to a new purpose three bays of a six-bay medieval building traditionally held to have been a monastic guest-house for impoverished pilgrims to the shrine of St Swithun.[1] As recent investigations have shown, the medieval building originally consisted of two halls built end to end, of three and two bays respectively, with a further single bay at the southern end.[2]

The larger hall, whose chief glory is its hammer-beam roof—the earliest surviving example of this technique—consists of three fifteen-foot (4.6 m) bays, enclosed by buttressed flint and rubble walls, and is now known as the 'Pilgrims' Hall'. It was restored as far as possible to its original state in 1959, having long served as the Dean's stable and coach-house.

The southern three bays appear, in the light of the most recent discoveries, to have been timber-framed.[3] There is no doubt, however, that the roof and, indeed, the entire timber structure of the complex is of one 'build': this is proved by the continuous longitudinal timbers of the roof and the consistent upper roof structure. The roof has recently been firmly dated to 1290 ± 5 A.D.[4] A considerable amount of its original timberwork has survived, encased within the walls of the seventeenth-century house.

---

1. For the full history of the house, see J. Crook, *A History of the Pilgrims' School*, Chichester, 1981, pp. 115–26.
2. J. Crook, 'The Pilgrims' Hall, Winchester', *Proceedings*, 38 (publ. 1982), pp. 85–101.
3. J. Crook, 'Was the southern end of the Pilgrims' Hall complex, Winchester, originally timber-framed?' *Hants. Field Club Historic Buildings Section Newsletter*, No. 2 (new series), Sept. 1984.
4. J. Fletcher and J. Crook, 'The date of the Pilgrims' Hall, Winchester', *Proceedings*, 40 (publ. 1984) pp. 130–33.

The smaller hall, in the timber-framed portion of the building, is important in the study of 'aisle-derivative' roofs, for its surviving central truss was of the type with curved blades and a short tie-beam generally known as a 'base-cruck': a system, like the hammer beam, of roofing a wide space without the use of aisle posts. To the south of this two-bay hall was a single bay which may have been a 'service bay': it was separated from the two-bay hall by a true aisled truss, with full-length aisle posts. This partition includes surviving original oak boarding at first-floor level, and similar boarding is evidenced at ground floor level.

The earliest certain documentary references to the building date from the beginning of the seventeenth century when the three-bay northern hall was in use as the 'Common Brewhouse' of the Dean and Chapter. In June 1626 Matthew Lidford, a Cathedral singing-man, obtained the use of the adjoining two-bay chamber as a dwelling-house.[5] It seems that at that time the southern 'service' bay was being used as the Dean's stable. The indenture of lease[6] locates the house 'between the Common Brewhouse . . . on the Northside thereof and on the Southside thereof the Deanes stable', and the dimensions quoted confirm that the demised property consisted of two seventeen-foot (5.2 m) bays, which Lidford seems to have extended westwards by means of a twelve-foot (3.7 m) extension, described in the document as his 'new building'.

The property passed, via Lidford's son-in-law, to John Woodman, the Parliamentary 'solicitor for sequestrations', who was responsible for administering the confiscated properties of the Dean and Chapter during the Commonwealth. At the Restoration the Chapter purchased the remaining term of the lease from Woodman, assigning the house, the adjoining service bay and the nearby outbuildings to Canon William Hawkins.[7] Following the death of a senior Canon, Nicholas Preston, which occurred while these arrangements were still being put into effect, Hawkins elected to move into one of the more desirable 'new brick houses' in Dome Alley. It was therefore necessary for him to change his Prebend, from the 7th to the 9th Prebend, in succession to Preston. Hawkins' own successor in the 7th Prebend, William Burt, became the first clerical occupant of No. 3, living there until his death in 1679. It was a convenient house for him in that he was Warden of Winchester College, and

---

5. He had already tried, unsuccessfully, to build a house in the Churchyard: see F. Goodman, ed., *The Diary of John Young*, London, 1928, p. 60.
6. LB XII fo. 33v (27 June 1626), renewed fo. 153 (23 June 1642).
7. CA 22 Sept 1663.

he obtained Chapter permission for a doorway to be pierced through the Close wall to facilitate his daily journeys across College Street.[8] The house appears to have been in a poor state of repair during Burt's tenure, but money was in short supply, and it was left to his wealthy successor in the house, Warden John Nicholas, to undertake the extensive improvements which gave to the building something of its present appearance.

John Nicholas was installed in April 1684 and work on the house appears to have begun almost immediately. The Treasurer's account roll of 1684–5 includes, for example, the large sum of £450 *ad aedificandum domus Dr Nicholas*. He also obtained grants of timber from Silkstead for flooring and other purposes. The work of reconstruction seems to have been completed by 1687, the date shown on the rainwater heads which adorn the handsome new front wing of the house, apparently a replacement built out to Lidford's original building line.

The Wainscot Book contains entries relating to the interior fittings installed by Warden Nicholas, notably the fine oak panelling on the ground floor executed by Valentine Housman, a renowned joiner who was responsible for the woodwork of many of London's City churches, and who had completed a new reredos, carved screen and panelling in College Chapel to the order of Warden Nicholas a few years earlier.[9] The fact that one of Wren's master craftsmen was involved in the rebuilding of No. 3 lends weight to the tradition that the alterations in this house were carried out under the direction of no less an architect than Sir Christopher Wren himself, at a time when the construction of Charles II's new royal palace brought Sir Christopher frequently to Winchester.

The 'Pilgrims' Hall' to the north of No. 3, no longer required for use as a Common Brewhouse, had been adapted to serve as the Dean's stable and coach-house. In November 1739, the then occupant of the house, John Morgan, entered into an agreement with the newly-appointed Dean, Zachary Pearce, by which a further half bay was added to No. 3 to form first-floor closets: a new brick wall was erected to mark the division between the stable and the house.[10] This alteration finds an echo in the pages of the Wainscot Book. Not recorded apparently is the date of the early eighteenth-century extension on the south side, joining the house (which until that time had been co-extensive with the medieval building) to a large

8. CA 16 Feb 1664/5.
9. See Appendix B under 'Housman'.
10. CA 26 Nov 1739.

outbuilding a few yards to the south-west: a building which seems to have served as a brewhouse and perhaps later as servants' accommodation. This part of the building was greatly altered again in the early nineteenth century with the creation of a first-floor drawing-room; but by this date, entries in the Wainscot Book relating to the house had been discontinued.

NO. 3, THE CLOSE

16   The House Next to the Dean's Stable.

Money layd out by Dr John Nicholas, one of the Prebends of the Cathedrall Church of Winchester, for wainscot in his prebends house to be repayd by his Successor, according to the Custome of the Church.

[May 28th 1686
For the Shelves & Dresser in the Kitchen,[79] & the Wainscot in the two Roomes[80] in his house in the Close.

For the Shelves in the Kitchen, & Drawers[81]	2	10	0][d]
For 55 yards & 2 foot at 2s 6d the yard	6	17	0
For 126 foot of Cornish at 1s the foot	6	6	0
For two Chimny peices[82]	2	3	-0
total summ	15	6	0

Joyners worke done by Valentine Housman.

For 69 yards of Wainscot in the Parlour at 6s 6d per yard[83]	30	11	0
For 49 yards of Wainscot in the withdrawing Ro[o]me[84] at 6s 6d per yard	22	10	6
Summ	53	1	6
For Carriage[85]	5	12	0
Summ total of the severall Bills	[75	19	6][d 86]
	73	19	6

This Bill hath been seen and approved of by the Dean and Chapter, 30th November 1687.
Thomas Cranley, Chapter Clerke.

20   The Charges of Dr Newey, One of the Prebends of the Cathedrall Church, to be repaid by his successor, a fourth parte to be deducted.

Paid to the Reverend Dr Cheney[87] the sume of forty one pounds twelve shillings and six pence	41	12	6
Paid more for work, as appeares by severall bills to Edward Butler	12	8	4
In all	54	0	10

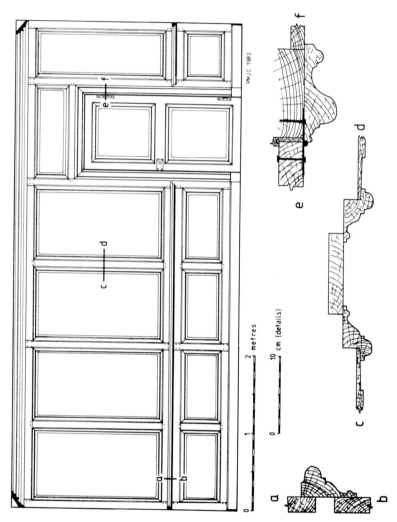

Fig. 14. South wall of 'Parlour' (present 'Old Library'), No. 3, The Close, Winchester, showing panelling installed by Valentine Housman in 1686–7 (WB p.16).

Paid by Dr John Cobb to the Executor of Dr Thomas Newey, deceased, the sume of Forty pounds tenn shillings and seven pence halfpenny 40 10 7

On the death of Dr John Cobb the summe of thirty pounds seven shillings and sixpence [was paid][i] on Mr Alsop's accession to the Abovemencioned House 30 7 6

On the death of Mr Alsop the sume of twenty two pounds fifteen shillings and seven pence halfpenny was paid by Dr Markland to Mrs Cobbe for the wainscott in the house above mencioned ..... 22 15 $7\frac{1}{2}$

November 23rd 1728
Received then of Dr Naylor by the hands of Mr Sturges[88] the summe seventeen pounds One shilling & eight pence halfpenny, in full of the wainscott money due upon the prebendall house of the late Dr Markland ..... 17 1 $8\frac{1}{2}$
Received, by me, A. Standish.

27th November 1728
Examined & allowed by the Dean and Chapter,
In presence of Charles Barton, Chapter Clerk.

35 The Charges of Mr Morgan in the prebendall house (near the Dean's stables) late Dr Naylors, to be repaid by his Successor (the fourth part being deducted).

30th June 1729
Paid by Mr Morgan to Dr Naylor for the Wainscott in the house abovemencioned (the fourth parte being deducted), the summe of twelve pounds sixteen shillings & three pence 12 16 3

This Accompt was examined & approved by the Chapter the 30th June 1729
In presence of Charles Barton, Chapter Clerk.

Expended more by Mr Morgan, as by bills produced and allowed in November Chapter 1739 for making two additional Closets to his house[89] 21 10 0

Note: the whole bills came to £31:10:0, out of which Mr Morgan
gave £10:0:0.
Witness, William Pescod, Chapter Clerk.

December 11th 1752
Expended more by Mr Morgan, by bills allowed   0   19   6
Witness, William Pescod, Chapter Clerk.

December 10th 1753
Expended more by Mr Morgan, by bills allowd   0   19   6
Witness, W. Pescod, Chapter Clerk.

36   July 8th 1760
Received of Dr Butler the sum of twenty seven
pounds three shillings & eleven pence on account
of Wainscot Money due, according to the Custom
of the Church of Winchester, to the Executors of
the late Mr Morgan, and received for their use
by me, Catherine Bourne   27   3   11
Witness, John Dison, Chapter Clerk.

November 1761
Expended more by Dr Butler for Wainscot &
Marble Chimney peice, as by bills produced &
allowed[90]
                                                     10   1   9
Witness, J. Dison, Chapter Clerk.

November Chapter 1762
Expended more by Dr Butler, as by bills produced
and allowed   12   4   4
Witness, J. Dison, Chapter Clerk.

November 1763
Expended more by Dr Butler for Wainscot &
Marble Chimney peice &c, as by bills produced
and allowed   58   6   2
Witness, J. Dison.

November 1764
Expended more by Dr Butler, as by bills produced
& allowed   23   14   0
Witness, J. Dison, Chapter Clerk.
                                                   ─────────────────
                                                    132   0   2
                                                     33   0   0½
                                                     98   19   11½

Of which sum £91 1s 6d was received of Mr Buller, being a Benefaction of the Bishop of Oxford for the use of the Church, by me, Peter Rivers Gay, Treasurer.

And the remaining part of the said sum £7 18s 5¾d was received of Mr Buller, for the use of the Bishop of Oxford, being Wainscot-money due to the House late Mr Hare's (see page 73) by me, J. Sturges.[91]

Total therefore paid by Mr Buller	98	19	11½
80 [Brought forward] Paid by Mr Buller	98	19	11½

1777, December 2nd
Expended for Painting, as allowed by Bill produced [& all]ᵈ — 0 8 6

1783, January 29th
Expended more, as per Walldin's [Stone Mason's]ⁱ Bill produced & allowed — 1 18 0½

1788, December 20th
Expended more, as per Hayes the Carpenter's Bill produced & allowed — 2 12 1

Expended more, as per *Ditto* — 2 5 0

December 22nd [1788]
Expended more, as per Walldin's Stone Mason's Bill produced & allowed — 5 8 1¼

Entered, J. Ridding, Chapter Clerk.	£111	11	8¼
Deduct one fourth	27	17	11
	£83	13	9

Which sum was paid by Mr Poulter to the Lord Bishop of Exeter by the hands of the Reverend Dr Sturges.[92]

J. Sturges.

Witness, J. Ridding, Chapter Clerk.

Deduct ¼	20	18	5
	£62	15	4

January 14th 1808
The sum of £62:15:4 was paid by Mr [de Grey]ᵈ Garnier to Mr Poulter.

J. Ridding, Chapter Clerk.

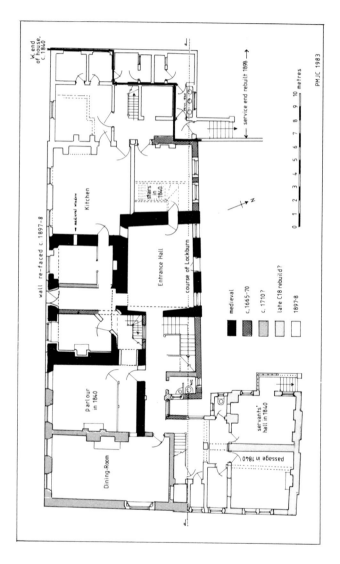

Fig. 15. Ground-floor plan, No. 4, The Close, Winchester, showing conjectural phases of construction. Based on plan dated Oct 1896, kindly made available by HRO (ref. 26M59-374-7), and incorporating evidence from a plan dated 1840-44 (MS, WCL).

No. 4, The Close

As with several other houses in the Close, the list of early occupants of No. 4 is established mainly by applying, as it were in reverse, that clause in the Cathedral Statutes which, until its repeal in 1670, required each Prebendary to move into the house of his predecessor.[1] The term 'Prebend' was, in fact, sometimes used as a synonym for a canonry house. Isolated early references to No. 4 serve to confirm, from time to time, an otherwise largely conjectural list of inhabitants, all of whom were, until 1701, Canons of the 2nd Prebend. The most important of these references are the *Narrative* of 1675 and the *Parliamentary Survey* of 1649.[2] The first document states that 'the house of Mr Halswell' (2nd Preb. 1641-73) was 'demolisht but in part' during the Commonwealth, and confirms that at the Restoration Halswell returned to his former prebend-house, which had been described in identifiable detail in the *Survey*.

The core of the house is undoubtedly medieval, as is suggested at first sight by the low ground-floor level, nearly three feet below the present Close. Indeed, isolated excavations in this part of the Close suggest that an important range of buildings extended along the south side of Dome Alley, and this conjecture is supported by the course of the monastic drain known as the 'Lockburn', which is apparently channelled so as to serve this range (Fig. 1).[3]

The buildings in question may have comprised the Infirmary of St Swithun's Priory; for reference is made in a Chapter Act of 1571 to the recently-demolished 'Fermery Hall', whose site, 'on the south side of the Little Cloister', was said to adjoin the newly-assigned

---

1. Statute *De Officio Thesaurarii*, published in G. W. Kitchin and F. T. Madge, eds., *Documents relating to the Foundation of the Chapter of Winchester (Cathedral Documents I)*, London and Winchester, 1889 (Hampshire Record Society), p.129 (translation, p.154).
2. Both printed in *Winch. Cath. Docs. II*, pp.158-70 and 75-93.
3. For the Lockburn, see J. Crook, 'Winchester's Cleansing Streams', *Record*, 53 (1984), pp.26-34 (Part I) and, especially, Part II, *ibid.*, (forthcoming).

prebendal house of Canon Robert Reynolds.[4] Reynolds' mid
seventeenth-century successor in the 11th Prebend was Lawrence
Hinton, whose house is indisputably located by the 1649 *Parliamentary
Survey:* it stood immediately north of Halswell's house (Fig. 1). Thus
the term 'Little Cloister' seems to refer to the area south of the
Refectory site, frequently called 'the Cloysters' in the 1649 *Survey*.

Successive alterations to No. 4 have left standing the medieval
walls in only a small area of the house, represented on the ground
floor by the butler's pantry, garden passage and housekeeper's
office, and the walls on the east and west side of the entrance hall
(Fig. 15). The front of the house, however, appears to have been
rebuilt in the mid seventeenth century, and further remodelled in
the eighteenth century. The medieval walls are concealed within by
plasterwork and, on the south side of the house, behind brick
refacing dating from the late 1890s; but one medieval feature was
recently uncovered: a narrow window in what was apparently an
external wall, lying between the present kitchen and the adjoining
office.

Whatever the purpose of the medieval structure represented by
these remains, it was allotted at the Dissolution as a house for the
Canon of the 2nd Prebend. No records relating to the accommodation of the earliest Canons of this Prebend have survived. No. 4
is first mentioned in 1582, when Thomas Bilson was granted the
'use and occupation of all that howse, sette and being nere unto
his . . . prebende aforesaide, called the Common Hall'.[5] Tempting
though it is to suppose that the 'Common Hall' was the surviving
Refectory or 'Frater' of St Swithun's Priory, one chance piece
of evidence suggests another possibility. In a seventeenth-century
calendar of Chapter leases compiled by that energetic and conscien-
tious Chapter Clerk, John Chase,[6] a tenement, which may be
identified from the Chapter's Ledger Books as comprising part of
the Prior's Hall, is referred to as *dom[us] D. le audit howse &
common hall in Clauso*. Unless John Chase had fallen victim to an
uncharacteristic aberration, this would indicate that the Prior's Hall
and the 'Common Hall' were one and the same. Added weight is
lent to this conjecture by the fact that when Bilson became Bishop
of Worcester, fourteen years later, a similar agreement[7] was made
with Canon Robert Bennett, who occupied the house adjoining

4. CA 5 Dec 1571.
5. CA 25 Nov 1582.
6. The *Book of John Chase*, MS, WCL. Transcription by F. Goodman, MS, WCL.
   The entry in question is found on fo. 59v.
7. CA 10 May 1596.

Bilson's former residence, occupied by Dr Hinton just before the time of the 1649 *Survey* (see Fig. 1). Both No. 4 and 'Hinton's' could reasonably be described as being 'nere unto' the Prior's Hall; but the Refectory site is too far from those houses to be comfortably described by such an expression.

The proximity of the houses in this part of the Close (Fig. 1) was a cause of frequent boundary disputes; and in 1619 Dean Young related in his *Diary* how he had smoothed over an argument between the respective successors of Bilson and Bennett, Theodore Price and Robert Kercher.[8]

The house was described in the 1649 *Survey* as 'built with stone and in good repayre, covered part with Lead and the rest with Tyle'. Indeed, the building had been retiled only in 1634, during the occupancy of Dr Halsey.[9] The main rooms were a hall, parlour and 'Dyninge roome', while the service rooms included a 'large roome to dry Cloathes in' over the kitchen, and 'A Washhouse with water cominge in through leaden pypes'. It was apparently quite an extensive dwelling, and was assigned to Sir Henry Mildmay, a Royalist politician turned Parliamentarian and not, it seems, a particularly attractive character, who can have had little use for the building and 'partially demolished' it,[10] presumably by removing the lead roofing which the surveyors of 1649 had valued at £64 17s 7½d.

It seems unlikely that No. 4 was rendered entirely uninhabitable. The *Account Book of Wm. Fletcher*[11] itemises a few repairs relating to the outbuildings of the house; and the sum of 9s paid on 18 Oct 1662 for 'Chimney Money' indicates that the house was not considered derelict at this time. Had the Treasurers' Accounts from the first eighteen months after the Restoration survived, they might have given details of repairs carried out, though at first the Close house repair programme seems to have been somewhat disorganised. In December 1661 the Canons noted that 'in the repayring of the said Church and buildinges belonging therto there have beene noe exacte accompte thereof brought in [whereby] great dammage hath come to the Dean & Chapter'.[12] It was to rectify this state of affairs that Richard Frampton was appointed to oversee the rebuilding of the Deanery.[13] A year later it was ordered that 'skilful surveyors'

---

8. See F. Goodman, ed., *The Diary of John Young*, London, 1928, p.64–5.
9. TR 1633–4. 3,600 tiles and 8 doz. ridge-tiles or 'Crests'.
10. *Narrative*, para. 2.
11. MS, WCL.
12. CA 7 Dec 1661.
13. See p.4.

should be appointed and 'models drawn' for building projects at various other houses, including 'the making up of the additions to Dr Haswells howse'.[14] Although this Act was subsequently deleted, the substance of it may have remained in force, for in 1664 a surveyor named William Taylor was appointed to supervise repairs at No. 4 at the agreed rate of £200.[15] Years passed, and the repairs were not carried out. In August 1668 Taylor was granted a further £50 for 'the full finishing of Mr Halswells house in all particulars included in his contract formerly made',[16] but by that time Halswell had been granted royal dispensation from his statutory residence in the Close 'by reason of his great age and the many infirmities & decayes of nature occasioned thereby'.[17] William Taylor declared himself bankrupt shortly afterwards, leaving the work unfinished, and No. 4 was left to decay further for a few years. In December 1672 the Chapter, learning that Taylor was 'much amended in the world and generally esteemed responsible for the summ he hath received', decided to take legal action if necessary in order to ensure the speedy completion of the work on Halswell's house.[18] As for Halswell, he was later criticized for his lack of careful concern 'in his owne and the Churches interest',[19] but by 1672 he can have felt little involvement in the affair, for he died a few days after the Chapter Act relating to his house was passed, and was succeeded by Thomas Sutton.

There can be little doubt that by this time the house was showing signs of neglect. Presumably a start had been made with the building work, and the brickwork on either side of the classical frontispiece of the north front of the house, with glazed headers and typically post-Restoration fenestration, may date from the time of Surveyor Taylor's operations; but the building was clearly incomplete, for in 1674 payment was made for 'a Load of peece straw for Dr Suttons house to stopp the windowes',[20] and in June it was ordered 'The windowes on the front of Dr Suttons howse to be glazed'.[21] The repairs were given a new impetus the following year, when the chimneys were repaired, new floorboards laid and planed, and at least part of the house re-roofed in slate.[22] At that time, however,

14. CA 1 Dec 1662.
15. As related in CA 16 Dec 1672.
16. CO 17 Aug 1668.
17. CA 17 Mar 1667/8.
18. CA 16 Dec 1672.
19. *Narrative*, para. 6.
20. TR 1673–4, fo. 8v.
21. CO 30 June 1674.
22. TR 1674–5, fo. 14.

the Chapter's building fund was seriously depleted as a result of Dr Gumble's 'illegal' building activities at No. 2.[23]

Few details have survived relating to work at No. 4 during the tenure of Sutton's successor in the house, who was probably Welbore Ellis, a conjecture justified by a reference to the pathway from No. 3 to 'Dr Ellis' corner'.[24] Ellis moved to No. 8, The Close on the death of Samuel Woodford, and was succeeded in No. 4 by Thomas Sayer, the first Prebendary whose name appears in connection with this house in the Wainscot Book.

The Wainscot Book provides a reasonably complete account of subsequent building operations at No. 4. The extensive works carried out for Dr Thomas Rivers, who lived in the house from 1710 to 1731, seem to have included rebuilding the south-east part of the dwelling and possibly adding a scullery at the west end; and the fine staircase, which is a feature of the house, was probably the one installed for Rivers at the Chapter's expense in 1711.[25] It is also possible that the north-east wing of the house was added during Rivers' tenure, or that of his successor, Alured Clarke; its present outline is shown on Godson's plan of 1750, but the brickwork shows evidence of rebuilding above first-floor level, and the wing may have been raised to its present three storeys later in the eighteenth century. This massive block is not one of the architectural glories of the Close.

The last Canon to appear in the Wainscot Book as an occupant of this house was George Pretyman, from whose tenure the earliest known plan of the building survives. On Pretyman's death in 1859 the 2nd Prebend was suspended, and the house was let to a series of lay tenants. In the 1860s the Dean and Chapter considered demolishing at least part of the building, and went so far as to obtain the necessary permission from the Ecclesiastical Commissioners;[26] but the house was selected three years later as the new Choir School premises.[27] The Cathedral Choir School remained at No. 4 until 1897 when it moved to a house outside the Close, in Colebrook Street: the Chapter had already negotiated a 99-year

23. See pp. 32–3.
24. CO 10 Dec 1697.
25. See Notes to Text, 94.
26. CA 25 Nov 1868. But CA 23 June 1870 has an apparently contradictory reference to letting 'The House late Mr Pretyman's for the Term of 5 years', and putting into effect the 'Order made at the November Chapter 1868 for pulling down No. 4'. It may be that the building had been divided into two parts at this time, of which only one, known as 'No. 4', was to be demolished.
27. CA 23 June 1871.

lease of the house to the County Council for use as a 'Judges' Lodgings' for the accommodation of judges on the south-western circuit. Extensive alterations and repairs took place, including the refacing of a large section of brickwork at the rear of the house and the addition of a new service wing at the west end of the building. Apart from the insertion of a floor above the kitchen, which is shown in 1896 plans as rising through two storeys,[28] the house has changed little since the end of the nineteenth century.

28. HRO 26M59 374-7.

NO. 4, THE CLOSE

19   The House over against the South Door of the Deanery.

The Charge of Dr Delanne.

Paid Dr Sayer	4	10	0
Expended more, as per bills	5	3	8
	9	13	8

30° Junii 1705
Examined & allowed by the Dean & Chapter,
In presence of Thomas Cranley, Chapter Clerk.

Dr Rivers Charge for the house late Dr Delanns.

Paid Mr Harris for the Thirds of the Wainscot of the said house[93]	7	5	3
Paid severall Bills[94] for work done by Butler and William Barefoot in & about the said house amounting to	43	18	3

30° Junii 1712
Examined & allowed by the Dean & Chapter,
In Presence of Thomas Cranley, Chapter Clerk.

June 29th 1712
I give to be standards for the Future the Irish Stich Hangings in the Chamber over the Kitchen,[95] and all the Locks and Latches upon all the Doors belonging to the house.
Thomas Rivers.

June 28th 1717
It was agreed by the Dean & Chapter that whereas the abovnamed Dr Rivers had layd out severall other sums of money over & above the sums above mentioned, that the said sums for his wainscott to be allowed him by his Successor shall be sixty pounds, his whole summe amounting to eighty pounds & upwards.[96]
In presence of Thomas Cranley, Chapter Clerk.

25   The Charges of the Reverend Dr Thomas Rivers, one of the Prebends of the Cathedrall Church of Winchester, for Wenscot in his house, to be repaid by his Successor, a fourth parte to be deducted.

Paid by Dr Rivers, the severall Bills following,[97] amounting to the summe of fifty one pound, three shillings and six pence (*vizt*):

Paid Roger Harris Esq for Dr Delanne[98] his thirds, seven pound five shillings & three pence	7	5	3
To Edward Butler for wainscoting the Dineing Roome[99]	20	0	0
To the same for Wainscoting the Kitchen-Chamber[100]	15	0	0
To the same for window shuts to the Brewhouse Chamber[101] window	1	13	9
To William Barfoot, Painter	4	14	6
To John White, Painter	2	10	0
In all	51	3	6

23ⁱⁱ Junii 1713
Examined & allowed by the Dean & Chapter,
Thomas Cranley, Chapter Clerk.

Standards to the said house.[102]

In the Brewhouse: the Pump.
In the Kitchen: the Bacon Rack, Two spitracks, One Iron bar in the Chimny, the Dressers & shelves.
In the Buttery next the Kitchen: the Dresser & shelves.
In the small beer Cellar: One hanging shelfe.
In the Buttery neere it: Two small Dresser tables & shelves.
In the Closett between the two Parlours: the Shelves.
In the Vault: the Stallders & shelves.

45   The Charges of Dr Alured Clarke in the prebendall house late Dr Rivers.

March 24th 1731/2
Then Received of the Reverend Dr Alured Clarke the summe of threescore pounds[103] on account of Wainscott Money due (according to the custome of the Church of Winchester) to me as Executrix to the late Dr Thomas Rivers, I say, received by me, Mary Rivers.[104] Examined *per* Charles Barton, Chapter Clerk.

Expended more by Dr Clarke for Wainscott, painting & varnishing, as by Bills produced & allowd att November Chapter 1732	37	18	0

Examined & allowd 9th December 1732,
In presence of Charles Barton, Chapter Clerk.

Expended more by Dr Clarke for Wainscott & Painting	2	18	0

Examined and allowed at Midsummer Chapter 1740,
In presence of W. Pescod, Chapter Clerk.

Expended more by Dr Clarke for Wainscott & Painting	2	14	10

Examined & allowed at November Chapter 1740,
In the presence of William Pescod, Chapter Clerk.

46 March 174[1/]2
The Reverend Mr Chancellor Hoadley paid to the Executor of Dr Alured Clarke the sum of seventy seven pounds, thirteen shillings and one penny halfpenny for the Wainscott money due upon the house late Dr Clarkes

	77	13	1½

Witness, William Pescod, Chapter Clerk.

December 1st 1744
Expended more by Mr Chancellor Hoadly for painting of New Wainscott[105]

	2	4	0

Witness, William Pescod, Chapter Clerk.

June 28th 1748
For the Wainscot in the Studys[106]

	7	7	0

Witness, William Pescod, Chapter Clerk.

December 10th 1748
Expended more, as by bill allowd

	2	17	6

December 11th 1752
Expended more, as by bills allowd
Witness, William Pescod, Chapter Clerk.

	2	6	5

December 10th 1753
Expended more, by bills allowde
Witness, William Pescod, Chapter Clerk.

	2	9	2
	94	17	2½

27th November 1760
Mr Sturges paid three fourths of the above sum to Dr Hoadly, being

	71	2	10½

Witness, John Dison, Chapter Clerk.

71   The House late Dr Hoadly, Now Mr Sturges's.

Brought forward	71	2	10½

November Chapter 1760
Expended more (& Allowed)   1   16   2
Witness, John Dison, Chapter Clerk.

November 1761
Expended more by Mr Sturges, as by bills pro-
duced & allowed   3   17   4

Standards in the above House received from Dr Hoadly by Mr
Sturges.[107]

In the Chamber over the Kitchen: Paper & Canvas Hangings.[108]
Nursery: Paper Hangings.
Brewhouse: The Pump.
Kitchen: The Bacon-rack, 2 Spit-racks, Dressers & Shelves, 1 Iron
    Bar in the Chimney.
Butler's Pantry[109]: Dresser & Shelves.
Pantry[110] next to the Small Beer Cellar: 2 small Dressers & Shelves.
Pantry near the Parlour[111]: Shelves.
Vault: Shelves.
Servants' Hall: The fixed Bench next to the Kitchen.
NB. The small-pannelled Wainscot taken down from the study,
when Mr Sturges put up his shelves there, has been employed in
repairing the Wainscot of the Hall & of other parts of the House.
Two large Doors of a Press which made part of it remain not
used.[112]
[The Wainscoting here is now replaced M.W.][i][113]

Expended more by Mr Sturges, as by several bills
produced & allowed   5   15   7
John Dison, Chapter Clerk.

November Chapter 1771
By Bills allowed   2   0   0¼
B. Burt, Deputy Chapter Clerk.

November Chapter 1774
Expended more (& allowed)   1   7   2½
W. Yalden, Chapter Clerk.   85   19   2¼

75   from Page 71, brought forward   85   19   2¼

1783 December 4th
Allowed for Bills for stuccoing Passage & Stair
case[114]   8   0   0

William Yalden, Chapter Clerk.

1793
Allowed for Messrs Hayes Bill, as per Allowance
of Chapter   4   4   10

1795, November Chapter
Allowed for Mr Hayes Bill   4   4   2
Ditto — Inglefield's —   0   15   3
Ditto — Lucas' —   0   18   0

                                £104   1 $5\frac{1}{4}$

Deduct $\frac{1}{4}$ 26   0 $4\frac{1}{4}$

                                £78   1   0

January 14th 1808
The above sum of £78:1:0 was paid by Mr North to [Mr *illegible*][d]
Dr Sturges Executors.
J. Ridding, Chapter Clerk.

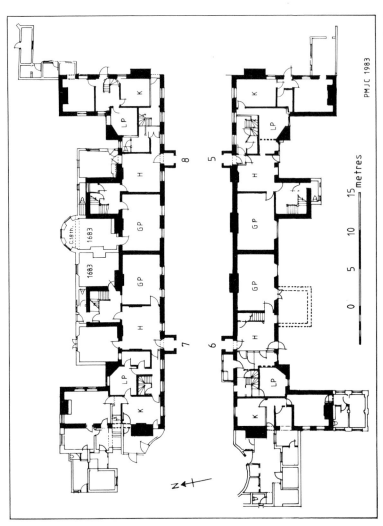

Fig. 16. Ground-floor plan, Nos. 5–8, The Close, Winchester. Original building (1661–2) shown in solid black. H: Hall. GP: Great Parlour. LP: Little Parlour. K: Kitchen.

Nos. 5-8, The Close

'THE NEW BRICK HOUSES'

One of the greatest problems facing the Chapter at the 'Return of the Church' in August 1660 was the shortage of accommodation for the Canons, each of whom, according to Statute, had to be provided with a dwelling within the Close wherein to fulfil his periods of statutory Residence. An early pre-Restoration Chapter Minute states that 'the Deanes howse & divers of the prebendes have beene in the late troubles utterly demolished',[1] and the *Narrative* of 1675 confirms that during the Commonwealth the houses of no fewer than seven of the Canons had been pulled down.[2] At their return, the Dean and Chapter immediately embarked upon a programme of building and repair. Fortunately, money was not lacking; a number of new leases of Dean and Chapter property were made in 1660, and the 'fines' relating to six such leases were immediately earmarked by the Chapter to be 'wholely imployed and bestowed in reparations of the Fabricke of the Cathedrall Church . . . and rebuilding of the howses belonging to the Deane & Prebendarys of the same Church and to no other use whatsoever'.[3]

Having decided to erect new houses in the place of those that had been demolished, the Chapter took the opportunity of rationalising the distribution of available land within the Close; for before the Commonwealth, when the houses tended to be huddled nearer together, in the neighbourhood of the former monastic buildings, an equitable distribution of land had been achieved by parcelling out 'garden plots', which often lay at some distance from the houses to which they belonged. Many of these outgardens lay in an area in the south-west corner of the Close, formerly known as the 'Great Garden';[4] it was here that the Dean and Chapter decided to build

1. CA 1 Dec 1662.
2. *Narrative*, para. 2.
3. MS, WCL, dated 14 Dec 1660.
4. CA 2 Dec 1663.

four new houses of brick, together with an access road (probably on the line of a former pathway to the outgardens) which would later be known by the name of 'Dome Alley'.

The work took place under the general supervision of William Fletcher, who may probably be identified with a former grocer and tenant of one of the Chapter's tenements on the site of what is now the garden at the corner of College Street and the approach to Kingsgate arch; he was also a Lay Vicar, became 'Sub-Sacrist' in 1642, and was appointed Clerk of Works at the Restoration, a post which he held until his death early in 1667. In view of the almost total absence of detailed building records from the early 1660s, it is particularly fortunate that an *Account Book* has survived, apparently in Fletcher's hand, itemising week by week the Chapter's expenditure on building materials and labour from November 1661 to November 1662; the period when the four 'brick houses' were under construction.[5] This valuable record shows that at least 97 workmen received payment for Chapter building projects during that year, though many of them were employed for only a few days during the height of the building season, which seems to have reached its peak in March-April 1662. The impression given is that of a small, permanent core of operatives assisted, as the need arose, by a large body of locally-recruited, casual labourers. Only five men worked for more than 100 days, seven worked between 50 and 100 days, fourteen worked between 25 and 50 days, and 43 worked for less than ten days.

Various details relating to the construction of the Dome Alley houses may be gleaned from this document. While William Fletcher was responsible for keeping the accounts, the joint foremen seem to have been Thomas George, one of an extensive family of masons employed both by the Cathedral and Winchester College, and John Clewer: they received several instalments of £150 a time for 'building the houses'.[6] The Purbeck Stone used for the footings was supplied by Samuel Tarry, although a certain amount of stone may have been re-used from the demolished buildings in the Close. The bricks were burned in the Close by Thomas Colly, 'the brickburner', using brick-earth bought from and delivered by Henry Crosswell. Thomas Colly appears to have had a house built for him, probably a temporary structure, within the Close or Churchyard; there is mention of a payment 'for straw and thatching the brick burners

5. MS, WCL. See also B. Carpenter Turner, 'The Return of the Church', *Record*, 29 (1960), pp.15-23.
6. Fo. 4v.

house'.[7] Colly did not, however, produce the 'specials' needed for the plinths and cornices of the houses, and these 'mould bricks', together with tiles (including 'crest tiles' for the ridges) were supplied by a number of outside manufacturers, notably Robert Cully (16,000 bricks, 69,900 tiles, 948 crests), Matthew Sidford (10,250 bricks, 19,600 tiles, 198 crests), John Berry (6,000 bricks, 5,000 tiles) and Ferman Goldfinch (400 bricks, 22,800 tiles). Timber was selected by Edward Collins, the Dean and Chapter's carpenter, and his assistant, Thomas Biggs. It was sawn in the Close by Richard Collis (who sawed no less than 10,880 feet of timber that year), assisted by John Barnard and John Cawt. The interior timberwork was painted by John Jerome, a renowned local painter, one of whose early assignments seems to have been to repaint the effigy of the 'Trusty Servant' at Winchester College,[8] and who was responsible for various works in the Cathedral at the Restoration, notably re-painting the vaulting above the Quire and painting the new choir-stall pinnacles.

The plan of the four houses (Fig. 16) is of interest as an early example of a type of architecture with which we are increasingly familiar today: a form of 'estate planning' with four dwellings constructed to a single basic pattern, the only difference being one of orientation. The two houses on each side of Dome Alley are mirror images of each other, symmetrically disposed about their party walls; but the lay-out of the houses is so conceived that the main rooms of all four houses enjoy a southerly aspect. Thus the main windows of the two houses on the north side of the Alley overlook the roadway: the houses on the south side present a blank wall to the road, and their main windows command a view of their gardens.

Each of the houses has had extra rooms added to it (No. 5 being the least altered), but they were originally of quite modest dimensions; just one room deep (4.6 m internally) and with a total length of about 23.5 m, this dimension including the width of a service wing, 5.2 × 10.7 m, returned at right-angles to the Alley at either end of each pair of houses. A small porch, with a closet above (removed in the case of Nos. 7 and 8 where the porches are now single-storeyed), gave into an entrance hall, more or less square on plan. Doors led out of the hall, on one side into a parlour and on the other into a passage to the service wing. At the rear of the

---

7. Fo. 14v.
8. Winchester College Muniments, quoted in T. F. Kirby, *Annals of Winchester College*, London, 1892, p.40: '*Hieronymo pictori pro reparanda effigie Dni. Fundatoris in aula et servi ante culinam*'.

house, with access from both the hall and the parlour, was a stair-turret. Three of these turrets have survived, complete with their staircases, which have interesting examples of flat balusters, similar to those of the staircase leading to the Cathedral Library. The stair-turret of No. 6 has vanished without trace; it was probably removed at the beginning of the nineteenth century, and is shown on Godson's map of 1750 but not on an architect's plan of *c.*1840.[9] A more modest staircase led up from the passage to the chambers on the first floor and ultimately to the servants' garrets, and down to the cellar beneath; while behind this stair-well, in the angle between the hall and the service wing, was a smaller room over the cellar, usually referred to in contemporary documents as the 'little parlour', complete with corner fireplace. This room seems to have served as a dining-parlour, conveniently situated near the kitchen. A little pantry between this parlour and the hall survived until recently in No. 7, and seems originally to have been common to every house except, perhaps, No. 8. The service wing consisted of a kitchen, a pantry or larder, a servants' hall and—apparently part of the main building—a brewhouse. The plan of the first storey echoed that of the ground floor, with bedrooms ('chambers') over each of the ground-floor rooms, while servants were presumably accommodated in the second-floor garrets.

Innovatory as the overall conception of the four houses may have been, the techniques employed in their construction were solidly traditional. The main walls, for example, owe their strength more to thickness and mass than to skill in brick-laying. The walls show a step-wise diminution in thickness: from 47 cm, up to the level of the first-floor wall-plate, to 33 cm, up to the main wall-plate at eaves level; and the brickwork of the gables is only one brick thick, 23 cm. The partition walls within this robust brick carcase are largely of timber-frame construction with brick infilling; this is especially clear in No. 5, where the framing of the service wing has been exposed as a decorative feature. The framing of the first floor is remarkable chiefly for the size of its principal timbers, explained no doubt by the ready availability of oak from the Chapter's estates; while the roof construction is typical of its period, with massive A-frame principal trusses, supporting butt-purlins into which the common rafters are tusk-tenoned. It is similar to that of the roof of the first phase of the Deanery rebuilding, dating from the early 1660s.

9. MS, WCL.

The main walls are laid in English Bond, like Phase I of the Deanery rebuilding (but unlike the Long Gallery, where Flemish Bond is used). In common with the Deanery, too, is the three-course *plate-bande* or string-course, at first-floor level. However, the detailing of the brickwork is in many ways more sophisticated, with its use of 'mould bricks' at the top of the plinth, its string-course at upper wall-plate level (two courses) and near the apices of the gables, and, above all, with its heavy, modillioned cornice, cut across rather aggressively by the barge-boards of the gables which are a feature of the Dome Alley houses. The former Cathedral Architect, T. D. Atkinson, was of the opinion that 'The gables were without question originally of curved outline', and published a suggested reconstruction in his book *Winchester Street Architecture*, showing the cornice as forming part of a continuous parapet.[10] While the suggested parapet is structurally just feasible, the Dutch gable hypothesis has been disproved during recent repairs, which revealed stub purlins tenoned to the outer face of the gable rafters. These purlins must be original, and their purpose was to support barge boards. If the gables had been of any other form than the present profile, the stub purlins would have protruded through the face of the gable by 12 cm. The existence of a continuous parapet is not justified by any surviving documents, nor by the general tendency towards structural and decorative diversity which the houses have shown since they were first built; and the notion is perhaps most tellingly dismissed by considerations of common sense: why, if a parapet originally existed, should it have been considered necessary to remove it at all?

Although many of the seventeenth-century windows were gradually replaced by more up-to-date 'sashes' in the eighteenth century, a small number of original windows have survived, lighting the service wings of the four houses. They owe their survival to the fact that their mullions and transoms, like their actual frames, are made of massive oak.

No description of the exterior of the Dome Alley houses would be complete without mention of the fine decorative leadwork, so skilfully restored in 1982–3. The rainwater heads are decorated alternately with the arms of the See of Winchester surmounted by a mitre, and a Tudor rose surmounted by a crown, with an added fig-leaf motif in each case. The straps attaching the down-pipes to the wall show the same fig-leaf motif and also the pomegranate. This use of Tudor motifs (the pomegranate was the device of

10. T. D. Atkinson, *Winchester Street Architecture*, Winchester, 1934.

Catherine of Aragon) led T. D. Atkinson to suggest that the leadwork 'evidently belonged to one of the destroyed buildings and [was] re-used here';[11] a conjecture which should perhaps not be accepted without further research.

The four new houses were allotted to their first occupants at an early date: many of them are referred to in the *Account Book of Wm. Fletcher* by the name of their intended occupant. Nos. 5–7 were assigned to three Canons whose prebendal residences had been 'totally demolished' during the Commonwealth; and the allocation seems to have been made in order of seniority (even though this was a matter of a few months' seniority at the most), with the house that eventually emerged as the most coveted, No. 7, being allotted to the most senior Canon, and the least attractive, No. 6, to the most junior. At this early date, the difference was simply one of the size of the respective gardens, and the distance of each house up the Alley. No. 8 was allotted to Dr Clarke, later Dean of Winchester, whose prebend-house, No. 11, had in fact been only 'partly demolished';[12] this move therefore entailed an interchange of the houses of the 10th and 12th Prebends. This was accomplished by means of an Act of Chapter dated February 1661/2, 'That Dr Clarke shal have the proffer of the 4th howse of the new build howses . . . and if he accept . . . then Doctor Dayrell shall have the howse that now Dr Clark hath'.[13] Such an interchange was, strictly speaking, contrary to Statute; but it appears that such moves were accepted while the complex housing arrangements were being reorganised.

The fact that the houses were allotted while still under construction allows many references in the *Account Book of Wm. Fletcher* to be identified with certainty. Some of these relate to items which would later appear in the Wainscot Book; such as the receipt, pinned into Fletcher's book, for the sum of £20 paid 'in part for wainscott to be put up in Dr Wafferers howse [No. 5]';[14] the payment to 'Henry Wickham for 49 yards of wainscott in Dr Prestons Howse at 2s 10d';[15] and the various entries relating to locks and catches in the four new houses. These two payments 'for wainscot' may indicate that Nos. 5 and 7 were built sooner than the other two houses, but are in a sense anomalous; for in December 1662 the Chapter

---

11. T. D. Atkinson, 'Winchester Cathedral Close', *Proceedings* XV (1941), p.22.
12. *Narrative*, para. 2.
13. CA 25 Feb 1661/2.
14. Fo. 22a.v (see Notes to Text, 115).
15. Fo. 23.

decreed 'That all manner of waynscott of the severall howses . . . shalbe made & finished at their owne proper charges respectively by the perticuler owner of every such howse . . .',[16] the Chapter Act which led to the creation of the Wainscot Book.[17]

The site of all new houses in the Close, and the various 'inter-changes' of sites that had taken place, were carefully set down in a Chapter Act of 2 December 1663, which was itself drawn up in response to an earlier Act in which it had been resolved that royal confirmation and approval of these changes should be obtained. It was the clause in this earlier Act relating to the cost and succession of wainscot which led to the creation of the Wainscot Book; and it is interesting to note that the four brick houses were among the first to be recorded under the new system. It is probably also true to say that these four houses show a greater rate of survival of fittings mentioned in the Wainscot Book than any other house in the Close.

16. CA 1 Dec 1662.
17. See p.xv.
18. CA 22 Sept 1663, which itself replaced the 'Deleted CA' of 1 Dec 1662.

NO. 5, THE CLOSE

17   First House [on the] Left Hand in Dome Alley.[115]

The Charges of Mr Abraham Markland, one of the prebends of the Cathedrall Church of Winchester, to be repayd by his Successor, according to the Custome of the Church.

August 14th 1682
Payd in money to Mr Seth Ward who was predecessor to the said Mr Markland,[116] for the Wainscot of his house (the fourth parte being deducted),
the summ of twenty four pounds twelve shillings,[117] as appeares by the acquittance under the
hand of the said Mr Ward   xxiiij £   xijs

This Bill hath been examined & approved of by the Vice-Dean & Chapter, 13th December 1687,
In præsentia Thomas Cranley, *Clerici Capituli.*

18   Standards in Mr Palmers house, late Dr Marklands, being the first house on the left hand of the four new houses.[118]

One Table, one Tressell with benches, 3 Shelves.
In the Hall: A forme now in one of the Garretts.[119]
In the Kitchen: One dresser & 4 Shelves round the wall, wooden racks for Spitts, The Iron bar in the Chimney.
In the Larder: one dresser or Table & Two Shelves [formerly in the Hall]^d
In the Wash house: A Leaden pumpe, the oven Lead.
In the Chamber over the Larder: A presse of fir & Cupboards over it.[120] A Fir Cupboard in the Wall by the Kitchen Stairs.[121]
In the Seller: Two greate Stands.

The Charges of Mr Samuel Palmer, one of the Prebends of the Cathedrall Church, to [be]^i repayd by his Successor, according to the Custome of the Church, for the house aforesaid.

Payd Dr Markland, who was predecessor to the
said Mr Palmer, in money for the Wainscot of
his house, a fourth part being deducted, as appeares by the acquittance under the hand of the
said Dr Markland, eighteen pounds nine shillings   xviij £   ixs

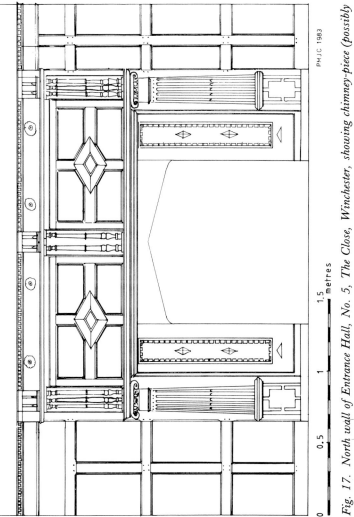

Fig. 17. North wall of Entrance Hall, No. 5, The Close, Winchester, showing chimney-piece (possibly re-used) and panelling dated 1661–2 (see Note to Text, 115).

Payd Robert Cole, the Joyner, & his Partner the
summ of seven pounds, nine & eleven pence for
Wainscot & Joyners worke done in the said house,
as by his Bill under the hand of the said Robert
Cole appeareth   vij £   ixs   xjd

This Bill was examined and approved [of]^i by the Vice-Dean and
Chapter, the 27th of June 1693,
In presence of me, Thomas Cranley, Chapter Clerke.

Memorandum. Paid by Mr Waple to Mr Palmer,
according to the custome of the Church, of which
a fourth part is to be deducted   19   9 $2\frac{1}{4}$

19   The Charge of Mr Lowth in the house late Mr Waples

Paid according to the Custome of the Church, a
fourth part being deducted   14   11   8

30° Junii 1705
Examined & allowed by the Dean & Chapter,
In Presence of me, Thomas Cranley, Chapter Clerk.

[The shelves in the Chamber over the Brewhouse & Servants Hall
Mr Lowth allowes as standards]^i

43   The Charges of Mr Lowth[122] in his prebendall house (being
the first house on the left hand in Dumb Alley) to be repaid by his
Successor &c.

Paid by Mr Lowth as in folio 19°   14   11   8

Expended more by him in painting, as per bill
produced & allowd att Midsummer Chapter 1730   3   0   10
                                                 17   12   6

This Account was examind & allowd, 29th June 1730,
In presence of Charles Barton, *Clerici Capituli.*

Paid by Dr Noyes to Mrs Lowth for the Wainscott
of the abovemencioned house (the 4th parte deduc-
ted)   13   4 $4\frac{1}{2}$

Examined & allowed att November Chapter 1732,
In presence of Charles Barton, Chapter Clerk.

February 7th 1740[/41]
Paid by Dr Maurice to Mr Whishaw[123]   7 8 6
Witness, William Pescod, Chapter Clerk.

Expended by Dr Maurice, as by bill allowd this
November Chapter 1741   4 3 0
Witness, William Pescod, Chapter Clerk
           11 11 6

December 1750
Paid by Mr Archdeacon Rolleston to the Executrix
of Dr Maurice (the fourth part Deducted)   8 13 7½
Witness, William Pescod, Chapter Clerk.

44 September 14th 1756
Paid by Dr Pyle to Mr Archdeacon Rolleston, the
fourth part deducted   6 10 2

7th March 1757   1 12 6
The above Sume paid by Mr Walton to Dr Pyle, 4 17 8
One fourth Deducted
Witness, John Dison.

[12th December 1759
Allowed Dr Pyle for Wainscott[124]   1 13 11][d]

12th December 1759
Allowed Dr Walton for First Painting, as by bill 0 4 1

28th June
Expended by Dr Walton, as by bills produced
and allowed by the Chapter   16 1 10½
Witness, John Dison, Chapter Clerk.

November Chapter 1760
Expended more (& Allowed)   3 10 6
Witness, John Dison, Chapter Clerk.

November 1761
Expended more by Dr Walton, as by bills pro-
duced & Allowd   15 7 0
Witness, John Dison, Chapter Clerk.

November Chapter 1763
Expended more by Dr Walton for painting, as by
bills produced & allowed—5:17:8½   0   5   0
Witness, John Dison, Chapter Clerk.

November Chapter 1765
Expended more by Dr Walton, as by bill produced
& allowd   9   16   3¼
Witness, J. Dison, Chapter Clerk.

                                                      50   2   4¾
                        the fourth part   12   10   7
                                                      37   11   9½

Which sum was paid by the Reverend Mr Ash to the Reverend Dr
Walton.
Witness, William Yalden, Chapter Clerk.

November Chapter 1776
Expended more by Mr Ashe, as by Bill produced
& allowed   1   0   5
Witness, William Yalden, Chapter Clerk.

                                                      38   12   2½

74   November Chapter 1778
Expended more, as by Bill produced & allowed   0   3   10
Witness, W. Yalden, Chapter Clerk.

                                                      38   16   0½
                        deduct the fourth part   9   14   0
                                                      29   2   0½

June 28th 1781
Which Sum was paid by Mr Woodford to the Executor of the late
Mr Ashe.
William Yalden, Chapter Clerk.

1783, December 4th
Expended for Chimney Piece   0   11   6
Mr Hayes's Bill for Doors & new Wainscott   1   16   11
Ditto for wainscot work & Shutters about new
sashes[125]   4   7   8
William Yalden.

Expended more for Wainscot Work & Shutters, as by Mr Hayes' Bill allowed November Chapter 1788	6	13	0
Expended more for Chimney piece, as per Mr Walldin's Bill allowed at same time	1	3	8½

J. Ridding, Chapter Clerk.

	£43	15	8
Deduct ¼ part	10	16	11
	£32	16	9

August 20th 1798
The above sum of £32:16:9 was paid by Mr Iremonger to Mr Woodford.

J. Ridding.

NO. 6, THE CLOSE

3 Uppermost House on the Left Hand of Dome Alley.[126]

March the 15th 1661[/2]
Received of Dr Bradshaw for the Wainscot of his little parlour & the Kitchin Chamber, fourteen poundes fower shillings six pence, in full, by me, Thomas Fawker.

The little parlour 47 yards at two & six pence the yard,[127] & the Chimney peice at thirty shillings. Thomas Fawker.

The money paid in the presence of William Fletcher,
                          Thomas Colpes.

March the 29th 1662
Received of Dr Bradshaw for Wainscott in the great Parlour, thirteene poundes five shillings.
For the Wainscott of the Hall, five poundes seaventeen shillings.
For the Chimney peice in the great parlour, two poundes five shillings.
For the bench in the Hall, eight shillings.[128]
For the Chimney peice in the Hall, one pounds five shillings, all which summes were received the day and yeare above written, by me, Francis Spender.

In the presence of William Fletcher,
                          James Petre, his marke.

May the 9th 1662
Received of Dr Bradshaw for the Wainscott of the Chambers over the great parlour and the hall, and setting it upp, twenty one poundes by me, Francis Spender.

In the presence of George Nicholas,
                          Thomas Colpus.

Summ totall of all the wainscot   58   4   0

8ᵛᵒ Decembris Anno Domini 1673
This bill is approved of by the Deane & Chapter and by their
Order entred accordingly into this wainscott booke.[129]
per me John Harfell *Clericum Capituli.*

4 The Charges of Dr Francis Morley, one of the Prebends of the
Cathedrall Church of Winchester, according to the Custom of the
Church, to be payd by his successor.

December 5th 1690
Paid by the said Dr Morley to Mrs Elizabeth
Hawkins,[130] Executrix of the Will of Dr Bradshaw,
Deceased, the summe of three & fourty pounds &
Thirteen Shillings for the Wainscott in the house
belonging to the Prebendary of the said Dr Brad-
shaw, deceased, one fourth part being deducted,
as appears by Acquittance   43   13   0

Standards belonging to the Church in Dr Morleys house.

In the Pantry: One Table, one Trussell with Benches.
In the Kitchin: Two dressers & all Shelves therein, wooden Racks
    for Spitts & the Iron barr in the Kitchin Chimney, & cupboards
    by the Chimney.
In the Larder: Five shelves & the dresser.
In the Wash house: the Leaden pump, the Iron barr in the
    Chimney, & the oven lead.
In the little Closett over the Porch[131]: the Shelves there.
In the Chamber over the Larder: A Presse of Fir & cupboard over
    it. A Firr cupboard in the Wall by the Kitchin Stairs.
In the Cellar: Two Great Stands.
In the Brewhouse: A Table formerly in the Hall.

9° Decembris 1690
Examined & allowed by Vice-Dean & Chapter,
In the presence of Thomas Cranley, Chapter Clerk.

The Charges of Mr Samuel Mews, one of the Prebendaries of the
Cathedrall Church of Winchester, to be payd by his Successor,
according to the Custome of the Church.

Payd to the widdow of Dr Morly the summ of
thirty two pounds fourteen shillings, a fourth part
being deducted   32   14   0

Examined & allowed by the Chapter, 12th April 1697
Thomas Cranley.

21 The Charges of Dr Charles Woodrofe for the house late Mr
Mews, to be repaid by his Successor, a fourth part being deducted.

Payd by the said Dr Woodrofe to Sir Peter Mews,
Executor of Mr Mews, late Prebendary, for the
wainscot of his house, a fourth part being deducted[132]   xxiiij £   xs   vjd

Out of which a fourth part being deducted, there
remains to be paid to Dr Woodrofe by his succes-
sor[133] at his leaving the said house   xviij £   vijs   xd   *ob.*

23io Junii 1715
Allowed & approved of by the Dean & Chapter,
In presence of Thomas Cranley, Chapter Clerk.

Februarii 19th 1724/5
Received then of the Reverend Mr Crosse for the
use of Mr Alsop, thirteen pounds & tenn shillings,
being in full for the Wainscott of the house in
which he succeeds him. I say, received by me,
John Cooke[134]   13   10   0

November 26th 1728
Received of the Reverend Dr Naylor, by the
hands of the Reverend Mr Sturges, tenn pounds
two shillings & sixpence, in full for the Wainscott
of the house in which he succeeded Dr Crosse. I
say, received for the use of the said Dr Crosse,
by me, Thomas Rivers[135]   10   2   6

November 27th 1728
Received then of Mr Morgan, by the hands of
Dr Hayley, the summe of seven pounds eleven
shillings & tenn pence halfpenny in full for the
wainscott money due upon the House in which
he succeeded Dr Naylor. Received, for Dr Naylors
use, by me, J. Sturges   7   11 $10\frac{1}{2}$

November 27th 1728
Examined & Allowd by the Dean and Chapter
In presence of Charles Barton, Chapter Clerk.

37   The Charges of Dr Hayley for Wainscott in the house late Mr Morgans (being the Uppermost house on the left hand in Dumb Alley), to be repaid by his successor (a fourth parte being deducted).

Paid by Dr Hayley to Mr Morgan for Wainscott in the Abovemencioned house (the fourth parte being deducted), the summe of Five pounds thirteen shillings & tenn pence half penny	5	13	10½

This Accompt was examined and approved by the Chapter, June 30th 1729,
In presence of Charles Barton, Chapter Clerk.

Paid by Mr Inett to Dr Hayley for the Wainscott of the house abovemencioned (the fourth parte being deducted), Four pounds five Shillings & fourpence	4	5	4

Examined & allowd (att November Chapter, the 9th December 1732),
in presence of Charles Barton, Chapter Clerk.

[Paid by Mr Shipley to Mr [*illegible*] the fourth parte deducted	3	4	0]^{d}
Paid by Mr Shipley to Mr Inett, the fourth part deducted Witness, William Pescod, Chapter Clerk.	3	4	0

December 1746 Expended by Mr Shipley for Wainscott & Painting, as by bill allowed	1	1	6
	4	5	6

38 Brought over	4	5	6
December 1747 Expended by Mr Shipley for Wainscott etc, as by bills allowd	4	10	11
December 11th 1749 Expended more by Mr Shipley for Painting, Wainscott & Chimney Peice, as by bills allowd	7	17	0

December 12th 1754

	£	s	d
Expended more by Dr Shipley, and bills allowd	5	10	4
	22	3	9
Deduct one fourth	5	10	$11\frac{1}{4}$
Remains, to be paid to Dr Shipley	16	12	$9\frac{3}{4}$

Paid by Mr Walton[136] to Dr Shipley the above sume

	16	12	$9\frac{3}{4}$
Deduct one fourth	4	3	$2\frac{1}{2}$
Remains, to be paid by Dr Ayscough	12	9	$7\frac{1}{4}$

July 10th 1758

Paid to Dr Ayscough *per* Dr Balguey	9	2	6

12th December 1759

Expended by Dr Balguy & allowed	7	18	0
	17	0	6
Remains, to be paid by Mr Sturges to Dr Balguy	12	15	$4\frac{1}{2}$

First painting Omitted, being 3 Quarters of 8s 9d[137]	0	6	2
Mr Sturges to pay to Dr Balguy	13	1	$6\frac{1}{2}$

27th November 1760

Mr Sturges paid the above sum to Dr Balguy.

Mr Ash paid Mr Sturges three fourths of the above sum, being	9	16	0

November Chapter 1760

Expended more by Mr Ash, as by bills produced & allowed	6	2	6

Witness, J. Dison, Chapter Clerk.

November Chapter, 1762

Expended more by Mr Ashe, as by bills produced & allowed	0	7	1

Witness, John Dison, Chapter Clerk.

	16	4	$7\frac{1}{2}$

Mr Mulso is to pay Mr Ash three fourths, being	12	4	$4\frac{1}{2}$

Witness, W. Yalden, Deputy Chapter Clerk.

73 February 2nd 1771
Received of Mr Mulso, by the hand of Mr Buller, the Sum of
Twelve pounds & four shillings. R. Ashe.

$\frac{3}{4}$th of	12	4	0
is	9	3	0

Memorandum, 10th March 1771.
The above sum of Nine pounds and three shillings was paid by the
Reverend Mr Nott to the Reverend Mr Mulso by the Hands of
Mr Buller.
Witness, William Yalden, Deputy Chapter Clerk.

December 14th 1771

$\frac{3}{4}$th of £9:3:0 is	6	17	0

The above Sum of six pounds seventeen Shillings was paid by the
Reverend Mr Rennell to the Reverend Mr Nott by the hands of
[the Reverend][i] Mr Buller.
Witness, B. Burt, Deputy Chapter Clerk.

November Chapter 1775

Expended more by Mr Rennell, as by Bills produced and allowed	6	16	$2\frac{1}{2}$

Witness, William Yalden, Chapter Clerk.

November Chapter 1776

Expended more by Mr Rennell, as by Bill produced and allowed	0	8	6

Witness, William Yalden, Chapter Clerk.

	14	1	$8\frac{1}{4}$
Deduct one fourth	3	10	5
Paid by Mr Hare to Mr Rennell[138]	10	11	$3\frac{1}{2}$
Deduct one fourth	2	12	$9\frac{3}{4}$

Midsummer Chapter 1777

Paid by the Bishop of Oxford[139] to Mr Hare	7	18	$5\frac{3}{4}$

Witness, W. Yalden, Chapter Clerk.

NO. 7, THE CLOSE

12   The Uppermost House on the Right Hand in Dome Alley.[140]

The charges of William Hawkins, Doctor of Divinity, one of the Prebendaries of the Cathedrall Church of Winchester, to be repayed by his Successor, according to the Custome of the Church.

Payd in money to Mrs Frances Preston,[141] widow, relict of Dr Nicholas Preston who was predecessor to the sayd William Hawkins (the 4th parte of the first price being abated), for his wainscott in his dwelling howse, the summ of Twenty seaven pounds twelve shillings fowerpence halfpenny, as appeares by bills & acquitance	27	12	4½

This bill hath been examined and approved of by Mr Deane and the Chapter, 28th day of November, *Anno Domini* 1676.[142]
In præsentia John Harfell, *Notarii Publici, Clerici Capituli.*

18th December 1685
A Note under Robert Coles hand.[143]
This is to testify that I, Robert Cole, together with my partner, Thomas Deverell, have received of Dr William Hawkins eleaven pounds for the wainscot of his new Parlour[144] by the yard, we finding also the materialls, & also that I have received of him, for the wainscoting the Roome over it,[145] as far as it is soe wainscoted, £2 14s 10d for worke, & that the materialls of Deale therein used was [*deletion*] valuable at twenty shillings, which comes in all to the summ of fourteen pounds fourteen shillings & tenn pence, as appeares by the originall Acquittance   xiiij £ xiiijs xd.

This Bill hath been examined & approved of by the Vice-Dean & Chapter, 13th December 1687.
In præsentia Thomas Cranley, *Clerici Capituli.*

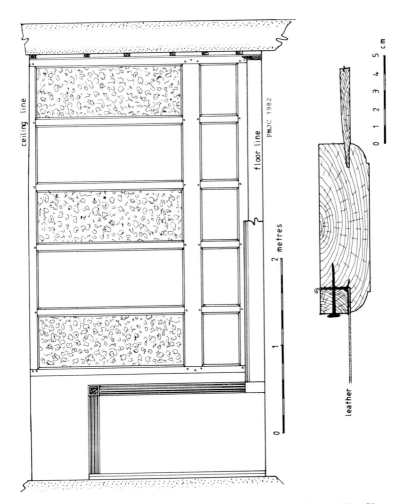

Fig. 18. West wall of first-floor room, 1683 extension, No. 7, The Close, Winchester, showing panelling, probably c.1730 (see Note to Text, 145). Leather panels evidenced by surviving fragments round edges of frames.

23ⁱⁱ Junii 1713

Payd by Dr West, who succeeded Dr Markland[146]
in the house abovesaid, xxiij £ xvjs vjd, a
fourth part to be repaid by his successor, according
to custom
                                                    xxiij £   xvjs   vjd.

Allowed & approved by the Dean & Chapter.
T. Cranley.

27 The Charges of Mr John Cooke for Wainscott in his prebendall
house.[147]

January 9th 1720/1

Received of the Reverend Mr John Cooke, successor to the late
Reverend Mr Spratt in his prebendall house att Winchester, thirteen
pounds seven shillings & nine pence,[148] in full of Wainscott money,
by the order & for the use of Mrs Frances Spratt, by me, Thomas
Rivers.

Received att the same time five pounds tenn shillings & three pence
for Additionall Wainscott sett upp by Mr Stone, by me, Thomas
Rivers.[149]

Paid more by Mr Cooke [more]ᵈ for painting and Addicionall
Charges in the house abovemencioned, nine pounds, as per bills
produced & allowed by Chapter, the 10th December 1724.
Ita Testor, Charles Barton, *Clericus Capituli.*

February 26th 1725/6.

Paid by Mr Cooke to John Earle, Carpenter, for 40 yards of
Wainscott in the Hall Chamber & Hall,[150] & for Window Shutts,
six pounds.

December 19th 1726

Paid also by him to Thomas Broadway, painter, for painters work,
three pounds five shillings and one penny.

The above mencioned [bills]ⁱ were produced and allowd att a
Chapter holden 18th March 1726/7,
In presence of Charles Barton, Chapter Clerk.

December 11th 1731

Expended more by Mr Cooke for Wainscott and painting, as per
bills produced & allowd att November Chapter 1731, thirteen
pounds.

Examined and allowd by the Chapter the 11th December 1731,
In presence of Charles Barton, Chapter Clerk.

53   The Charges of Mr John Cook for Wainscott in his Prebendal
house.[151]

December 3rd 1737
Expended by Mr Cooke for two moveable Win-
dow shutters for the Chamber over the Hall   0   11   0

Examined and allowd by the Chapter, 3rd December 1737
In presence of William Pescod, Chapter Clerk.

December 8th 1738
For Seven yards of New Wainscott and repairs of
Wainscott in the Drawing roome   1   4   6

Examined and allowd by the Chapter, 8th December 1738.
Witness, William Pescod, Chapter Clerk.

December 7th 1739
Expended more for the New Wainscott and Paint-
ing, as by bills produced and allowd   1   16   4

The Great Seat in Mr Cooks garden is allowd to be a Standard.
William Pescod, Chapter Clerk.

Expended more by Mr Cook, as by bill allowd
this November Chapter 1741   0   17   6
Witness, William Pescod, Chapter Clerk.

December 4th 1742
Expended more by Mr Cook for Wainscott, as
by bill allowd   0   8   6
Witness, William Pescod, Chapter Clerk.

54   December 10th 1744
Dr Cheyney[152] paid the Executrix of Mr Cook,[153]
one fourth being [deducted] from the summe of
£54:19:11   41   5   8½
Witness, William Pescod, Chapter Clerk.

November 29th 1746
Expended more by Dr Cheyney for Wainscott
& Painting, as by bills allowd and produced,

November Chapter 1746	1	3	0
Witness, William Pescod, Chapter Clerk.			
	42	8	8½
Deduct one fourth	11	2	2
Remains	31	6	6

Which Sume was paid by Mr Whisshaw to Dr Cheyney.

December 1748			
Expended more by Mr Whishaw	0	17	0

December 1750			
Expended more by Mr Whishaw for Wainscott &			
New Painting	3	19	7½
Witness, William Pescod, Chapter Clerk.			

December 1751			
Expended more by Mr Whishaw for a Chimney			
[Pece]^d Slabb and a Corner Cupboard	3	18	0
Witness, William Pescod, Chapter Clerk.			

December 10th 1753			
Expended more by Mr Whishaw, by bill allowd	4	1	8

December 12th 1754			
Expended more by Mr Whishaw, by bills Allowed	8	18	3
Witness, John Dison.			

65　Brought on from folio 54.			
Mr Whishaws House	51	1	0½

7th March 1757			
Expended more, as by bills allowed	3	1	6
	54	2	6½
Deduct One fourth	13	10	7½
Remains	40	11	11

Which Sum was paid by [Mr Pyle to]^d Dr Shipley [now Dean, at Midsummer Chapter 1761]^d to the Executors of Mr Whishaw.[154]

Deduct One fourth of	40	11	11
Being	10	3	0
Remains	30	9	0

	£	s	d
Which sum of 30£ 9s 0d was paid by Mr Pyle[155] to Dr Shipley, now Dean, at Midsummer Chapter 1761	30	9	0
1761 Expended by Mr Pyle for first painting, as by bill produced & allowed Witness, J. Dison, Chapter Clerk.	1	19	0
November 1764 Expended more by Mr Pyle, as by Bill produced & allowed Witness, J. Dison, Chapter Clerk.	14	1	0
November 1773 Expended more by Mr Pyle, as by Bill produced & allowed Witness, William Yalden, Chapter Clerk.	2	2	0

	48	11	0
Deduct ¼	12	2	9
	£36	8	3

The above Sum of £36   8s   3d was paid by Dr Hook to Mr Pyle's Executors.

	9	0	0
	£27	0	0

The said sum of £27 was paid to Dr Hook by Mr F. Iremonger.

Deduct fourth	6	15	0
Mr C. North to Dr Hook[156]	20	5	0

NO. 8, THE CLOSE

5   First House on the Right Hand in Dome Alley.

Goods in Mr Paynes howse, February the twenty sixth *Anno Domini* 1665[/6] (*Stylo Angliæ*):[157]

In the Pantry: One table there on tressells with benches.
In the Hall: A firr table, a forme & a bench.
In the Kitchin: the [2][i] dressers and all shelves herein, Woodden racks for spitts, and the yron-barr in the kitchin chymney, & An ovenlead.
In the Larder: Five shelves & the dresser.
In the Wash-howse: The leadne pump, the yron barr in the Chymney, And the ovenlead.
In the little Clossett over the doore: the shelves there.
In the Chamber over the larder: A presse of firr & a cupbord over it, A firr cupbord in the wall by the kitchin stayres.
In the Seller: Two great stands.

These are upon the account of the Church.
Attested by Walter Syms.

April the 13th 1666.
Layd forth by the said Mr William Payne as followeth:[158]

For the Oaken wainscott in the great Parlour being eightie eight yards, to Thomas Dalley, Joyner	11	14	4

December the 22th 1666

For the deale wainscott in the little parlour[159] being 56 yards, to Nicholas Bates, Joyner	8	13	0
[For a copper furnace, bought of Cropp, brasier	4	12	0
For setting it upp	0	12	6
The Cover of the furnace	0	4	0

86

The Oaken wainscott	[*illegible*][160]
The deale wainscott	[*illegible*][161]
The furnace	[*illegible*][162]

6 The partition in the gallery for the study,[163]
with severall shuts & shelves   2   10   0
The Rowler in the garden   0   16   0][d164]

Dr Payne further left as a standard One Bech Table, as also The
Shelves in the study [*deletion*] by him built.
Samuel Woodforde.

The Charges of Dr Samuel Woodford, one of the Prebends of the
Cathedrall Church of Winchester, to be repayd by his Successor,
according to the Custome of the Church.

Payd to the Executor of Dr William Payne,[165]
who was predecessor to the said Dr Woodford,
for the wainscot of his house (the 4th part being
deducted) the summ of fifteen pounds one shilling
& tenn pence[166]   xv £   js   xd

Examined & allowed by the Vice-Dean & Chapter,
In the presence of Thomas Cranley, Chapter Clerke.

The Charges of Dr Welbore Ellis, one of the prebends of the
Cathedrall Church of Winchester, to be paid by his successor,
according to the Custome of the Church.

Payd to the Executors of Dr Woodford, who was
predecessor to the said Dr Ellis, for the wainscott
of his house, the 4th parte being deducted, the
sume of Eleaven pounds fifteen shillings and Eleaven pence halfpenny[167]   11   15   11½

November 6th 1713[168]
Received then of Captain Brewer the summe of six pounds twelve
shillings & Nine pence in full for the Arrear of Wainscott due for
the house that is now Dr Hammonds in the Close of Winchester,
according to the Register of the Chapter Clerk, I say, received *per
me*
Thomas Cheyney.[169]

31 The Charges of Dr Manwaring Hammond, one of the prebendaries of the Cathedrall Church of Winton in his prebendall house

(being the first house on the right hand in Dumb Ally), to be repaid according to the custome of the Church.

The Carpenters bill for 93 yards of Wainscott att 2s 6d per yard[170]	11	12	6
The painters bill	2	12	4
	14	4	10

Examined & approved by the Chapter, December 12th 1728, In presence of Charles Barton, Chapter Clerk.

Paid more by Dr Hammond on Account of Wainscott in this house as in folio 6[171]	6	12	9

December 27th 1731
Received then of Mr Barton[172] the summe of Fifteen pounds thirteen shillings two pence farthing for wainscott money due according to the Custome of the Chapter to the House late Dr Hamonds

per me Elizabeth Brewer.	15	13	$2\frac{1}{4}$

December 1733
Paid by Mr Bourne to Dr Barton for the Wainscott of the above-mencioned House (a 4th parte deducted)

	11	14	$10\frac{1}{2}$

Expended more by Mr Bourne for Wainscott & painting as by bills produced & allowd at June Chapter 1734
Charles Barton, Chapter Clerk.

	0	19	6

59 Brought over from Folio 31	12	14	$4\frac{1}{2}$

Expended more by Mr Bourne as by bills allowd for Wainscott & Painting, November Chapter 1740

	2	18	$11\frac{1}{2}$
	15	13	4

December 5th 1740
Paid by Dr Cheyney to Mr Bourne,[173] one fourth deducted
Witness, William Pescod, Chapter Clerk.

	11	15	0

December 10th 1744
Paid by Mr Rolleston to Dr Cheyney, one fourth
deducted   8   16   3
W. Pescod, Chapter Clerk.

Paid by Mr Redding[174] to Mr Rolleston, one
fourth part deducted   6   4   0¾

Expended by Mr Redding, as by bill allowd
December 10th 1745   12   8   2½
William Pescod, Chapter Clerk.

Expended more by Mr Ridding for New Painting
as by bill allowd November 25th 1746   2   10   6
William Pescod, Chapter Clerk.

December 1748
Expended more, by bill allowd   0   9   6

December 1750
Expended more by Mr Ridding in new Painting   2   17   0
Witness, William Pescod, Chapter Clerk.

December 10th 1752
Expended more by Mr Ridding   0   8   6
                                                            ────────────
                                                            24   17   9¼

60 December 12th 1754
Expended more by Mr Ridding, by bills allow'd   0   13   3
Witness, John Dison.

November 1761
Expended more by Mr Ridding, as by bills pro-
duced & allowed   8   16   8½
Witness, John Dison, Chapter Clerk.
                                                           ─────────────
                                                           34   7   8¾
          Deduct One fourth, being   8   11   6
                                                           ─────────────
                                                           25   16   2

Which Sum was Paid by Sir Peter Rivers[175] to the Administratrix
of Mr Ridding.
Witness, John Dison, Chapter Clerk.

November 1766
Expended by Sir Peter Rivers, as by bills produced
and Allowed   36   8   0
John Dison, Chapter Clerk.

November 1771
Expended more by Sir Peter Rivers, as by Bills
allowed   1   5   0
Witness, William Yalden, Chapter Clerk.

November 1773
Expended more by Sir Peter Rivers, as by Bills
allowed   8   15   0
Witness, William Yalden, Chapter Clerk.

November 1774
Expended more by Sir Peter Rivers, as by Bills
allowed   11   2   0
Witness, William Yalden, Chapter Clerk.

November 1775
Expended more by Sir Peter Rivers, as by Bills
allowed   6   7   6
Witness, William Yalden, Chapter Clerk.

November 1777
Expended more by Sir Peter Rivers, as by Bills
allowed   7   0   0
Witness, William Yalden, Chapter Clerk.
                                                    _____
                                                    96   13   8

79   Brought from Page 60   96   13   8

November Chapter 1779
Expended by Sir Peter Rivers Gay, Bart., as by
Bill produced for Painting   0   16   6

Ditto by Mr Biden's Bill   9   9   1

December 1781
Ditto by Mr Walldin's Bill   6   6   10
Ditto by Mr Hayes' Bill   39   0   0
Ditto by Mr Willis' Bill   1   5   8

May 1788
Ditto by Mr Hayes' Bill   2   10   10

October 1788
Ditto by Mr Cave's Bill
J. Ridding, Chapter Clerk.

	0	6	6

	156	9	1
Deduct one fourth	39	2	$3\frac{1}{4}$
Leaving the Balance of	£117	6	$9\frac{3}{4}$

Which sum was paid by Dr Warton to Lady Rivers.
M. Rivers
Witness, J. Ridding, Chapter Clerk.

Brought down	117	6	$9\frac{3}{4}$
Deduct	29	6	$11\frac{3}{4}$
$\frac{1}{4}$ [of]	£87	19	0
	21	19	11
	£65	19	11

November Chapter 1800
The above Sum was paid by the Reverend J. Garnett to the Account
of Dr Warton's [Executors]^d Administrators at Messrs Waller.
J. Ridding, Chapter Clerk.

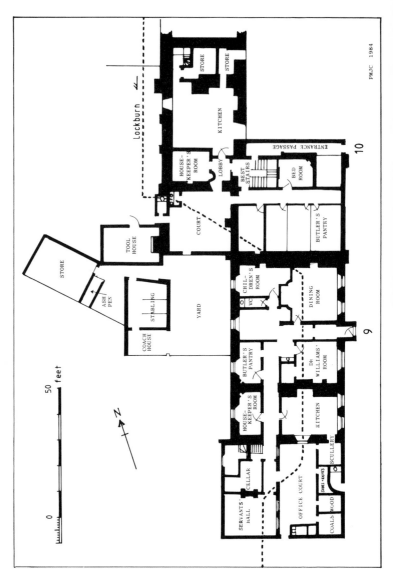

Fig. 19. Ground-floor plan of Nos. 9 and 10, The Close, Winchester, based on two plans dating from 1840–44 (MSS, WCL). Rooms labelled as they appear on the original plans. Details of doors and windows largely conjectural. Course of 'Lockburn' as depicted in old plans; though it may, more logically, pass below the ground-floor W.C. of No. 9.

No. 9, The Close

This imposing house, built of blocks of Quarr and Binstead stone, much of which may have been re-used, dates from 1661–4 when it was erected for William Lewis,[1] one of seven Canons who returned to the Close at the Restoration, the other five having died during the Commonwealth. Lewis' original house had been taken down by 1646 and does not therefore figure in the *Parliamentary Survey* of 1649 except with regard to the adjoining property, Mr Crooke's,[2] which was described as including four rooms which had been 'parte of Dr Lewis his howse, the rest fallen downe'. As Mr Crooke's house was later demolished in its turn, it is not possible to identify the exact location of Dr Lewis'. The house probably lay approximately at the south end of the present No. 9 and, as the *Survey* makes clear, had a garden to the east, bounded by the 'Cloysters'. The surveyors seem here to have meant the 'Little Cloister' (see pp. 49–50 and Fig. 1), rather than the monastic cloister garth. This last was often referred to in earlier documents as the 'Great Cloister', but is described in the *Survey* merely as 'a faire greene Court leading to the Cathedrall Church'. Virtually no evidence has survived as to what Lewis' house was like. It was retiled in 1634 and 1637,[3] and seems to have been built in stone, which, when the building was demolished, was used in repairs at the Castle Hall. A contemporary document, dated Feb—Sept 1646, mentions a payment of 14s. for 'the Carridge of 12 load of stone from Doctor Lewses'.[4]

The main evidence that Dr Lewis' house was rebuilt more or less on its former site (though probably incorporating the site, and possibly even the remains of the west wall, of Mr Crooke's) is a

1. 8th Prebend, 1627–64.
2. 9th Prebend, 1640–45.
3. TR 1633–4 (7,000 tiles used) and 1636–7, p.6.
4. B. Lib. Add. MS 24861, fo. 7.

Chapter Act of December 1661 by which the Chapter sought to exercise tighter control over the somewhat anarchical rebuilding programme which had started in the Close. In accordance with the terms of this Act, Dr Lewis appointed 'Anthony Gosling, Clerke, to Oversee and Order in all things in repayring & building the Prebendes howse & edifices belonging to him the saide William Lewis in the Close'.[5] There is no evidence to suggest that Lewis' house was rebuilt on a new site; furthermore it is generally true that each 'new' prebendal house built at the Restoration was erected either on the site of the former house or in one of the outgardens thereunto belonging; and such changes of site that did occur were defined by a number of Chapter Acts. It is true that the site of Dr Lewis' 'New Stone House' was defined by an Act of 2 Dec 1663, but this Act seems to be more concerned with the changed boundaries of his gardens than with an entirely new site for his house.

Apart from his appointment as 'Surveyor', the name of Anthony Gosling appears no more in Chapter documents, and it may well be that the actual building of the house was entrusted to the Clerk of Works, William Fletcher. Certainly his surviving *Account Book* records payments of £600 in approximately six-weekly instalments between 9 May and 12 Nov 1662 'for Dr Lewis' building', and the Treasurer's Roll of 1662–3 records the payment of a further £250 in four instalments 'To Mr Fletcher towards Dr Lewis his building'. The work appears to have been completed by the end of 1664, and a final Treasurer's entry, dated 10 Dec 1664, notes the sum of £3 paid 'To Jerome the Painter for arreares about Dr Lewes his howse'.[6]

William Lewis resigned his Prebend in 1664 and died three years later. He was succeeded by Henry Beeston, but though the *Narrative* of 1675 refers to 'the house of Dr Lewis now in the possession of Dr Beeston', the few references to the house in contemporary Cathedral documents add little to our knowledge of the building during that period. The next two inhabitants in the table of occupants, Dr Harris and Dr Eyre, are conjectural.

No. 9 appears to have been entered in the Wainscot Book for the first time in 1710, with the arrival of Dr Layfield in the house.[7] It must be admitted that the entries are the least interesting of any house in the Close. Furthermore, the building has been subject to

5. CA 7 Dec 1661.
6. TR 1664–5, fo. 3v.
7. 4th Prebend, 1687–1715.

considerable changes during the present century, owing to its use from 1926 to 1931 as the Cathedral School, and subsequently as the Diocesan Offices, and few of the original internal fittings seem to have survived.

NO. 9, THE CLOSE

23 The House over against the West side of the Deanery.

The Charges of Dr Charles Layfeild,[176] One of the prebends of the Cathedrall Church of Winchester, to be repayd by his Successor.

For part of the Wainscott in the Little parlor	3	12	0
For an Addition to it and the Carpenters Worke	9	14	0
For Wainscotting the Study	3	10	0
	16	16	0

This Bill hath been examined & approved by the Dean and Chapter, June 27th 1710,
In Presence of Thomas Cranley, Chapter Clerke.

Paid by Mr Roger Harris[177] to Dr Layfeild on Dr Delannes coming to this house	12	12	0
More expended by Mr Harris for New Wainscott	5	2	0
total	17	14	0
Paid by Dr Crosse to Mrs Harris as Per receipt produced	13	5	6

Examined & approved by the Chapter, 12th December 1728, In presence of Charles Barton, Chapter Clerk.

Paid by Dr Crosse to Thomas Broadway for painters work etc	1	13	9
Paid more by him to Walter Goodsall for Joyners work & materialls etc	5	12	2

Examined & allowd by the Dean & Chapter, the 28th June 1729. Charles Barton, Chapter Clerk.

47 The Charges of Dr Hayley in his prebendall house (late belonging to Dr Crosse) to be repaied by his Successor, according to the Custome of the Church.

July 1st 1732
Received then of Dr Hayley the summe of Fifteen pounds eight shillings and sixpence three farthings in full for the Wainscott money due upon the house of the late Dr Cross, received for the use of Mrs Cross by me, J. Sturges[178]   15   8   6¾

Examined & allowed att June Chapter 1732
Charles Barton, Chapter Clerk.

Expended More by Dr Hayley for Wainscott & painting as by Bills produced and Allowd at a Chapter held the 7th of June 1734	6	4	9

Examined & allowd
In presence of Charles Barton, Chapter Clerk.

Paid by Dr Cheyney to the Executor of Dr Hayley one fourth deducted	16	5	0

December 3rd 1740
Paid by Mr Hoadley to Dr Cheyney,[179] one fourth deducted — 12 3 9
Witness, William Pescod, Chapter Clerk.

48 Paid by Mr Whishaw[180] to Mr Hoadly, 4th deducted — 9 12 9$\frac{3}{4}$

Paid for Wainscott and painting as by bills allowd — 4 6 5
Enterd by Mr Morgan, December 1747.

Total — 13 9 2$\frac{3}{4}$

June 30th 1748
Paid per Mr Exton to Mr Whishaw — 10 1 11
William Pescod, Chapter Clerk.

December 10th 1748
Expended more, as by bills allowd — 39 16 0

— 49 17 11

December 12th 1754
Expended More, as by bills allowed — 1 10 0
Witness, John Dison

— 51 7 11

12th December 1759
Paid by Dr Balguy to Dr Exton, Executor of the late Mr Exton Deceased — 38 16 3

Expended more by Dr Balguy and Allowed — 2 2 3$\frac{1}{2}$
Witness, John Dison, Chapter Clerk.

November 1761
Expended more for Wainscot, as by bills produced
& allowed   3   16   6
Witness, John Dison, Chapter Clerk.

November 1763
Expended more by Dr Balguy   0   7   11
Witness, John Dison.

November 1769
Expended more by Dr Balguy, as by bill allowed   0   11   10
Witness, John Dison, Chapter Clerk.

December 5th 1770
Expended more by Dr Balguy   1   7   0
Witness, William Yalden, Chapter Clerk.

December 3rd 1770
Expended more by Dr Balguy, as by bill allowed   0   4   6
Witness, William Yalden.

	47	6	$3\frac{1}{2}$
deduct $\frac{1}{4}$	11	16	$6\frac{1}{2}$
	£35	9	9

The Sum of Thirty five pounds nine shilling Ninepence was paid
by Mr Barnard to the Executors of the late Dr Balguy.
J. Ridding, Chapter Clerk.

81 Brought From Folio 48	35	9	9
Willis Painter's Bill	4	10	$3\frac{1}{2}$
Lucas Bricklayer	7	13	$6\frac{3}{4}$
Walldin Stonemason	1	19	$1\frac{3}{4}$
Hayes Carpenter	12	4	$11\frac{1}{2}$
Inglefield Plumber	0	9	0
	£62	6	$8\frac{1}{2}$

The above Bills allowed April 5 1796.
J. Ridding, Chapter Clerk.

Dr Williams having paid for Fixtures in the above house, no further
charge remains for Wainscott money on this house.[181]

No. 10, The Close

The original purpose of the medieval remains incorporated within this house has long exercised the minds of researchers on the Cathedral Close. For the antiquary John Milner,[1] the thirteenth-century undercroft that is a feature of the northern part of the building was the conventual kitchen of St Swithun's Priory; for Vaughan, it was an ambulatory beneath the monks' infirmary.[2] Both theories seem to be invalidated by surviving documentary evidence. The building known variously as the 'Old Kitchen of the Pryory'[3] and the 'Old Bake-house',[4] used, according to the 1649 *Survey*, as a stable shared by Dr Hinton and Dr Lewis, is said to have stood somewhere near the south end of the Prior's Hall,[5] while the 'Fermery Hall' of the Infirmary range appears to have been located near No. 4.[6] It seems more likely that, in common with other Benedictine houses, the east range of the main cloister was the domain of the 'Cellarer'; this, however, is a question outside the scope of the present study.

The *Narrative* of 1675 states that the house was one of three to be 'preserved entyrely whole' during the Parliamentary occupation of the Close. It was therefore the good fortune of the pre-Commonwealth occupant of No. 10, Edward Stanley, who held the 3rd Prebend from 1639-62, to be able to return, at the Restoration, to his former dwelling in the Close. Earlier records confirm that this house was occupied by successive Canons of the 3rd Prebend; there are two references in the Treasurers' Rolls to a 'Tampin'—the term appears to denote a kind of pivoted gate—between the gardens of the three houses to the west of the former cloister garth: No. 10 (then

---

1. J. Milner, *History of Winchester*, 1798 (3rd edn. 1838) Vol. II, p.138.
2. J. Vaughan, *Winchester Cathedral Close*, London, 1914, pp.53-6.
3. *Protest of Henry Foyle*, MS, WCL, printed in *Winch. Cath. Docs. II*, pp.138-9.
4. LB VII fo. 61v dated 7 Dec 1592.
5. CA 26 Sept 1663. This could have been the Prior's kitchen, however.
6. See pp.49-50.

in the possession of Dr Barlow), No. 11 (occupied by Dr Hurst) and the house which was fore-runner of No. 12 (Dr Wickham's and later Dr Goade's). This 'Tampin' was repaired in 1618 and again in 1625.[7] The 1649 *Survey* confirms that the successors of Barlow, Hurst and Goade occupied those same houses until their expulsion from the Close *c*.1645. This is exactly what one would expect, for, as explained elsewhere,[8] the succession of prebend-houses was laid down by Statute, and until 1670 Canons were not at liberty simply to choose any house that might fall vacant.

In this way it may be shown that Dr Ralph Barlow, who held the 3rd Prebend from 1611 to 1631, was the occupant of No. 10 during that period, rather than Abraham Browne, (8th Prebendary from 1581 to 1627), as supposed by Vaughan on the evidence of the Browne crest (an eagle displayed, with two heads) as the central feature of the Jacobean overmantel in the first-floor 'Oak Room', and 'the initial of his surname, a big "B", . . . carved in stone on a cartouche outside the new [south] window'.[9] It is true that the Browne family crest is such a device (always assuming that the said Abraham came from an armigerous branch of the family), but the crest is shared with over forty other families. It is conceivable that the overmantel was salvaged from Dr Lewis' house when this was demolished in 1646. As for the *cartouche,* which has now disappeared, the letter 'B' could refer equally to Barlow or his predecessor in the 3rd Prebend, John Bridges.[10] There can be little doubt that Abraham Browne's residence in the Close was in fact the house which Dr Lewis occupied after him until its demolition at the beginning of the Commonwealth.

The only identifiable reference to No. 10 to have survived from the period of tenure of Barlow's successor, Benjamin Lany,[11] is a Treasurer's Roll entry relating to roofing work in 1633-4.[12] Lany was in turn succeeded by Edward Stanley, who had occupied the house for some six years when he was dispossessed of the Prebend at the time of the sequestration of Close properties by the Parliamentarians, following Cromwell's capture of Winchester in October 1645.

The *Survey* of 1649 states that the house was assigned to 'Colonel Norton', who appears to have lived there, and thus preserved it

---

7. TR 1617–8, p.4. and 1624–5, p.17 (called 'a gate').
8. See pp.xviii–xxi.
9. *op. cit.* in Note 2, pp.56–7.
10. 3rd Prebend, 1565–1611.
11. 3rd Prebend, 1631–9.
12. TR 1633–4. 3,000 tiles were used.

during the Commonwealth. Richard Norton was one of two officers
from the Parliamentary garrison allotted houses in the Close during
this period. It is not easy to relate the Parliamentary Surveyors'
description of the house to the present building. It is confusingly
described as lying 'betweene the Garden [of the house] and Orchard', a phrase which led T.D. Atkinson to situate Stanley's house
well to the west of No. 10.[13] In fact, the 'Garden' of the *Survey*
must surely refer to the old Refectory site, and the area formerly
occupied by the 'Little Cloister', to the east of the house. This part
of the Close is shown as a garden in Godson's Plan of Winchester,
dated 1750; and the 'Court' immediately east of No. 10 was,
indeed, thrown into the Close only in 1795.[14]

One searches in vain for a reference in the 1649 *Survey* to the
medieval undercroft. Unfortunately, the Surveyors did not concern
themselves with antiquities. Thus it is that the splendid medieval
roofs of the Prior's and Pilgrims' Halls are dismissed with the
laconic epithet 'well-timbered'. The Winchester *Parliamentary Survey*
is a document of limited value compared with, for example, those
taken at the same time at Lincoln or Gloucester, which describe
the houses in the Cathedral Closes of those Cities in some detail,
complete with their dimensions.[15]

Building activities at Dr Stanley's house at the Restoration seem
to have been confined to minor repairs. The *Account Book of
Wm. Fletcher* (1662) shows a few small payments; for example, 'for
bricks & sand used at Doc. Stanleys Howse 7s 3d',[16] and for various
bolts, locks and catches; and five labourers appear to have worked
for a fortnight at his house in March 1662.[17] Little more than
necessary maintenance seems to have been involved, but the Chapter
was anxious that 'those Prebendaries whose houses were preserved
whole & entyre should not in their good fortune repyne at the
rebuilding those which were totally demolished, upon the common
charge', and ensured that 'whatsoever was in the least degree out
of repayre in their houses also was at the same tyme amended,
even unto curiosity, which Dr Gulston and Dr Stanley, unto whom

13. Unpublished *Notes on Close Houses*, MS, WCL.
14. CA 17 Mar 1795.
15. It should perhaps be emphasised that there can be no doubt that Stanley's house
    was indeed No 10: this is shown initially by the position of the house in the
    Survey, where the houses are itemised in a clockwise direction, working round
    the Close (just as they are numbered today). See also p.108.
16. fo. 2.
17. fos. 12–12v.

two of the forementioned houses did belong, tooke sufficient care for themselves'.[18]

Edward Stanley did not live long to enjoy the house thus put into full repair, for he died on 22 August 1662 and was succeeded by Dr Richard Hyde. The house of Dr Hyde was mentioned as a reference point for the adjoining properties in an important Chapter Act of 2 December 1663, but there was no need to define the site of No. 10 itself as no change of site or Prebend was involved. The Act mentions the 'Lane leading to the house of Dr Hyde' from Dome Alley and implies that this was the main approach to the building. The lane survives as a parking area to the west of No. 9.

Dr Hyde was Treasurer in 1662–3, and again from 1664–5; and recorded various improvements and alterations to the house: 'To the Tiler for 2 daies for himself and his man for the wall & house of office in Dr Hyde's Garden';[19] 'To the brickburner for 1500 of bricks for my parlour & stable wall';[20] 'For a cart to carry rubbish [rubble] out of my backside [yard] 2 dayes';[21] 'To a mason to set up a fornace in my brewhouse'.[22] But all these works did not prevent the house from being described as 'like to fall' in 1674 when it was repaired 'with mazons worke & Carpenters worke'.[23] By that time, it had passed to George Beaumont, as the *Narrative* of 1675 makes clear, with its reference to 'the house of Dr Stanley now in the possession of Dr Beaumont'.[24] Beaumont was succeeded in No. 10 by Francis Morley, after which the occupancy is somewhat uncertain until the arrival in the house of Robert Eyre, as recorded in the Wainscot Book. Shortly after his arrival, it was ordered that his house 'bee view'd by the proper officers, & Repair'd according as they shall see occasion'.[25] Thereafter, the pages of the Wainscot Book provide a complete list of inhabitants of the house until the beginning of the nineteenth century.

18. *Narrative,* para. 3.
19. TR 1662–3, dated 22 Aug 1663.
20. TR 1664–5, entry for 19 July 1665.
21. *ibid.,* 17 Nov 1665.
22. *ibid.,* 21 Nov 1665.
23. TR 1673–4, fo. 8v.
24. *Narrative,* para. 2.
25. CO 24 Feb 1700/1.

NO. 10, THE CLOSE

24 The House at the South-West Corner of the Mount.

The Charges of Dr Robert Eyre,[182] one of the prebends of the Cathedrall Church of Winchester, for Wainscot in his house, to be repaid by his Successor, a fourth part to be deducted.

For wainscotting the Roomes below staires & the
Parlour & bed-Chamber above staires[183]   xxx £

November Chapter 1710.
Examined & allowed by the Dean & Chapter,
In presence of Thomas Cranley.

The Charges of Mr Sturgis, one of the prebends of the Church, in the House above mencioned, late Dr Eyre's.

December 7th 1724
Received then of Mr Sturges the summe of twenty
two pounds and tenn shillings in full for Wainscott
Money due upon the house late Dr Eyre,
Received by me Elizabeth Eyre.   22   10   0

Examined and allowed by the Dean and Chapter, 10th December 1724,
In presence of Charles Barton, *Clerici Capituli.*

December 12th 1727
Received then of the Reverend Mr Soley the summe of sixteen pounds seventeen shillings & sixpence, Which (after fourths deducted) is in full of the Wainscott Money due upon my late house. Received by me, J. Sturges.

Examined & allowed 12th December 1727
Charles Barton, *Clericus Capituli.*

49 The Charges of the Reverend Mr Christopher Eyre in his prebendall house (late Mr Soleys) to be repaid by his Successor, according to the Custome of the Church.

July 14th 1732
Received of the Reverend Mr Eyre twelve pounds thirteen shillings for Wainscott Money due upon my late House,
Received by me, J. Soley   12   13   0

Examined & allowd 25th July 1732
In presence of Charles Barton, Chapter Clerk.

Expended More by Mr Eyre for painters work, as by Bill produced and allowd att Midsummer Chapter 1733 Charles Barton, Chapter Clerk.	2	5	7
Expended more by Mr Eyre, as by Bill produced & allowd at November Chapter 1733 Charles Barton, Chapter Clerk.	4	1	2
Expended more by Mr Eyre [for painting]ⁱ as by bill produced and allowd at November Chapter 1737 William Pescod, Chapter Clerk.	1	7	8
Expended more by Mr Eyre for Window Shutters and Painting, as by bill produced and allowd this 5th of December 1739 William Pescod, Chapter Clerk.	1	8	1

50   December 1st 1742

Expended more by Mr Eyre, as by bill allowd for Wainscott and a Beam set and shelves in Mr Eyre's study &c William Pescod, Chapter Clerk.	6	4	0

August 18th 1743

Then Mr Shipley paid to Mr Philip Eyre, Executor of Dr Christopher Eyre deceased the Sume of twenty pounds nineteen shilling and seven pence halfpenny for Wainscott money due upon the late Mr Eyre's house Witness, William Pescod, Chapter Clerk.	20	19	7½

1745

Then Mr Rolleston paid the Reverend Dr Shipley the summe of Fifteen pounds fourteen Shillings & seven pence for the Wainscott money due to his House Witness [blank]	15	14	7

November 28th 1750
Then   Mr Lechmere   paid   the   Reverend
Mr Rolleston the summe of Eleven pounds sixteen
Shillings for the Wainscott Money due to his
House   11   16   0
Witness [blank]

December 1750
Expended more by Mr Lechmere by Bills Allowed
the summe of four pounds fifteen shillings & Nine
pence   4   15   9
Witness, William Pescod, Chapter Clerk.

December 10th 1753
Expended more by Mr Lechmere, by bills allowd,
the sume of twenty three pounds three shillings   23   3   0
Witness, W. Pescod, Chapter Clerk.

12th December 1758
Expended more for Wainscot & Marble Slab   3   6 10

Expended more by Mr Lechmere, November
1763   0   11   9
Witness, J. Dison.

72   Brought forward from page 50   43   13   4

November Chapter 1764
Expended more by Mr Lechmere, as by bills
allowd   3   18   8
Witness, J. Dison, Chapter Clerk.

November Chapter 1765
Expended more by Mr Lechmere, by bills pro-
duced and Allowed   8   10 11
Witness, J. Dison, Chapter Clerk.
                                                       _____
                                                       56   2 11
             Deduct ¼ being   14   0   8¾
   Remains to be paid by Mr Mulsoe   42   2   2

Received, 13th December 1770, of The Reverend Mr Mulso[184] per
Mr Buller forty two pounds two Shillings.
T.G. Waller.[185] Executor to Mr Lechmere.

             from the above Sum of   42   2   2
             deduct one fourth   10   10   6½
                                                       _____
                                                      £31   11   7½

Which Sum of 31:1:7½ was paid by Mr Poulter to the Representatives of the late Mr Mulso.
J. Ridding, Chapter Clerk. January 2nd 1792.

deduct one fourth	7	17	11
£23	13	8

2nd February 1793
The Sum of 23:13:8 was paid by Mr Garnett to Mr Poulter.
J. Ridding, Chapter Clerk.

Deduct ¼th	5	18	5
£17	15	3

The Sum of 17:15:3 was paid by Mr Barnard to Mr Garnett.
J. Ridding, Chapter Clerk.   [*less*] ¼   4   8   3
                                          £13   7   0

June 3rd 1795
The Sum of Thirteen Pounds seven shillings was paid by Dr Turner to Mr Barnard.
J. Ridding, Chapter Clerk.   [*less* ¼]   3   6   9
                                          £10   0   3

December 12th 1795
The Sum of Ten Pounds & Threepence was paid by Mr Legge to Dr Turner.
J. Ridding, Chapter Clerk.

72v   Brought from Folio 72   10   0   3
                             ¼   2   10   0
                                          £7   10   3

The Sum of £7:10:3 was paid by Mr Iremonger to Dr Turner's Executors. J. R[idding]
                             ¼   1   18   0
                                          £5   12   3

The Sum of £5:12:3 was paid by Mr Pelham to Mr Iremonger.
                             ¼   1   8   0
                                          £4   4   3

December 12th 1799
The Sum of £4:4:3 was paid by Mr Heathcote to Mr Pelham.
Witness, J. Ridding, Chapter Clerk.

Deduct ¼	1	1	0
£3	3	0

November Chapter 1800
The Sum of £3:3:0 was paid by Mr Garnier to Mr Heathcote.
Witness, J. Ridding, Chapter Clerk.[186]

No. 11, The Close

Like the better-known 'House of Thomas Ken', the building known, until its demolition in the mid nineteenth century, as 'No. 11' fell victim to the progressive reduction in the number of Canons from twelve to five recommended by the Ecclesiastical Commission.[1] Apparently in a poor state of repair, the house was ordered to be pulled down by a Chapter Act of 13 March 1842, when the Chapter Seal was set to a scheme drawn up at the previous November Chapter meeting. Some demolition took place immediately, and the Treasurer's Roll of 1841-2 mentions 'old lead from house No. 11', which was re-used. The garden of No. 11 was quickly annexed to Nos. 10 and 12. Part of the house, however, remained standing for a time, for it was originally intended that this should be added to No. 10; a scheme that was later abandoned when the latter house became no longer required as a prebendal residence.[2] The house to the north, formerly '12', was renumbered '11' from 1842.

As with the other Close houses, the 1649 *Survey* is a useful starting point for investigations, and one may retrace the history of the building by following the well-proven premise that, in accordance with Statute, the house was duly occupied by successive holders of the same Prebend, in this case the 10th. The earliest references in the Cathedral muniments provide little more than the names of the occupants, but certain Treasurers' Roll entries prove that the premise holds true for No. 11. The Roll of 1617-8, for example, mentions a structure called the 'Tampine'—probably no more than a gatepost, as the term seems to indicate a 'great hinge' or 'pivot'— between 'Mr Hearst's,[3] Mr Treasurer's [Ralph Barlow][4] and

1. Stat. 3 & 4 Vic. c.113 s.10. See J.M. Horne, ed., *John Le Neve's Fasti Ecclesiae Anglicanae,* London, 1974, p.107.
2. CA 26 Mar 1845.
3. Christopher Hurst, 10th Prebend, 1614-28.
4. Ralph Barlow, 3rd Prebend 1611-31 and Treasurer in 1617-8, as shown in MS version of Dean Young's Diary, MS, WCL, p.11 '6 Feb 1617-8 . . . I receaved of Mr Dr Barlo Threasourer . . .'

Dr Wickham's';[5] and the Roll of 1624 mentions again the 'Tampen' between Dr Barlow's [6] and Mr Hurst's. The 1624 Roll itemises a further payment for 'making the gate' between Hurst's premises and that of Dr Goade, who had succeeded Wickham in the adjoining house to the north. These entries thus confirm the relative positions of the three houses which the 1649 *Survey* locates to the west of the old cloister garth: No. 10, which survived the Commonwealth virtually intact; No. 11, which survived 'in part';[7] and the house to the north, totally demolished, and rebuilt at the Restoration as 'No. 12'.

Christopher Hurst was succeeded by Dr John Harris. Anthony Wood praised him as a preacher 'second only to St Chrysostome' and called him 'so admirable a Grecian'. He became Warden of Winchester College in 1630, and indeed has been called 'The greatest of all Wardens'.[8] His house in the Close is referred to as 'formerly belonging to Dr Harris' in the 1649 *Survey* but the description of the house in that document is not particularly informative, consisting merely of a catalogue of the rooms. The house is described as 'built with Stone Walls covered with Lead', which suggests that it was originally a monastic structure. It enjoyed the benefit of a back entrance from the Churchyard, a passage which passed through the back yard of the adjoining house to the north;[9] and the gate referred to in the Treasurers' Rolls already discussed probably lay between the two properties, and was related to this back entrance.

John Harris was deprived of his house in around 1645, and it was allotted to a certain William Withers.[10] However, Warden Harris probably felt the loss of his Prebend less strongly than his fellow-Canons in the Close. His religious persuasions seem to have inclined towards a mild form of Puritanism, and during the Civil War he sided with the Presbyterians, which enabled him to retain his Wardenship. He did not entirely abandon his interest in the Cathedral Church, however, for in 1654 he contributed £5 towards its repair. He died in 1658, thereby missing the Restoration of the Monarchy by two years.

When the members of a much-altered Chapter returned to the Close in 1660, No. 11 was found to have been 'demolished in part'.

---

5. Edward Wickham, 12th Prebend, 1609–21.
6. Then occupying No. 10.
7. *Narrative*, para. 2.
8. See G.E. Aylmer, 'Seventeenth-Century Wykehamists' in R. Custance, ed., *Winchester College Sixth-Centenary Essays,* Oxford, 1982, p.307.
9. See Notes to Text, 228.
10. As shown in the MS of the Survey at HRO, ref. 59492 (fos. 4–19 for Close).

No doubt it was because of this that Dr William Clarke, who had succeeded Harris in the 10th Prebend, was allowed one of the new 'brick houses', No. 8, The Close. By a Chapter Act of 25 Feb 1661/2, it was ordered that 'Dr Clarke shal have the proffer of the 4th howse of the new build howses to accept or refuse the same. And if he accept . . . then Dr Dayrell shall have the howse that now Dr Clarke hath'. Dr Clarke evidently did accept, and by a further Act, dated 1 Dec 1662, it was decided 'That the scite of Dr Darells howse be there where Dr Harris his howse [*illegible*] adjoyning the roome now standing to that part which [is] to be built new, and that he have Doctor Lewes and Dr Harris backsides gardens [*illegible*] layde to it'. This Act was, however, annulled and deleted, and by the superseding Act of 22 Sept 1663 the house was allotted to John Ryves.[11] It is clear that by this date Dr Darell had decided to have a new house built in the 'North-West Corner. of the Mount'. The Wainscot Book shows this house, 'No. 12', to have been completed by 1665. Darell was, however, allowed to continue to live in No. 11 'till his owne house [was] built'.[12] These new arrangements were confirmed three months later, and No. 11 was assigned 'to Mr John Ryves, and to his successor for ever'.[13]

No.11 appears to have been uninhabitable both when Ryves held it as his prebend-house and during the tenure of his successor, Dr Robert Sharrock. According to a Chapter Act of 9 December 1668, Bishop Morley had promised Sharrock a house 'upon the next avoidance', and by the same Act it was ordered that various houses, including Sharrock's, should be surveyed, in order that the sum of £900 set apart for repairing those houses should be wisely spent. The following year, however, Sharrock exchanged Prebends with Thomas Ken, who became the new occupant of No. 11; and thus the *Narrative* of February 1675 refers to 'The house of Dr Harris now in the possession of Mr Ken'.[14] By 1671, a considerable amount of work had been ordered: 'The foote of the stayres turned into the house, the stayrecase lathed and plastered and made close. A door to be made at the [Northern?] End of the house in the place of the window. The loose wainscot to bee sett up in the lower roome: A wall of bricks to bee made from Mr Archdeacon's corner [Darell— in No. 12] to the Close wall with a gate-way in it. The wall next the close to be coped as far as the high part of it. And a house of

---

11. 4th Prebend, 1660–5.
12. CA 22 Sept 1663.
13. CA 2 Dec 1663.
14. *Narrative*, para. 2.

office to be made in the place prepared for it next Mr Archdeacons.'[15] There seems to have been some delay in building the garden walls, for in September 1673 it was ordered 'that Mr Ken's . . . walls be covered immediately to prevent further Ruin'.[16]

As shown by the table of occupants, many of whom are conjectural until the period covered by the Wainscot Book, No. 11 appears to have been the least coveted of all the Close houses, and tended therefore always to fall to the most junior Canon, who moved into more desirable premises as soon as another house was vacant. In 1681 the house, though nominally a prebendal residence, was inhabited by the Clerk of Works, John Baskerville; for a Chapter *Memorandum* notes that 'Dr Woodford makes choyce of the house late Mr Marklands where Mr Baskerville now lives'.[17] Samuel Woodford was responsible for substantial additions to the outbuildings of the house: a woodhouse and a wash-house were built there at Chapter expense,[18] and a new 'payer of backstayres' installed, leading out of the buttery.[19] A study 'over the wash-house' was added by a subsequent occupant, Giles Thornborough.[20] In this way each successive occupant—and there were many of them—added somewhat to the desirability of the dwelling.

The first reference to No. 11 in the Wainscot Book is an isolated inventory of fixtures in 'the little House at the West-End of the Church lately inhabited by Mr Lowth, Feb 21 1704-5'. The phrase used to locate the house is misleading, and it is small wonder that the compiler of the title page was baffled when he added the table of contents to the Wainscot Book in around 1760. Lowth was undoubtedly the holder of No. 11 from 1696 to 1704, however— this can be proved by a process of elimination—and the lay-out and rooms of the house as they appear from the inventory tally with what may be discovered about the house from other contemporary documents, which are discussed in the notes relevant to this page of the Wainscot Book.

The house is fully recorded in the Wainscot Book from 1724, by which date the house seems to have risen in favour somewhat; and the entries show that a number of Canons elected to move into No. 11 from other houses in the Close. It is by analysing such changes

15. CO 11 May 1671.
16. CO 27 Sept 1673.
17. CO 30 Nov 1681.
18. CO 30 Nov 1681.
19. CO 1 Dec 1682.
20. CO 12 Mar 1685/6.

of prebend-house, given here in the Table of Occupants, that one can gain some idea of the relative status of the twelve Close houses during the period of the Wainscot Book.

Although the 1705 Inventory gives a little detail, the other entries provide few indications as to the nature of the building, and the information gleaned from the pages of the Wainscot Book is largely restricted to a list of occupants. It is unfortunate that no records, plans or drawings appear to have survived, for details of the plan of this vanished house would doubtless add considerably to our knowledge of the lost monastic buildings of St Swithun's Priory, part of which would seem to have been contained in No. 11 itself.

NO. 11, THE CLOSE

[The Middle House on the West Side of the Mount][187]

22 An Account of the Standards belonging to the little House at the West-End of the Church lately inhabited by Mr Lowth: taken February 21st 1704/5.

In the Wash-House[188]: a Pump.

In the Bake-house: 2 shelves.

In the Kitchen : a Dresser Board, [a Tressel under the Dresser][i] & Shelves all along one side, & a Rack over the Mantletree.

In the Larder : a Hanging Shelf, two Dresser Boards, a short shelf.

In the Cellar[189]: a partition of lattice & two shelves.

In the little Closet within the Parlour : 4 shelves.

In the Chamber over the Kitchin, the [Blue][i] Hangings of the Room.

In the Closet within that Chamber : 2 Shelves.

In the Closet on the left Hand of the Dining-Room : 2 shelves.

On the top of the 2nd pair of Stairs[190]: a cubbard with several shelves.

A Partition between the two Cock Lofts.

A Coal-Pen in the Wood-yard.[191]

32a[192] The Charges of Mr Crosse in his prebendall House (being the little house next to Dr Woodroffes).

Expended by him for Wainscott, Painting and other charges, as appears by workmens bills produced and allowed by the Dean and Chapter att November Chapter 1724, the sume of eleven pounds *Ita Testor,* Charles Barton, *Clericus Capituli.*	11	0	0
Paid by Mr Clarke to Mr Crosse for the Wainscott in the House abovemenconed (the Fourth part being deducted)	8	5	0
Expended more by Mr Clarke in Wainscott, Painting etc, as per Bills produced and allowed att June Chapter 1727 *Ita Testor,* Charles Barton, *Clericus Capituli.*	14	15	11
	23	0	11

Expended more by Dr Clarke for Wainscott,
painting etc, as by bills produced & allowd att
June Chapter 1728.   20   17   1½

Memorandum. The Shelves in the Study were not included in the
above mencioned Bills.[193]
Charles Barton, Chapter Clerk.

33 The Charges of Dr Alured Clarke in the house (late Dr
Crosse's) for Wainscott, to be repayd by his Successor (the 4th
parte being deducted).

Paid to Dr Crosse   8   5   0

Expended more by Dr Clarke as by bills produced
& allowed att June Chapter 1727   14   15   11½
Ita Testor, Charles Barton, *Clericus Capituli.*

Expended more by Dr Clarke for Wainscott,
painting &c, as per bills produced & allowed att
June Chapter 1728   20   17   1½

Memorandum. The Shelves in the Study were not included in the
Abovemencioned bills.
Charles Barton, *Clericus Capituli.*

Expended more by Dr Clarke for Wainscott and
painting, as by Bills produced and allowd att
Midsummer Chapter 1731   6   1   0
                                              In toto   49   19   1
Ita Testor, Charles Barton, *Clericus Capituli.*

May 12th 1732
Received then of the Reverend Mr Soley the summe of thirty seven
pounds nine shillings on account of Wainscott Money (due according
to the Custome of the Church of Winchester) by me, Alured Clarke.

Examined & allowed July 25th 1732.
In presence of Charles Barton, Chapter Clerk.

55 The Charges of Mr Soley for Wainscott in his Prebendal
House.

Paid by Mr Soley to Dr Clarke   37   9   0

	£	s	d
Expended more by Mr Soley for Wainscott and painting, as by bills produced and allowd, November Chapter 1737	11	2	4
	48	11	4
Examined and allowed the 3rd of December 1737, in presence of William Pescod, Chapter Clerk.			
Paid by Mr Chancellor Hoadly to the Executrix of Mr Soley	36	8	10
Expended more by Mr Hoadley [as by bills]^d for making a New Passage from the Kitchen to the Brewhouse, as by bills allowd this 5th December 1739 William Pescod, Chapter Clerk.	4	2	11
Expended more by Mr Hoadley for painting, as allowd November Chapter 1740 Witness, William Pescod, Chapter Clerk.	1	11	0
1741 Mr Whishaw paid Mr Hoadley[194] Witness, William Pescod, Chapter Clerk.	31	12	3
Mr Nash paid Mr Whishaw	23	14	2¼
1742 Expended by Mr Nash for repairing Wainscott as by bill allowd	0	6	9¼
December 1746 Expended more, as by bill allowd for Wainscott	2	9	10
December 1748 Expended more, as by bill allowd, for a Chimney Peice in the Parlour	1	17	0
	28	7	9¾
56 Brought over	28	7	9½
December 10th 1753 Expended more by Dr Naish, by bills allowd Witness, William Pescod, Chapter Clerk.	5	19	0
December 12th 1754 Expended more by Dr Naish, by bills allowed Witness, John Dison.	1	18	10

January 25th 1758
Dr Ayscough paid the Executrix of Dr Naish, one
4th being deducted out of the above payment   27   4   0
Witness, William Pescod, Chapter Clerk.

November 1763
Expended more by Dr Ayscough   0   16   7
                                                          £28   0   7

10th September 1764. Received of the Reverend Mr Buller, one of
the Prebends of Winchester, The Sum of Twenty One Pounds,
being the money coming to Dr Ayscough deceased, late one of the
Prebends of Winchester, from the Wainscot Book, I say, received
by me, sole Executrix of the said Dr Ayscough, £21:0:0. Anne
Ayscough.

Mr Buller paid to the Executrix of Dr Ayscough
(One fourth being deducted out of the above sum)   21   0   0

November 1769
Expended by Mr Buller, as by bill producd &
allowd   7   2   9
John Dison, Chapter Clerk.
                                                          28   2   9
                                                           7   6 $2\frac{1}{4}$
                                                          20 16 $6\frac{3}{4}$

The Locks & Dressers given to the House, the Bishop of Oxford
having done so to the House Mr Buller succeeded to.[195]

December 8th 1777. Received of the Reverend Mr Hare, The
above Sum. [of W]^d William Buller.

March 23rd 1779
Expended more [as]^d by Mr Hare, as by Bill
produced & allowed   2   14   7
William Yalden, Chapter Clerk.   £23   11 $1\frac{3}{4}$

76 Brought over   23   11 $1\frac{3}{4}$

March 16th 1786
Expended by Mr Hare, as by Bills produced &
allowed at the last November Chapter   2   5 $10\frac{1}{2}$
J. Ridding, Chapter Clerk.

	£	s	d
1793. Lucas' Bill for Repairs allowed	5	17	5
Hayes *Ditto*	4	10	10½
1794. Willis *Ditto*	3	17	2

J. Ridding, Chapter Clerk.

	£	s	d
¼ [of]	40	2	5¾
	10	0	5¾
	£30	2	0

Which Sum of Thirty Pounds two shillings was paid by Dr Turner to Mr Hare, 12th December 1795.
J. Ridding, Chapter Clerk.

November Chapter 1797

	£	s	d
Lucas Bill for [Alterations &]^d Repairs allowed	17	17	11
Hayes' Bill for *Ditto*	55	19	8

J. Ridding, Chapter Clerk.

	£	s	d
	£103	19	7
Deduct one fourth	25	19	11
	£ 77	19	8

Paid Lucas : £17:17:11 [Received] Henry Lucas
Paid Hayes : £55:19:8 Received Edward Hayes
Paid Messrs <u>Waller</u> : £4:2:1

£ 77   19   8

The above Sum of £77:19:8 was paid by Mr Iremonger to the Executors of Dr Turner as above.

J. Ridding, Chapter Clerk. ¼	19	9	11
	£57	9	9

The above Sum of £57:9:9 was paid by Mr Pelham to Mr Iremonger.
J. Ridding, Chapter Clerk.

[November Chapter 1798			
Walldins Bill allowed at this Chapter	2	18	3
	60	8	0]^d

	£	s	d
1798. Hayes Bill for Repairs	10	11	9½
Waldins *Ditto*	2	18	3
Weddell *Ditto*	3	8	6½
	74	8	4
[deduct] ¼	18	12	1
	£55	16	3

July 14th 1803
The Sum of £55:16:3 was paid by Mr North to The Bishop of Bristol.[196]
J. Ridding, Chapter Clerk.

Deduct ¼	13	19	0¾
	£41	17	2¼

January 14th 1808
The above sum of £41:17:2 was paid to Mr North
by Mr Salter.
J. Ridding, Chapter Clerk.

82 Brought from [page] 76	41	17	2
Deduct ¼	10	9	2
	£31	8	0

which sum of £31:8:0 was paid by Mr Charles Augustus North to the Executrix of the late Mr Salter, November Chapter 1812.
J. Ridding, Chapter Clerk.[197]

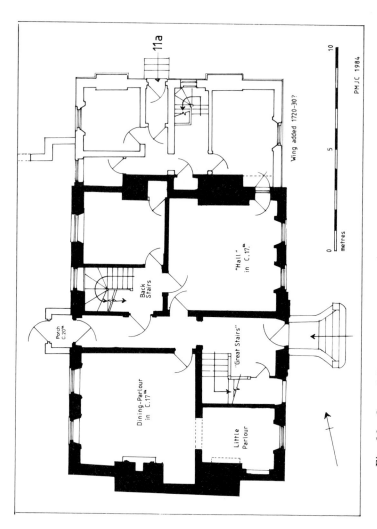

Fig. 20. Ground-floor plan, No. 12, The Close, Winchester (now 'No. 11').

No. 12, The Close

This house, known since the demolition of the adjoining premises southwards in 1842 as 'No. 11', has received even less attention from students of Winchester's canonry dwellings than the other houses in the Cathedral Close. The late T. D. Atkinson, confusing the building with No. 1, supposed it to have been constructed in 1727, a view which threw into some confusion his analysis of the buildings adjacent to the two houses which he had thus interchanged.[1] The Wainscot Book, however, confirms what is evident from other sources; that the house was erected soon after the Restoration, more or less on the site of the earlier house associated with the 12th Prebend.

This earlier house is referred to in the *Survey* of 1649 as 'The Howse lately belonging to Doctor Goade', although Thomas Goade[2] had in fact by that date been long succeeded by John Oliver, who survived the Commonwealth, dying in October 1661. Goade's predecessor was Edward Wickham,[3] and good documentary evidence, already discussed with reference to No. 11, confirms that Wickham was the occupant of the building at the beginning of the seventeenth century.[4] He appears to have left the house in a poor state of repair, however, and Dean Young recorded in his *Diary* how he 'moved [the Canons] in my Lord Bishops name in the behalfe of Dr Goad for healping towards the reparing of his house'.[5] The request appears to have fallen largely on deaf ears, though some timber was granted towards the repairs.

1. T. D. Atkinson, 'Winchester Cathedral Close', *Proceedings of the Hampshire Field Club,* XV (1941), pp. 20-1; and his unpublished 'Notes on Close Houses', MS, WCL.
2. 12th Prebend, 1621-38.
3. 12th Prebend, 1609-21.
4. See pp.107-8.
5. F. Goodman, ed., *The Diary of John Young,* London, 1928, p. 72.

The best description of the original house occurs in the *Parliamentary Survey,* which implies that the house was not set back from the old cloister garth, as is the present No. 12, but aligned with Nos. 10 and 11: it probably formed part of the same west range of buildings and, like No. 11, is described as being built of stone and roofed with lead. The *Survey* makes particular mention of the right-of-way from the Churchyard to No. 11, which passed behind Dr Goade's house; this passage was preserved at the Restoration, and re-routed in a more logical fashion only in 1765.[6]

During the Commonwealth the house was assigned to Captain Thomas Bettsworth, a Parliamentary officer, and he appears to have had it demolished for the value of its materials, notably the lead, estimated at £183 13s 6d. Following the Restoration, the Dean and Chapter obtained from Bettsworth a written authorisation for their agents to enter 'any such of the gardens or grounde which I now possess in the Close . . . which are or shalbe . . . designed for Prebends howses to be built upon and to Laye the foundations & build such howses there . . . '[7] Apparently the Chapter was taking no chances over the matter of reclaiming their confiscated property.

No mention is made of Dr Oliver in the cathedral documents of the immediate post-Restoration period, and it may be that he did not need a prebendal house. A considerable amount of reorganisation of prebendal residences occurred in order to suit the needs of those Canons who had returned to the Close, and in 1662 Oliver's successor, Walter Darell,[8] was at first allotted No. 11, whose statutory occupant, the 10th Prebendary, Dr Clarke, had been offered one of the new brick houses, No. 8.[9] This arrangement was confirmed by the Chapter Act of 1 Dec 1662, subsequently deleted; but by September 1663 housing requirements had changed somewhat, and it was ordered that Darell was to live in No. 11 (referred to as 'the howse late of Dr Harris') only as a temporary measure 'until his owne house is built'.[10] This implies that by this date Darell's new house, the present 'No. 12', was under construction; a supposition supported not only by the *Narrative,* which explicitly states that Darell's house was habitable by 1663–4, but also by the pages of the Wainscot Book, which show that the interior painting of the building was completed in 1665.

6. See Notes to Text, 228.
7. MS, WCL, dated 24 Jan 1660/1.
8. 12th Prebend, 1661–84.
9. CA 25 Feb 1661/2.
10. CA 22 Sept 1663.

The two pages relating to the original internal decoration of this house are particularly rich in detail, and it is therefore a matter of special regret that so much of the panelling installed in this house in the 1660s should have been destroyed by subsequent remodellings. Indeed, the only features which may with certainty be ascribed to this period are two fine staircases: the magnificent stairway leading out of the entrance hall, and a more modest service stair at the rear of the building.

This small but elegant house, to which a further wing was added in the early 18th century, was conceived with a *piano nobile,* approached by a short flight of steps or *perron,* and with basement service rooms. The appearance of the east façade is surprising, as both the fenestration and the brickwork appear to date from the early eighteenth century: the other external walls, in rather rough bricks in various hues of red and purple, laid in English Bond, are typical of the 1660s. It seems, then, that the front of the house was complete refaced from ground (though not basement) level upwards, but the date of this is uncertain as the windows may be consciously archaic in their proportions. The lead rainwater pipes were evidently re-used.

NO. 12, THE CLOSE

7 The House at the North-West Corner of the Mount.

An Inventarie of the waynscott and other ioyners worke and paynting in the Prebend howse of the right worshipful Walter Darell, Doctor of Divinity, One of the Prebendaries of the Cathedrall Church of the Holy Trinity of Winchester.

The Joyners Bill

Imprimis: for nynty yardes of wainscott in the Dyning[198] roome at seaven shillings & six pence the yard

33 15 0

For the Architrave moulding about the doorecases, lyning, making good the posts, & furring, at sixpence the foote, one hundred foote

2 10 0

For one hundred fifty two foote of cornish,[199] at fifteene pence a foote

9 10 0

For a Chimney peice in the Dyninge roome, the cornish & all the ornament to it

5 0 0

In the Little parlour:[200]

For fourty nyne yards of wainscott [and] the cubberde in the waynscott,[201] the trouble of the worke being more then the wainscott, at five shillings a yard

12 5 0

For a chimney peice in the same roome, with the cornish belonging to it

4 0 0

For thirty eight foote of Cornish at fifteene a foote[202]

2 7 6

For thirty fower foote of architrave moulding at sixpence a foote

0 17 0

In the Hall:[203]

For fifty yards & five foote of Waynscott at fower shilling a yard

10 2 0

For a mantlepeice

2 0 0

For thirty five foote of architrave worke, a six-pence a foote	0	17	6
For two payre of dowble doores[204] at fourty shillings a payre	4	0	0
The Carvers bill amounts to	6	0	0
	93	4	0

8 The Worke done at the said Doctor Darells howse by Nicholas More, paynter Stainer, *Anno Domini* 1665.[205]

For one hundred thirty & seaven yards in the Dyning roome at 2s 6d the yard	16	2	6
For the playne worke in the stayer-case & great gates & outer doores & back stayers, eighty fower yards & an halfe	4	4	6
For the two doores in the dyning-roome, sixteene yards at 14d the yard	0	18	8
In the doores next the back-stayers, nyne yards[206]	0	10	6
In the fronticepeice or screen,[207] sixteene yards at 14d the yard	0	18	8
In the hall, fourty seaven yards[208] at 16d the yard	3	2	8
In the fower doores upon the great stayers,[209] 28 yardes at 16d the yard	1	17	4
	27	14	10

15 The Charges of Dr William Harrison, one of the prebendaryes of the Cathedrall Church of Winchester, to be repayd by his successor, according to the Custome of the Church.

Payd to Mr Beniamini Whitear,[210] Legatee of Dr Darell who was predecessor to the said Dr Harison (the fourth parte of the first price being abated) for his wainscot in his dwelling house, as appeares by acquittances, the summ of sixty nine pounds eighteen shillings	lxix£ xviijs
payd him more for wainscot upon the side of the Study[211] & behind the bookes	v£ xs
for Mouldings & Cornish on the Crosse beames in the Chamber over the Parlour & round the Roome[212]	iiij £

A paire of window shutts in the Chamber over
the Hall   vs

Two paire of window shutts in the little Parlour   xs

           summm   lxxvj £   iijs

This bill hath been examined & approved of by Mr Dean and the
Chapter, the 30th of June 1684.
Thomas Cranley, Chapter Clerke.

Paid by Dr Fulham to the Executors of Dr Harison
for the Wainscot above mencioned, a fourth part
being deducted   57   2   3

Out of which a 4th parte being deducted which is
£14 5s 6d there remains forty two pounds sixteen
shillings viijd *ob.* which was payd by Dr Sayer to
the Executors of the said Dr Fulham his prede-
cessor   xlij £   xvjs   viijd   *ob.*

The Window shutts in the Chamber over the hall & the Window
shuts in the Litle Parlour being included in the said Account as
standards.[213]

10th December 1703
This Account was examined & approved of by the Dean & Chapter,
in the presence of Thomas Cranley, Chapter Clerke.

14   More Dr Sayers house.[214]

For 18 dayes & an halfe, Mr Cole in Wainscotting
the Stair Case[215]   1   19   0
For 18 dayes & an halfe for his boy the same   0   17   6
for 98 foot of whole Deale board   0   16   4
for 201 foot of sleet Deal board   1   0   11
         summe   4   13   9

Examined and approved by the Dean and Chapter, December 10th
1705.
In presence of Thomas Cranley, Chapter Clerke.

Paid by Dr Layfield to the Executor of Dr Sayer
for the wainscot of his house, a fourth part being
deducted[216]   35   12 $9\frac{3}{4}$

5th October 1711
Examined & allowed by the Dean & Chapter
In presence of Thomas Cranley, Chapter Clerk.

An agreement made by Dr Layfield and Dr Woodroffe as Followeth:[217]

Whereas in the Wainscot book of the Cathedrall Church it is Registred that Dr Layfield hath paid to the Executrix of Dr Sayer for the wainscott of the house late in his possession Thirty Five pounds Twelve Shillings and Ninepence three farthings, Now be it remembered that in fact and by agreement between the said Dr Layfield and Dr Woodroffe the said Dr Woodroffe shall discharge the said Dr Layfield from the payment of the said money and hath taken upon him to pay the same, But upon Mrs Sayers continuance in the said house 'tis agreed that the same shall be unpaid till her amovall from thence, And on her said removall the said Dr Woodroffe doth hereby promise to pay to the said Mrs Sayer the said Thirty five pounds Twelve Shillings & Ninepence three Farthings for the purpose aforesaid.
Dated this sixth day of December, *Anno Domini* 1711.
Witness Charles Layfield, D.D.   Charles Woodroffe
        Thomas Cranley, Notary Public.

The Charges of Dr Charles Woodrofe for the house late Dr Layfields & before Dr Sayers to be repayd by his successor, a fourth part being deducted according to the Custome of the Church.

Paid by the said Dr Woodrofe to the Executors
of Dr Layfield, a 4th part of £35 12s 9¾d being
deducted for Dr Layfields taking the said house[218]

                                    xxvj £   xiiijs   vijd   *ob.*

23rd June 1715
Allowed & approved of,
In presence of Thomas Cranley.

26 The Charges of Dr Woodroffe for Wainscott.

Mr Butlers Bill.
November 29th 1720
For Wainscotting a Roome conteining 53 Yards
att 3s per Yard[219]   7   19   0

November 1724
paid more by Dr Woodroffe For Wainscott and
Painting as appeares by bills produced at this
Chapter twelve pounds   12   0   0

Seen, examined & allowed by the Chapter, 10th December 1724.

Paid by Dr Woodroffe to the Executors of Dr
Layfeild as appears in folio 14°   26   14   7½

October 24th 1727
paid by Mr Sturges to Mr Brideoake,[220] the
Executor of Dr Charles Woodroffe, for the Wainscott of the said Dr Woodroffes house (the 4th
parte being deducted)   34   19   9

December 2nd 1727
paid more by Mr Sturges to Walter Goodsall for
Wainscott done in the same house, as per
Goodsalls bill   6   15   0

paid more by Mr Sturges to Thomas Broadway
for painting the past Mencioned wainscott, as per
his bill.   0   18   0

The abovemencioned Bills & receipts were produced & allowd att
November Chapter 1727
Ita Testor, Charles Barton, *Clericus Capituli.*

January 1st 1740/1
Paid by Mr Bourne to the Executrix of Mr Sturges
for the Wainscott of the said Mr Sturges house,
the fourth parte being deducted[221]   31   9   6¾
Witness, W. Pescod, Chapter Clerk.

61   Mr Bournes house the late Mr Sturges's

Brought over from Folio 26, paid to the Executrix
of Mr Sturges[222]   31   9   6¾

Paid by Mr Inett to the Executrix of Mr Bourne
for the Wainscott of the said Mr Bournes house,
1 4th part being deducted   23   12   1½

Paid by Dr Sykes to Mr Inett   17   14   0

December 11th 1749			
Expended per Dr Sykes in Bills allowed	9	13	0
Witness, William Pescod, Chapter Clerk.			
	27	10	3

July 5th 1757			
Paid by Dr Pyle to Mrs Sykes, as [per]^d her receipt appears below	20	10	3
Expended by Dr Pyle, bills allowed	3	11	6
June 1758. William Pescod, Chapter Clerk.			

July 5th 1757. Received of Dr Pyle twenty pounds ten shillings & three pence in full for Wainscot money of the Prebendal House late Dr Sykes's.
£20:10:3 by me, E. Sykes.

1758. Standards in the House.[223]

In the Kitchen : Dressers & Drawers & all shelves & the Bacon Rack.

In the Scullery : The Pump with the Leaded Trough under it. All Shelves & the Dresser.

In the Pantry adjoining : All Shelves &c.

In the Pantry out of the Kitchen : All Shelves &c.

In the Butler's pantry at the Foot of the Kitchen Stairs: Lattice Doors & Rails within for Bottles.

In the Stable[224]: 2 stalls [now 4, 1765]^i. [deletion]. Racks & mangers throughout.

In the Servants Hall[225]: Benches.

In the Closet or Pantry out of That : Shelves & Dresser.

In the Brewhouse : The Pump, & wooden Shutters to the windows.

In the Vault : all Bins.

Top of the Backstairs : a Large Press, or Cupboard, with shelves in one half of it, & pins for hanging Cloth[e]s in the other,

62 And a Partition of Deal, which makes a Passage from the 'fore Chamber to the little Chamber next the Garden.[226] Given by Dr Pyle to go with the other Standards. E. Pyle. (see below†)

Brought over	24	1	9

12th December 1759			
Expended & allowd for Wainscott, as by bill	1	13	11
Ditto More for first painting	1	9	3

November Chapter 1760
Expended more by Dr Pyle & allowd by 2 bills   2   13   0
Witness, John Dison, Chapter Clerk.

November 1761
Expended more by Dr Pyle for a Mantlepiece
[*and* a marble Hearth in the Fore Chamber][i] &
painting, as by bills produced & allowed   3   6   11
Witness, John Dison, Chapter Clerk.

November 1762
Expended more by Dr Pyle, as by bills produced
& allowd.   14   8   3
Witness, John Dison, Chapter Clerk.

November 1763
Expended more by Dr Pyle, as by bills produced
& allowd   6   2   1
Witness, John Dison.

†Dr Pyle gives also as standards, The partition of Boards put up in
the small beer Cellar (at the foot of the Back-stairs) for the more
convenient stowage of Coals. And the Partition of Boards put up
cross the Passage that Leads to all the Garrets. He also gives all
the Hangings of Paper throughout the House, whether put on
Canvass or pasted to the Walls or ceilings.[227] And all Locks, bars,
bolts, shelves &c. N.B. Whereas the Occupier of the *next* house to
this (now Mr *Buller's,* 1765) hath customarily brought Coals &
Wood in Carts thro' the Green yard adjoining to *This* House, [no][i]
such conveyance of Coals or Wood is allowed for time to come; a
passage for this Purpose to Mr Buller's House, by a door [*deletion*]
into the little Close or Mount, being made by consent of Parties
[at Dr Pyle's expence][i] and confirmed by order of Chapter [at][i]
Midsummer 1765.[228]

November 1766
Expended more by Dr Pyle, as by bills produced
& allowed   1   10   0

December 1770
To Bill allowd   0   8   4¾
Witness, William Yalden, Deputy Chapter Clerk.

November 1771
By Bills allowed   3   7   8
B. Burt, Deputy Chapter Clerk.

November 1774			
By Bills Allowed	6	2	1
B. Burt, Deputy Chapter Clerk.			
63 Brought over	65	3	3¾
To Bill allowed	0	4	6
Witness, W. Yalden, Chapter Clerk.			
	£65	7	9¾

Received, 21 March 1777 of the Reverend Thomas Rennell per James Rivers Esq., forty nine pounds and ten pence for The Executors of the Reverend Dr Pyle. T. G. Waller.[229]

	49	0	10
Deduct fourth part	12	5	2½
Due from Mr Rennell Junior to his Father	36	15	7½
November 1786			
Two Marble Chimney Pieces	17	4	0
Hayes Carpenter's Bill on Account of Mouldings to Chimney Piece in the Dining Parlour	2	15	0
Ditto on account of Mouldings &c to the Chimney Piece in the Drawing Room	3	18	0
A new Door	1	7	4
Two new Window Shutters	2	1	0
Lucas for 75 Feet of Cornish with two Inrichments at 11d per Foot	3	8	9
	£30	14	1
as above	36	15	7½
Witness, J. Ridding, Chapter Clerk.			
	£67	9	8½
deduct ¼	16	17	5
Paid by the Reverend Mr Williams to Mr Rennell	£50	12	3½
J. Ridding, Chapter Clerk.			
deduct ¼	12	13	0¾
Paid by Mr Vaux to the Executors of Mr Williams	£37	19	2¼

Notes on the Text

1. This table of contents was first compiled in the mid 18th century and maintained by subsequent Chapter Clerks. At the same time the pages of the WB were renumbered (the erased original pagination is illegible) and headings added to each page filled by that date; a date bracket of 1760-64 may be obtained, and the hand is the same as that of the inventory on WB pp.61-2, which is dated 1758. This hand has not been identified, but it is not that of John Dison, then Chapter Clerk.

The houses are ordered into three groups:
a) The Deanery and five houses near it (Nos 1,2,3,4, & 9).
b) The houses west of the cloister garth (Nos 10,11 & 12).
c) The four houses in Dome Alley.

2. The term seems to refer to the 13th-century porch, which is called the 'Gate-way' to the Deanery in the *Notebook of Dean Zachary Pearce* (MS, WCL) p.2 dating from 1739-48.

3. The three bays of the medieval building now known as the 'Pilgrims' Hall' were used as the Dean's stable and coach-house from the Restoration to the 20th century.

4. The heading of WB p.51 has the variant 'The Dean's Great Garden'. The area now comprises the Deanery vegetable garden and orchard.

5. *sine numero*. This seems however to have been an erroneous entry.

6. In the mid 18th century the term 'the Cloister' denoted the passage underneath the Cathedral Library; it had been called the 'Dark Cloyster' as early as 1683 (TR 1682-3 and CO 10 Dec 1689). The passage is similarly named in CA 25 Nov 1766, relating to the footway from No. 1, The Close to 'the Cloister', and in a later Act (CA 25 Nov 1809) referring to the 'archway underneath the Library known by the name of the Cloisters'.

7. The term 'The Mount' or 'Mound' to denote the site of the monastic cloister garth dates from the late 17th century: e.g. TR 1682-3, 'repairing the Mound walls' and CO 6 Dec 1695, 'the Way cross the Mount to be pitched'. The name fell into disuse at the end of the 18th century. T. D. Atkinson has suggested that 'there was possibly something of a mound in the middle which has spread over the whole' ('Winchester Cathedral Close', *Proceedings*, XV (1941), p.13). The late date of the term would seem to exclude any derivation from a lost monastic feature such as a Calvary. It

is equally unconnected with the mound in the garden of No. 12, The Close (now No. 11), which was excavated in 1962–3 (M. Biddle, 'Excavations at Winchester 1962–3', *Antiquaries Journal*, XLIV (1964), pp.188–219).

8. The name 'Dome Alley' is not attested in documents before the 18th century. CA 2 Dec 1663 refers simply to 'The Pav'd way leading to the fower new Brick houses'. Only in 1727 is an order found 'to amend Dumb Alley' (CO 11 Dec 1727), while in November of the following year the Chapter Clerk, Charles Barton, inserted a title in the margin on WB p.21 'The Uppermost House on the left-hand in Dumb Alley'. The lane is also called 'Dumb Alley' on Godson's plan of Winchester (1750). The present form of the name is first found in CA 22 Feb 1764, an order that the south side of the way 'leading to the Houses in Dome Ally' be paved. The fact that 'Dome' is apparently a corruption of 'Dumb' must argue against a possible derivation from *domus* as occasionally suggested. The name may rather be synonymous with 'Blind Alley', i.e. a *voie sans issue*.

9. This title, which appears on WB p.22, evidently baffled the compiler of the title page, who therefore omitted it. There can be little doubt that the building referred to is No. 11 (see Note 187).

10. This list of 'standards' dates from 1665, when Hyde was nominated Bishop of Salisbury.

11. i.e. rebuilt after the Commonwealth. Only the first phase was complete, hence the rooms later created in the Prior's Hall are not mentioned.

12. See Fig. 8. The position of this room is confirmed by the subsequent reference to the 'Chamber over the Hall'. It continued to be called the 'Hall' as late as the 1740s, when the dimensions of the 'bedchamber over the hall' were entered by Dean Pearce in his *Notebook* (see Note 2, above). The wainscot in this room, now an office, has not survived.

13. The wainscot, which has survived, consists of small-square oak panelling of Jacobean type, which continued to be used throughout the Close in the 1660s. The overmantel appears to date from the same period.

14. A few 17th-century fittings have survived in this room (now used as an office), notably the small cupboard by the great hearth in the west wall and, possibly, the iron hooks in the ceiling. A small area of tall panels, probably 17th-century work, remains on the south wall.

15. Until the Commonwealth the buildings of the Close enjoyed the benefits of the water supply inherited from St Swithun's Priory: a stone conduit carried water from the Conduit Head near Easton to Water Lane. It was piped from there to a cistern situated in the NW corner of the Close and distributed in smaller lead pipes to the various houses. The main feeder pipe and the smaller branch pipes were dug up for their lead during the Parliamentary occupation of the Close, and from the 1660s until the mid 19th century each house was supplied from an individual well; hence the frequent mention of pumps in inventories of Close houses during this period.

16. Shutters were still regarded as 'wainscot work' as late as 1788 (WB p.74), and it is interesting that they were not considered to be part of the architecture of the house at that late date. Half of one such 'wainscot

shutting' appears to have survived in the west wall of the 'chamber above the Hall' (see Fig. 8), the window behind it having been bricked up (for the hinges of this leaf, see Fig. 7c). The wainscot in these chambers consists of small-square oak panelling, which has suffered much alteration since it was first installed.

17. The Audit House, first mentioned in a document of 1592 (LB VII fo. 61v), comprised the first-floor rooms above the 13th-century porch of the Deanery. It has been suggested that it was adapted from the Prior's private chapel at the Dissolution (B. Carpenter Turner, '1548; The last Prior and the first Deanery', *Record*, 42 (1973), pp.12–21). The Wainscot Book entry implies that the present division into two rooms (a 'roome' and a 'closett') dates from Hyde's rebuilding of the Deanery. The surviving wainscot of the inner room consists of rather tall rectangular panels, with stiles and rails of the section associated with small-square oak panelling.

18. The cellarage beneath the Prior's Hall was the subject of a drawn-out dispute between the Dean & Chapter and their Steward, Henry Foyle (see p.5). The location of the two cellars mentioned here is uncertain, but by 1681 Dean Meggott had full possession, and Thomas George paved the cellars in brick at a cost of £5 5s 6d, using 3,400 specially-ordered paving bricks (TR 1680–1 p.11).

19. Until 1645 the Canons used the ancient 'Pilgrims' Hall' as a 'Common Brewhouse' (see p.40), but individual brewhouses were built for each canonry house from 1660, and the Pilgrims' Hall was adapted for use as the Dean's stable and coach-house. The 'Brewhouse' referred to here is probably the long building on the east side of the Deanery kitchen yard, now known as the 'Old Bakehouse'. Surprisingly, this building is omitted from Godson's plan of 1750. For vocabulary used in this section, see Glossary.

20. See Fig. 9 for the surviving lead pump in the brewhouse, which is possibly the one referred to here.

21. Probably located on the ground floor of the North Gallery. 'Square planck' is a curious term to denote a long piece of wood, presumably square in section.

22. Alexander Hyde (see Note 10). This shows that Hyde's expenses for 'wainscot' amounted to £59 5s 4d. Exceptionally, this wainscoting seems to have been included with the 'standards' listed in the Inventory of 1665.

23. The second phase of the rebuilding, including the remodelling of the Prior's Hall and the addition of the Long Gallery. Dean Clarke's additions were admired by Celia Fiennes who visited Winchester at the end of the 17th century and noted the Dean's 'Good old house' with 'a dineing drawing room and bed chamber very good' and its 'long gallery' (C. Morris, ed., *The Illustrated Journeys of Celia Fiennes*, London, 1982, p.66).

24. This entry seems to suggest that a staircase originally led out of the room known as the 'Hall'; it was possibly removed or modified when the main staircase (greatly altered in the early 19th century) was built in the entrance hall.

25. The *loggia* beneath the Long Gallery. This door replaced the former window in the east wall of the parlour.

26. cf. Note 24

27. This window appears to have been replaced by an alcove, which is lined with small-square oak panelling.

28. i.e. local joiners. cf. the (superior) 'London Joiners'.

29. Virger & Janitor from 1666 (CA 25 Nov 1666). Clerk of Works in succession to Giles Lamphire by 1673. Died 1694.

30. The meaning of this term is uncertain. 'West' seems unlikely. Possibly a type of 'rough wainscot' behind textile hangings. The London joiners wainscoted only the 'Chimney side' in this room, which was formed from the two southernmost bays of the medieval 'Prior's Hall'. See Note 37 below.

31. The two galleries mentioned here are the new 'Long Gallery' and the earlier 'North Gallery' (Fig. 8). The North Gallery is referred to simply as 'the Gallery' in CO 17 Aug 1668. The two galleries were conceived as a continuous promenade passing through the three 'chambers', where a measure of temporary privacy, or warmth, could be obtained by closing the 'double doors': these, however, have been replaced. Celia Fiennes wrote, in the late 17th century, 'A long gallery runns through the house and opens into the garden by a descent of several stone steps . . .' (*op. cit.* in Note 23, p.66).

32. The sense of this phrase is unclear. The present windows in this room date from 1808, when the entire south wall and gable of the Prior's Hall were rebuilt.

33. The sum entered in the Wainscot Book, £11 6s 8d, was the total of one of the London joiners' bills, and the Chapter Clerk no doubt kept the 'acquittance' justifying the Dean's expenditure. However, because this bill included wainscot work in the Long Gallery, for which the Wainscot Book system did not operate (see pp.5–6), an adjustment had to be made for this non-eligible work.

34. A further adjustment had to be made because Dean Clarke's alterations involved removing a certain amount of wainscoting set up at Dean Hyde's expense, and replacing it by the four 'double doors', which were apparently located in the 'chambers between the two galleries'.

35. The deal panelling installed in the Dining-Room and Great Bedchamber formed the most expensive part of Dean Clarke's bill. While the Canons were content with small-square panelling, installed by local craftsmen (the 'country joiners', as they are called here), the Dean required something more up-to-date in his main reception room. Much of the panelling in the Dining-Room (known now as the 'Prior's Hall') may be attributed to Dean Clarke; with the exception of the upper two-thirds of the east wall, where the wall above chair-rail height has been plastered, and large panels defined by means of applied, wooden mouldings. The south wall (Fig. 10) is typical of the period, with a heavy bolection moulding both for the framework of the panels, and for the fireplace surround itself. There are signs of alteration to the cornice, however, and to the doors; these appear to be the original

doors, cut down to fit the altered door-frames—probably, on the evidence of the door-furniture, during the extensive operations of 1808.

36. Textile hangings were not always considered suitable for use in dining-rooms (they tended to hold the smell of food); but Celia Fiennes' description (see Note 23) shows that the room was conceived as a dual-purpose 'Dining/Drawing-Room'. The hangings were probably suspended on the east wall, opposite the windows; and the present large panels and hooks, though certainly not themselves original, may at least represent the original scheme.

37. The large double chimney which separates the Great Bedchamber from the Dining-Room was built *c*.1663 (see 'The Protest of Henry Foyle', MS, WCL, printed in *Winch. Cath. Docs. II*, pp.138–9). The chimney-piece in the Bedchamber is virtually identical to that in the adjoining Dining-Room. The London joiners appear to have wainscoted only the 'Chimneyside', while the remaining walls were covered with textile hangings. As noted earlier, this less prestigious work had been entrusted to Willis, a local joiner.

38. This entire bill was subsequently disallowed (see Note 43) as relating to 'Ironwork', which was not eligible for entry in the Wainscot Book. The entry is of interest, giving the cost of these items; but none seems to have survived. For discussion of the vocabulary, see the Glossary.

39. Probably the door from the parlour to the *loggia*.

40. See Note 26.

41. i.e. four double doors in the chambers between the two galleries, one double door in the 'New' [Long] Gallery, and two double doors in the North Gallery.

42. Deal wainscoting was invariably painted. This entry proves that the present-day colour scheme is historically correct. Samuel Master's bill was for 300 square yards of painting. The total wall area of these two rooms, making due allowance for windows, fireplaces etc., is about 320 square yards, which appears a tolerable agreement. This item was subsequently disallowed (see Note 43).

43. When Dean Clarke's expenditure was finally reckoned, two items were disallowed by Order of Chapter: 'Upon examination of the bill of Dean Clarke entred in the booke to be payd by his successor they did finde fifteene poundes for painting and six poundes fifteene shillings & tenn pence for Ironworke, both which by the rule & custome of this Church are not to be brought in for Income nor be allowed by the successor' (CA 6 Dec 1679). The bill for 'Gimmers etc.' in fact comes to only £5 16s 4d. It is however clear that this is the bill referred to in the Chapter Act, for if this bill and the sum of £15 for painting are excluded, Dean Clarke's total expenses (including the sum of £39 19s 0d paid to his predecessor) amount to £110 13s 10d. After the customary deduction of 25% (i.e. £27 13s 5½d), the sum payable by his successor amounts to £83 0s 4½d, as correctly calculated in the Wainscot Book. The matter of Dean Clarke's wainscot expenses was a matter of further dispute: see the letter from Dean Meggott to Bp. Morley 'concerning the appeale made by the Executors of his predecessor etc.' (MS, WCL (Morley Papers—misc.)).

44. It was customary for the arms of the reigning monarch to be displayed in grand houses. The WB entry may refer to the arms of the House of Stuart (probably of Charles II) above the east door of the Prior's Hall.

45. The calculation is inexact. The sum due to Mrs Meggott was in fact £64 7s 7d. Thomas Cranley appears to have had difficulty in manipulating Roman figures in his calculations, which are frequently inaccurate (see also Notes 147 and 166).

46. It is not clear in what this modification consisted. It may have involved the removal of pediments. 'Great Chamber'—the great bedchamber.

47. One alteration to the Deanery wainscot which took place during the time of Dean John Wickart (1692–1722) was not eligible for entry in the Wainscot Book: 'Ordered that some wenscot be allo'd to the Dean for a square room near his parlor & not to be laid on the income of the Deanery to be taken out of the Gallery Wenscot' (CO 22 Apr 1701). The wording implies that the cost of workmanship was borne by the Chapter but that the panelling itself was simply moved from the Long Gallery. The total for 'wainscot money' paid by Dean Trimnell to Wickart's executors shows that no other wainscot work was allowed to Wickart: the sum is however only approximately correct (see Note 45), and should in fact be £48 12s 9d.

48. It is possible that this entry relates to the wainscoting of the small extension north of the 'Parlour', referred to in the *Notebook of Zachary Pearce* (MS, WCL) as 'The passage to the Parlour'. It is unfortunate that the bills mentioned so often in the Wainscot Book were not retained after they had been 'approved', for this would have resolved such uncertainty. The Windsor 'Income Book' (see p.xxi) provides a much more detailed coverage of wainscot work, and workmen's bills are generally transcribed in full.

49. The rules concerning painting were changed shortly after this (see p.xvi).

50. The wainscot of the 'Great Staircase' was probably removed during the enlarging of the entrance hall in 1808. This work removed most of the 'passage to the three chambers', now represented merely by a landing. The passage in question ran east-west along the south side of the main 1660–65 block, effectively linking the two galleries.

51. The 2nd storey, below the medieval roof of the Prior's Hall, was considerably altered *c*.1960, and no 18th-century work survives. Marks on the principal trusses show the level of a former ceiling. The term 'garret' usually implies servants' accommodation, and the wainscot itemised here may have been of the simplest kind.

52. The room 'over the kitchen' would appear to be 'new' in function rather than fabric, and this entry probably relates to alterations to the former 'chamber over the kitchen' for a new purpose. This room is currently used as a dining-room, but Dean Pearce's alterations, which included installing a fine chimney-piece (Fig. 11), may have been intended to form a new reception room.

53. The *Notebook of Zachary Pearce* (MS, WCL, p.3) proves that the term 'Hall' was still applied to the ground-floor room between the Kitchen and the Parlour (Fig. 8), and not to an entrance hall.

54. The wainscot of the north gallery, now used as a flat ('Deanery Cottage'), has not survived.

55. This item, in the room now used as the Dining-Room, has survived (Fig. 11). There is a similar chimney-piece in the 'Long Gallery'. Marble chimney-pieces were deemed eligible as Wainscot Book items at the very Chapter meeting when this entry was approved. By an earlier Chapter Order, provision had been made for making good damage caused by the removal of such chimney-pieces in the Canons' houses (CO 11 Dec 1731— see p.xvii), and by a further Act of November 1747 it was agreed that this order was 'to extend to the Deanry . . . and that in case the Dean or any Prebendary be be not willing to take away any Marble Slab or Marble Chimney peice with the carved or plain Mantle-tree, Mouldings and other appurtenances to the same . . . he may cause the same . . . to be enter'd in the Wainscot book subject to the same deduction as the Wainscot is' (CA 25 Nov 1747).

56. The above Act now permitted the private transaction between Dean Pearce and Dean Naylor's executors (d. June 1739) to be entered in the Wainscot Book.

57. It is not possible to identify with certainty any of Dean Cheyney's (1748-60) many expenses for 'wainscot work'.

58. Jonathan Shipley (Dean 1760-9) was enthroned Bp. of Llandaff in February 1769 and was translated to St Asaph in September 1769.

59. 'New' in the sense of 'rebuilt'. 'The Cloyster'—see Note 6.

60. It is not possible to identify with certainty all the rooms mentioned in this summary of Woodroffe's wainscot bills, and the labelling of the ground-floor plan, Fig. 12, is therefore partly conjectural, though the identification of particular rooms is justified in the notes which follow. It seems clear that the three main rooms listed—the Great Parlour, the Drawing-Room and the Study—lay on the east side of the building, while the two wings at the 'back' of the house contained service rooms.

61. The use of small-square oak panelling in the room at the NE corner of the house is a strong argument in favour of its being the 'Study' mentioned here. Though such panelling, decidedly out of date by 1727, would not have been considered suitable for the main reception rooms, it was evidently deemed acceptable for the more private rooms. The oak panelling may well have been salvaged from the earlier building. The north and east walls of the study are wainscoted in this panelling, while the window shutters, cornice and certain other fittings are typical of the reign of Queen Anne—a somewhat incongruous mixture.

62. The drawing-room (see Fig. 12) was panelled in a manner more in keeping with the intimate nature of such a room. The large plain panels on the west wall (281 × 188 cm), above the fireplace and on the north wall were probably designed to receive textile hangings. Being movables, these are not recorded here. The other panels are similar to those of the adjoining

'Great Parlour' (Fig. 13). The wooden cornice is identical to that of the other two ground-floor reception rooms. It is possible that there was originally access from the Parlour into the Drawing-Room, but this doorway now forms a cupboard and the panelling on the Parlour side, though in poor condition, shows no certain signs of having been rebuilt.

63. There can be no doubt that the 'Great Parlour' was the large room at the centre of the house, which retains its high-quality deal panelling (Fig. 13). Its principal function would have been that of a dining-room.

64. The wainscot referred to has not survived. In view of the low price, it may have consisted of re-used 'small-square oak panelling', like that installed in the next room mentioned.

65. The south wall of this bedroom is wainscoted from floor to ceiling in small-square oak panelling, including two contemporary 'oak-wainscot' doors, with original hinges; the panelling may have been salvaged from the earlier building, which would explain its low cost. The other three walls are similarly panelled up to chair-rail height only.

66. It will be noted that no charges are quoted here for wall-coverings in the other two large first-floor rooms on the east side of the building. Perhaps these were wainscoted with the 'rough wainscot' mentioned here, which was covered by textile hangings.

67. The relatively large charge for painting reflects the 18th-century taste for painted deal panelling. All the surviving small-square oak panelling in the house is now similarly painted, though it is unlikely that this was the original treatment.

68. The vault is situated in the older part of the house (dating from 1699), and probably formed part of it. It consists of a brick, barrel-vaulted cellar, oriented east-west. The bins for wine storage possibly sat on the three-foot-high brick ledges on either side of the cellar. The hanging shelf was presumably mounted on the end wall, for the vault seems always to have had only one entrance, from the corridor.

69. This room also contains a large 18th-century kitchen cupboard: a rare survival of a piece of domestic furniture in its original situation.

70. This room and the following 'Butler's Room' appear to have been situated in the 1699 wing. They were thrown together to form the present dining-room, probably in the late 19th century.

71. This room has not been identified, but may have been situated in a lean-to against the south wall of the house, behind the kitchen chimney. Excavations in this area have revealed at least three earlier brick buildings on the site of the present boiler-room.

72. An interesting reference to a purpose-made ironing board.

73. This *memorandum*, in the hand of the writer of the other entries on this page, dates from 1728 but was later cancelled by the second *memorandum* in Woodroffe's own hand, which is written in the left-hand margin and partly covers the 1728 entry. It was the 1728 *memorandum* that eventually led to marble chimney-pieces being considered as Wainscot Book items. At the November Chapter of 1731 it was resolved that if Woodroffe or any other

prebendary should elect to remove a marble chimney-piece from his house, then the sum of 30s per chimney piece should be paid to the succeeding prebendary in that house 'to be applyed towards putting up a Stone chimney piece in the place thereof or otherways making good the same' (CO 11 Dec 1731). By a further Act of 25 Nov 1747, any Dean or Canon not wishing to remove a marble chimney-piece in this way was permitted to enter its cost in the Wainscot Book, subject to the same rules as true wainscot (see Note 55). Woodroffe duly entered the cost of his two marble chimney-pieces on 11 Dec 1749 (WB p.30), but seems to have changed his mind in December 1762, when he added the second *memorandum*, which denied all possibility of the chimney-pieces remaining as part of the house after his death. The cost of the chimney-pieces was duly subtracted from Woodroffe's total wainscot expenses when the final reckoning was made (WB p.30).

74. It was apparently felt that in view of Woodroffe's exceptionally lengthy tenure, a larger depreciation than the normal 25% should be made. The sum of £15, over and above the regular 25%, was presumably fixed by negotiation between the Chapter and Woodroffe's executors.

75. This change is also recorded in the *Insurance Memorandum* of November 1740: 'Dr Maurice's house (now Dr Sykes) is situated between Mr Woodroffe's and the Dean's lower garden. [The house is] insured for 300£, Outhouse 20£, Brewhouse 30£ and Stable 50£.'

76. By CA 26 Nov 1739 only the painting of new wainscot, or the first repainting of old work by a new occupant were eligible for the Wainscot Book (see p.xvi). Entries relating to painting after this date often specify 'New' or 'First', therefore.

77. The sum erroneously entered was not expended on any other house at about this time and the 'mistake' probably involved the entering of a charge later disallowed by the Chapter.

78. The entry demonstrates how a Canon set about having an item entered in the Wainscot Book at one of the two main Chapters of the year.

79. In the basement. The room above it is part of a *mezzanine* floor.

80. The site of these 'two rooms' is uncertain. The wainscoting costed here has not survived.

81. Such items were not eligible for the Wainscot Book and were therefore deleted.

82. Two wooden chimney-pieces with heavy, wooden bolection mouldings have survived, in the 'Parlour' and in the room over the 'Withdrawing Room'.

83. This important example of late 17th-century oak panelling, installed by one of Wren's master craftsmen, has survived (Fig. 14), although a large section (occupying a complete wall) and several smaller pieces were transferred to the present entrance hall at the end of the 19th century, when the 'parlour' was turned into a library. The room was drastically altered, at that time, by the addition of a bay-window. However, the total wall area of the original room amounts to approximately 65 square yards: an adequate agreement.

84. The panelling in this smaller room has fared better, despite the ingenious insertion of a 19th-century cupboard behind one of the panels, and the disastrous application of white gloss paint in the present century. The door, like that of the parlour, retains its original hinges. The windows are 18th-century replacements (many panes of crown glass survive), complete with fold-away shutters.

85. The entry implies that the mouldings and panels may have been prefabricated elsewhere and transported to Winchester.

86. An error possibly caused by the entering of the cost of the kitchen shelves, though the sum is still out by 10s.

87. The wainscot money transaction between Dr Thomas Cheyney Sr. (Headmaster of Winchester College 1700-24 and father of Dr Thomas Cheyney Jr., 8th Preb. 1739-48) does not appear here. The missing calculations are as follows: Dr Nicholas' total: £73 19s 6d less 25% (£18 9s 10½d) = £55 9s 7½, paid by Dr Cheyney to Dr Nicholas. Less 25% (£13 17s 4d) = £41 12s 3½d, paid by Dr Newey to Dr Cheyney. (cf.£41 12s 6d, recorded in the Wainscot Book.) This shows that no wainscot work eligible for inclusion was left by Dr Cheyney whose tenure lasted for only a few months.

88. John Sturges (12th Preb. 1721-40) had been elected Treasurer for 1728-9 at this November Chapter.

89. The 'Closets' were formed out of half a bay of the Pilgrims' Hall, which Morgan obtained by the exchange of 'a part of his woodhouse and hayloft over it' for 'one part of the Dean's stable' (the Hall itself). According to CA 26 Nov 1739: 'Mr Morgan having lately built a Brick Wall between Mr Dean's stables and that part of his prebendal house where his closets adjoyn to the said stables, agreed that Mr Morgan . . . shall be reimbursed for the same [wall], he declaring at the same time that he would give Ten pounds towards the buildings of the Closets, and enter the remainder only on the Wainscot Book'. The Note relating to this transaction is entered in the left-hand margin of the Wainscot Book.

90. Although the Wainscot Book provides only the barest details of Dr Butler's improvements to the house in 1761-4, which were evidently extensive, it seems likely that the work included the surviving wainscot of the upstairs rooms, which has large, unfielded, deal panels with a simple ovolo moulding surround. This work, which is of typical mid 18th-century type, has survived in two rooms, but the 'marble chimney-pieces' have disappeared.

91. John Butler, who was enthroned as Bp. of Oxford in 1777 but held his Winchester Prebend *in commendam* until his translation to Hereford in 1788, appears to have waived his claim to almost all the wainscot money due to him as outgoing occupant of No. 3, claiming only the sum of £7 18s 5d which he himself owed to Robert Hare, his predecessor in No. 6, into which house he had just moved. The remainder of the wainscot money was given to the Cathedral as a 'benefaction'. Dr Butler also gave 'the Locks & Dressers to the House', as noted on WB p. 56 (see Note 195).

92. William Buller (12th Preb. 1763-92) was enthroned Bp. of Exeter in 1792.

93. Roger Harris was Dr Delanne's tenant in No. 4, and moved to No. 9, Delanne's new prebendal residence, in June 1719 (see Note 177). His rôle in the payment of wainscot money was simply that of an intermediary between Dr Rivers and Dr Delanne. This is made clear on WB p.25, where Dr Rivers' two payments are set forth again, in greater detail.

94. These 'several bills' were entered again on WB p.25 a year later. Thomas Rivers was responsible for a number of alterations at No. 4 which cannot be positively identified. In December 1710 he was allowed materials 'to build where his kitchen now is, the workmanship to be att his owne expense' (CO 11 Dec 1710); this probably involved extending the kitchen westwards by adding a scullery (see Fig. 15). A few months later, having undertaken to spend £100 of his own money on improvements (in the end he spent £105), it was ordered 'that a New Stair Case be built for him at the Expense of the Church' (CO 21 March 1710/11). There can be little doubt that the fine main staircase dates from this period, and was possibly the one mentioned here.

95. References to textile hangings are rare in the Wainscot Book. For the term 'Irish Stitch' see Glossary. At a later date, these hangings were replaced by 'paper & canvas hangings' (WB p. 71). There is little reason to suppose that the kitchen was then situated anywhere other than in its present position; and the removal of the floor, so that the kitchen rose through two storeys, seems to have been a late Victorian phantasy, carried out when this end of the house was 'modernised' in 1898.

96. As its date shows, this *memorandum* was added after the entries on WB p.25. The estimated sum of £80 was probably intended to include the cost of a further building operation (not recorded in the Wainscot Book) undertaken by Rivers in 1714 and referred to as 'Rebuilding the old part of his house' (CO 27 Feb 1713/4). For this he was again allowed materials but not labour costs. The part of the house referred to here was probably that represented on the ground floor by the Dining-Room and adjoining Parlour (see Fig. 15). The panelling and chimney-pieces of these rooms are consistent with an early 18th-century date, as is the fenestration.

97. It is not clear why these bills, which had been approved and entered at the June Chapter of 1712 (WB p.19), should have been examined, allowed and entered a second time, a year later.

98. See Note 93.

99. Probably the room in the south-east corner of the house marked 'Dining Room' in the surviving architect's plan of 1840–44 (MS, WCL), and still used for that purpose. The deal panels are fielded, in an ovolo moulded frame, with a typical early 18th-century chair rail and cornice. They have unfortunately been 'improved', by being covered with hardboard, with modern, applied mouldings around the edge of each panel.

100. Unidentified. This room is perhaps the same as the 'Chamber over the Kitchen'.

101. cf. CO 10 Dec 1701: 'A brewhouse to be made at Dr Sawyers house'. This may be the 'scullery' of the 1840 plan, but there is no reason to suppose that the brewhouse was not an independent building.

102. A probable first draft of this inventory survives (MS, WCL, dated 29 June 1712), and includes Rivers' *memorandum* about the 'Irish Stitch' hangings: this dates the WB version to June 1712. The MS shows some variants: two dressers are specified in the kitchen; the Iron Bar is referred to as 'The Iron Barrs for the Pot-hangers'; the Buttery is called 'the Pantery within the Kitchin'; the Closet between the two parlours is described as 'dark' (no windows); an additional reference is found to a 'little Closet in the Old Buildings' (see Note 96).

103. See Note 96.

104. Died 28 Oct 1755, aged 74 (Monument, Winch. Cath.)

105. See Note 76.

106. Later referred to as 'small-panelled Wainscot' (WB p.71). See Note 112.

107. The inventory of *c.*1761 offers a useful comparison with the earlier inventory (WB p.25) of June 1712. Many 'standards' had survived unchanged.

108. See Notes 95 and 100. It is interesting that the hangings, though paper, should be listed as 'standards', implying the possibility of removal.

109. The 'Buttery next the Kitchen' of the 1712 inventory.

110. The 'Buttery neere [the small beer Cellar] of 1712.

111. The '(dark) Closett between the two Parlours' of 1712.

112. See also Note 106. The 'small-panelled Wainscot' appears to survive on the north wall of the entrance hall. It is now painted and the wood used is not identifiable: possibly oak. The panels are narrow (approx. 9 ins) and relatively tall (approx. 18 ins.).

113. The date of this entry is unknown, but the initials M. W. are those of Matthew Woodford (2nd Preb. 1780–1807), who was Treasurer from Nov 1786 to Nov 1798.

114. A solitary example of plasterwork allowed as a Wainscot Book item.

115. This house was first allotted to Myrth Waferer (6th Preb. 1660—80), as shown in CA 2 Dec 1663: it is referred to as 'Dr Waffer[er's]' as early as May 1662, in the *Account Book of Wm. Fletcher* (fo. 16v). Two months later the following receipt is found: 'July 2nd 1662. Received then of Wm Fletcher twenty pounds . . . in part for wainscott to be put up in Dr Wafferers howse . . . *per me* Francis Spender' (*ibid.* fo. 22a *verso*), and a further payment of £3 19s 0d is recorded on 30 Aug 1662 'Pd. Wm. [*sic*] Spender for wainscott in Dr Wafferers Howse' (*ibid.* fo. 23v).

116. cf. CO 30 Nov 1681: '*Memorandum* that Mr Markland at this Chapter chuses Mr Wards house . . .'

117. Ward's final wainscot total, before deduction of 25%, amounted therefore to £32 16s 0d, which implies that a further £20 was spent by Waferer in wainscoting his house.

118. Similar inventories were taken of the 'standards' in Nos. 6 and 8, and offer an interesting comparison. For vocabulary, see Glossary.

119. These garrets were presumably used as servants' accommodation and are sufficiently spacious to serve today as independent flats.

120. These fitted cupboards were a feature of the Dome Alley houses. Good examples survive in No. 6, The Close.

121. These deal wall-cupboards have also survived in Nos. 5, 7, 8. They are situated in the wall at the head of the first flight of the service stairs. For their hinges, see Fig. 7.

122. Chapter expenses during Louth's tenure include the cost of materials 'to make a new door out of his Hall into the Great Parlor' (30 June 1718).

123. In margin at this point in MS: '1 fourth 3:6:1'. However, details of the payment of wainscot money from Whishaw to Noyes have been omitted. The calculation is as follows: Dr Noyes' total: £13 4s 4½d less 25% (£3 6s 1d) = £9 18s 3½d, paid by Mr Whishaw to Dr Noyes. Less 25% (£2 9s 7d) = £7 8s 8½d, paid by Dr Maurice to Mr Whishaw (£7 8s 6d in Wainscot Book). The change in tenure is recorded in CA 1 July 1740: 'This day Mr Whishaw by a Letter to the Dean Declared his choice of the house late Dr Noyes's and Dr Maurice succeeded him in his Prebendal house'. See also CA 25 Nov 1740 (*Insurance Memorandum*): 'Mr Whishaw's House (Now Dr Maurice's) is Scituated at the East end of the South Side of Dome Alley'.

124. This was entered in error under the wrong house. It relates in fact to No. 12, where Pyle was living in 1759, and was correctly entered on WB p.62 after its deletion here.

125. Many of the 17th-century mullioned and transomed windows in the Close were replaced by sash windows during the 18th century; this was paid for by the Chapter, and counted as a 'repair' (CA 23 June 1798). No. 5 has some good example of early 19th-century Classical Revival sash windows on the south side, but these are later than the work itemised here.

126. Of the four brick houses, No. 6 has been subject to the most alteration. The hall was drastically altered probably c.1800, when a new stair replaced the stair-turret, which was demolished. No panelling survives in the hall or 'great parlour', or the rooms above them. The 'little parlour', on the other hand, received more kindly treatment.

127. The surviving small-square panelling in this room is amongst the finest of its type in the Close. Its surface area is indeed 47 square yards, though the panelling of the entire east wall was moved when the room was enlarged by incorporating the closet between the little parlour and the hall. The total cost of the panelling amounted to £5 17s 6d, as appears from Fawker's bill. The cost of the 'chimney peice' may relate merely to fitting it, as the overmantel itself seems to be a re-used Jacobean overmantel dating from earlier in the 17th century.

128. This bench or 'forme' was apparently common to all four Dome Alley houses. cf. WB p.18, where the 'forme' in No. 5 had been moved from the hall to one of the garrets. cf. also the 'tablebord' at No. 7 (see Note 142).

129. The date of this entry shows that the bills had been retained for some years. The Canons were apparently expected to keep bills justifying their expenses for 'wainscot work' (cf. Note 78).

130. Mrs Elizabeth Hawkins, widow, sister of Dr Bradshaw (but not the wife of Wm. Hawkins), is named as Bradshaw's Executrix in his will (HRO B Wills 1690), together with Dr Hawkins and Richard Harris.

131. The porches of Nos. 5 and 6 have survived as two-storey structures, while those of Nos. 6 and 7 have been cut down and now consist merely of a ground-floor porch. Alterations to the brickwork at first-floor level, together with the reference to 'the little Clossett over the doore' at No. 8 (WB p.5), prove that the porches of Nos. 6 and 7 were formerly two-storeyed, with a 'Closet' approached from the bedchamber over the hall.

132. Though this transaction must have taken place in 1706, it was not entered in the Wainscot Book until 1715 when the entries relating to the house were brought up to date. Although no further entries were made during Woodroffe's tenure, the Chapter Books contain the entry 'That a Window in Dr Woodroofs Study & beddchamber be repaired, or else timber allowed to make a New Sash Window' (CO 11 Dec 1710). This appears to be the earliest reference to a sash window in the Cathedral archives. See Note 125.

133. Anthony Alsop (4th Preb. 1715-26). In 1719 the Dean and Chapter sought the advice of their Visitor, Bishop Jonathan Trelawney, on the subject of Alsop's residence; he was in prison for debt at the time and could not fulfil his statutory obligations. The Bishop concluded that as Alsop's imprisonment was unavoidable, he should be excused his residence (MS, WCL, 19 Dec 1719).

134. John Cooke, Treasurer at this date, appears to have acted as intermediary between the new occupant, Mr Crosse, and Anthony Alsop—still unavoidably absent.

135. John Sturges was Treasurer in 1728-9 and Thomas Rivers was Receiver from 1723-30. The use of intermediaries in both Dr Naylor's payments suggests that his tenure of No. 6 was merely nominal; it cannot have lasted for more than a few months (see Table of Occupants). A chain of house-moving took place at this time, due to the successive deaths of Delanne and Markland. These entries, recorded at the November Chapter meeting of 1728 and spread over two days, bring the Wainscot Book up to date during a time of considerable change in housing.

136. A similar rapid reshuffle took place in the second half of 1756, involving Nos. 5,6,7 and 12.

137. This rather clumsy adjustment was necessary because the 25% deduction had been entered before it was realised that the amount for 'first painting' of Dr Balguy's new wainscot had been omitted.

138. This entry dates from January 1777.

139. John Butler (see Note 91). TR 1779-80 shows that James Rivers Esq was his tenant in No. 6 at that time.

140. Several entries relating to building 'Dr Preston's' appear in the *Account Book of Wm. Fletcher*, including 'Aug: 16th 1662 paid Henry Wickham for 29 yards of wainscott in Dr Prestons Howse at 2s 10d: £6 18s 10d' (fo. 23). Dr Preston's total wainscot bill appears to have amounted to £36 16s 6d before

the 25% deduction. The wainscot installed was slightly more expensive than that of No. 6 (2s 6d per yd.) (WB p.3).

141. Mrs Frances Preston (d.17 Sept 1689—Monument Winch. Cath) was a daughter of Dr Francis Alexander (4th Preb. 1613–58).

142. William Hawkins had moved to No. 7 around Sept 1664. An entry relating to a fixture installed during his tenure appears in TR 1664-5 fo. 4v: 'To 2 joyners for a tablebord for Dr Hawkins hall £1 2s 0d'.

143. These bills relate to the addition of an extension on the north side of the house, traditionally said to have been built by Dr Hawkins for use by his father-in-law, Izaak Walton. A similar extension was added to No. 8 at the same time (see Fig. 16). In June 1682, Dr Hawkins, 'having represented a designe of building two additionall roomes to his house for the better convenience thereof to himselfe & his successors', was granted up to four or five tons of timber from Crondall woods, 'And the like order then made for Dr Payne for the like Addition to his House' (CO 26 June 1682). A date-stone inscribed 'W.H.1683' marks the completion date of Hawkins' wing. Izaak Walton died in December of that year. See J. Crook, 'Izaak Walton and Winchester', *Hampshire Magazine*, Vol. 23, No. 9 (July 1983), pp. 40-43.

144. The wainscot of the 'New Parlour' appears to have been replaced in the 18th century. The present panelling consists of large, unfielded deal panels with very plain, ovolo-moulded surrounds. The chimney-piece is apparently contemporary. The decoration in this room appears to date from the second quarter of the 18th century.

145. The panelling in the 'room over the parlour', recently revealed when layers of wallpaper and hessian were stripped off, and finally removed in 1983, is of great interest (Fig. 18), It consisted originally of alternate panels of deal and gilt-leather or *Guadameci*; but the leather panels had unfortunately been cut out, presumably when the panelling was covered over with hessian for papering. Though, as John Waterer has shown (*Spanish Leather*, London, 1971), *guadameci* was being produced in London as early as 1600, the ovolo mouldings of the deal framework of the panelling of this room are undoubtedly of early 18th-century type. They are in fact identical to those until recently surviving in the room over the hall, the 'Hall Chamber', shown by WB p.27 to date from 1726 (see Note 150). The bills of Robert Cole quoted in the Wainscot Book do not relate to this work therefore and the panelling was probably installed *c*.1726. A large number of London leather gilders were still in business at this date. The leather is too fragmentary for the appearance to be determined; but it seems to have consisted of gilt flowers on a green ground, with some unidentifiable cream passages: the colour decorating a pattern embossed in very low relief.

146. The wainscot money paid by Abraham Markland to William Hawkins is not recorded in the Wainscot Book. The calculation is as follows: Hawkins' total: £42 7s 2½d, less 25% (£10 11s 9½d) = £31 15s 4d, paid by Markland to ?Anna Hawkins, widow, in July 1691. Less 25% (£7 18s 10d) = £23 16s 6d, paid by Dr West to Dr Markland, as shown in the Wainscot Book.

147. John Cooke (5th Preb. 1712–1744) succeeded Thomas Spratt (d.10 May 1720) as appears in the Wainscot Book. The payment of wainscot money by Spratt to West was not recorded in the Wainscot Book. The calculation is as follows: West to Markland £23 16s 6d, less 25% (£5 19s 1½) = £17 17s 4½d, paid by Spratt to Dr West. Less 25% (£4 9s 4d) = £13 8s 0½d, paid by John Cooke to Mrs Spratt, widow. The small discrepancy between this sum and the actual amount recorded in the Wainscot Book (£13 7s 9d) seems to result from Thomas Cranley's poor arithmetic (cf. Note 45). John Cooke was responsible for a considerable amount of building and decorative work at this house, as the Wainscot Book shows. He had been in No. 6 for only a few months when it was ordered 'that Mr Cooke have a new floor laid in his Great Parlour and liberty to make use of such of the old materialls taken upp as shall be thought by him to be usefull elsewhere about his house' (CO 10 Dec 1720). In view of all this building activity, it therefore seems likely that the early Georgian panelling found in several of the rooms of this house (including 'Hawkins' Wing') may date from his tenure, though it is not possible to relate the details given in the Wainscot Book to surviving features.

148. This amount is expressed in figures in the left-hand margin, as are all other payments entered on this page. The figures are written a second time at the foot of the page, in the form of a sum totalling £50 2s 1d.

149. This 'additional wainscot' must have been set up during the tenure of Thomas Spratt; and the amount paid by Mr Cooke was the total after 25% deduction. The full cost of the wainscot was therefore £6 17s 0d.

150. The wainscoting in the 'chamber over the hall', which has partially survived, consisted of large unfielded deal panels surrounded by a simple quadrant or 'ovolo' moulding, similar to that in the first-floor room of the 1683 extension (see Fig. 18 and Note 145). The panelling above chair-rail height was subsequently removed, by sawing through the stiles. The subsequent reference to 'moveable window shutters' in the chamber over the hall (WB p.53) implies that the 'window shutts' mentioned here were installed only in the hall, and not, at this stage, in the chamber.

151. In LH margin: 'Bt. over 50:2:1' (see Note 148) and further sums.

152. Dr Thomas Cheyney Jr. (8th Preb. 1739–48). He was the son of the former headmaster of Winchester College (1700–24), who had lived as a tenant in No. 8 and No. 3 (see Notes 169 and 87).

153. Mrs Elizabeth Cooke, who, as the *Repair Book, I* shows, continued as a tenant in No. 7 until at least 1748. She died 14 Sept 1758 (Ledger stone in Winch. Cath.).

154. The errors in this sentence indicate that in June 1761 John Dison set about up-dating the Wainscot Book entries relating to No. 7, and at first inadvertently omitted the Shipley-Whishaw payment, confusing it with the payment then due from Mr Pyle to Dr Shipley.

155. In November 1804 it was ordered 'that Mr Pyle's house be surveyed by the Carpenter and Bricklayer' with a view to repairs (CA 25 Nov 1804). He died before these could be carried out, but a substantial amount of alteration and repair seems to have occurred during the tenure of his

successors. It seems likely that the reeded neo-classical architraves, with their characteristic *paterae* at the corners, date from this period (one such doorway is shown in Fig. 18). £281 0s 8d was paid for 'repairs' in 1808 (Treasurer's Book 1805–22 p.99), £143 2s 5d in 1818 (*ibid.* p.397) and £138 14s 8d in 1820 (*ibid.* p. 461).

156. In error for 'Mr Iremonger'. The last two lines of this page are entered in pencil.

157. This inventory was taken about three weeks after the installation of William Payne as 10th Prebendary on 3 Feb 1666. Another copy in Payne's own hand survives, entitled 'A note of the Particulars left by Dr Clarke in his Praebend House, taken by Dr Darrell the Vice Dean & Dr Burt Treasurer and Mr Wa: Syms the 26 day of February 1665 [/6]' (MS, WCL). Apart from minor differences of spelling, the significant variants are: 'Kitchen: 2 dressers & shelves over them'; 'A Firre cupbord in the wall going up staires'.

158. These bills, including the lengthy deleted section, are noted on the verso of the Inventory.

159. This may be the deal panelling which has survived on the east wall of this room and below the window. It is framed in the same way as small-square panelling, but the muntins and rails are unmoulded, 10 cm wide, and the plain panels, recessed by 1 cm, are 58 cm high and 51 cm wide (23 × 20 ins). The area quoted implies that there was no adjoining pantry, as at No. 7, and the present wall on this line is modern. This was the only 'Little Parlour' to be wainscoted in deal, those of the other three Dome Alley houses being wainscoted in small-square oak panelling.

160. £11 14s 4d in Inventory.

161. £8 13s 0d in Inventory.

162. £5 8s 6d in Inventory: the sum of the three items relating to the 'furnace'.

163. It seems likely that the 'study' was formed by partitioning off the room above the 'little parlour' thereby forming a 'gallery'. A similar modification appears to have been made at an early date at No. 7.

164. This entire section was deleted as the items mentioned had already been entered. The 'copper furnace' is probably synonymous with one of the 'oven leads'. The wainscot details had already been entered, and in greater detail. The study fixtures are subsequently entered as 'standards', and the garden roller appears to have been disallowed.

165. An important addition to the house during Payne's tenure, not mentioned in the Wainscot Book, was the erection of a new wing in the angle of the stair-turret, adjoining the similar wing built by William Hawkins, occupant of No. 7. By CO 26 June 1682, Payne was granted up to 4 or 5 tons of timber from Crondall woods for this 'Addition to his House', under the same terms as Hawkins (see Note 143). The ground-floor room of this extension was apparently not wainscoted until 1700, when Samuel Woodford (6th Preb. 1680–1701) was granted, out of the Chapter's store of timber, 'sufficient to Wainscott the roome joyninge to the great parlour in his House, Provided the setting it up bee not charged

on the income of the house' (CO 29 June 1700). This latter proviso explains why the operation is not entered in the Wainscot Book.

166. The calculation is inexact and should be as follows: Payne's total = £20 7s 4d, less 25% (£5 1s 10d) = £15 5s 6d. Thomas Cranley, whose poor arithmetic has already been noted, appears to have inadvertently entered the unit pounds, shillings and pence of the 25% discount.

167. Starting from the (incorrect) total of £15 1s 10d, and deducting 25% (£3 15s 5½d), Ellis should have paid £11 6s 4½d. The correct amount is in fact £15 5s 6d less 25% (£3 16s 4½d) = £11 9s 1½d. Cranley's second error brings the total nearer to the correct amount!

168. The last figure of this date is badly formed and may read 1712.

169. The sum entered in this transaction shows that one occupant is unrecorded in the Wainscot Book. By a process of elimination, this was probably Alexander Forbes (5th Preb. 1704-12). The calculations are as follows: Ellis to Woodford, £11 15s 11½d, less 25% (£2 19s 0d) = £8 17s 0d, paid by Forbes to Ellis, less 25% £2 4s 3d) = £6 12s 9d, paid by Captain Brewer (for Hammond) to Thomas Cheyney (for Forbes). Cheyney and Brewer appear to have been tenants: Dr Thomas Cheyney Sr., Headmaster of Winchester College (1700-24), and father of the 8th Preb. of the same name, occupied No. 8 from 1706 until Feb 1712, when he moved to No. 3 (WB p.20 and Note 87). His successor, as tenant of No. 8, was Captain Thomas Brewer (d. 11 July 1724, as shown in the *Burial Register* (MS, WCL)), whose widow, Elizabeth, eventually received the wainscot money due on the house from Hammond's successor there, Philip Barton (WB p.31). It is uncertain whether the tenants actually paid the wainscot money themselves (but see Notes 171 and 177).

170. Unidentified.

171. This entry, repeating the last item of WB p.6, seems to suggest that the tenants, Cheyney and Brewer, actually paid the wainscot money due for the house, even though it was nominally the prebend-house of successive Canons.

172. Philip Barton B.C.L. (8th Preb. 1731-3). The courtesy title 'Dr' in the entry dated Dec 1733 may have served to distinguish him from Charles Barton, Chapter Clerk.

173. This change is reflected in the *Insurance Memorandum* of Nov 1740, where the house is referred to as 'Mr Bourne's, now Dr Cheyney's'. The *Repair Book I* shows that in Nov 1743 the house was occupied by a tenant, Mrs Molineux.

174. Thomas Ridding (3rd Preb. 1745-66), during whose tenure it was ordered that 'The Treasurer do get the back building (now shor'd up) of Mr Riddings house repaired . . .'

175. As the large number of unspecified entries in the Wainscot Book indicate, Sir Peter Rivers, Bart. (known as Sir Peter Rivers Gay from 28 July 1767) was responsible for an important amount of decorative or constructional work at No. 8. Apart from the entries here, the Treasurers' Rolls show payments for 'sash frames': two in 1766-7, two in 1772-3, a 'sash window' in 1773-4, six 'sashes' in 1781-2.

176. It is not possible to determine with certainty the date when Charles Layfield (4th Preb. 1687–1715) succeeded to No. 9. A considerable number of changes of tenancy occurred about 1710, but few of these are recorded in extant documents. A Chapter Order of 1 July 1709, 'that thirty pounds be payd out in pitching [flint paving] in the Close between Dr Layfield's garden Wall & his Court yard wall', may relate to paving work in the approach to Dome Alley; for No. 9 had a garden opposite the house, on the south side of the Alley.

177. This, and the following entry, show that Roger Harris was a non-Canonry tenant in the house, who paid wainscot money on behalf of the nominal prebendal occupant, Dr Delanne, and also paid for the installation of certain wainscoting. His widow continued to live in the house until 1744, as *Repair Book I* (MS, WCL) shows, with its entry for November 1744 referring to 'Mr Whishaw's (Mrs Harris)'. Roger Harris had been Delanne's tenant in No. 4 (WB pp.19, 25 and Note 93) and moved from No. 4 to No. 9 in this capacity.

178. John Sturges was Receiver from 1731–34, and received this sum of wainscot money in that capacity.

179. This change of occupant is mentioned in the *Insurance Memorandum* of November 1740, which states that 'Dr Cheyney's (now Mr Hoadly's) has a Great Court before it, on the West Side of the Deanry, and joins to the South end of Mr Eyre's.'

180. By a letter dated 'Sarum, Nov 1 1740 (MS, WCL), Thomas Whishaw announced that he had 'resolv'd upon succeeding Dr Cheyney if he quits his present House; where the Ladies [Mrs Harris—see Note 177] are very welcome to continue Tenants'. In fact, John Hoadley (Whishaw's senior as Prebendary by two years) seems to have exercised his right of first option, and Whishaw did not become the occupant of No. 9, actual or nominal, until 1742.

181. The Wainscot Book system had been discontinued in 1798, shortly after the preceding bills were entered. Dr Williams' payment was therefore the last to be made for this house.

182. The list of occupants of No. 10 before Dr Robert Eyre (6th Preb. 1701–22) is highly conjectural, and it is possible that he had moved into this house well before this entry of 1710.

183. None of this wainscoting, probably in the southern portion of the house (now 10a) appears to have survived.

184. The end of the 18th century saw the beginning of interest in the antiquities of the Close, and Mulso's house was described by the anonymous author of the *History and Antiquities of Winchester* of 1773 (possibly the Revd Richard Wavell), who noted the undercroft—'several apartments with arched stone-roofs'—and 'the traces of two windows, remarkably long and narrow, discernable in the east end [of the southern part, now 10a] of the Prebendal House'. These features have now disappeared, but Wavell and, 25 years later, Milner, identified four round-headed arches under the present lean-to entrance passage to 10a as 'Walkelin's work': the present arched windows appear, however, to date from the 17th century. For

further details of Mulso's career, see B. Carpenter Turner, '"Dear Gil" and a Close Correspondent' *Record* No. 39 (1979) pp. 25–9.

185. Thomas Godridge Waller (d.3 Feb 1806) had married Rebecca, niece of Nicholas Lechmere (9th Preb. 1750–70), as appears on her ledger stone in Winch. Cath. The Wallers, whose bank was located in nearby Minster House, acted for the Dean & Chapter at the end of the 18th century.

186. By 1798 the house 'late Mr Mulso's' was described as 'considerably out of Repair, having been for some years uninhabited, & having passed through various Hands'.

187. This title is editorial, for the mid-18th century compiler of the 'Table of Contents' and the page headings (see Note 1) was evidently unable to identify the house in question. This is hardly surprising in view of the phrase used to locate it, which demands a knowledge of early 18th-century occupants of the houses—information not available at the time. A close study of the known occupants of the Close houses at the end of the 17th century shows that William Lowth held No. 11, and this fact, together with a comparison of certain features mentioned in the inventory with entries in Chapter Minutes and Treasurers' Rolls, confirms that the 'Little House at the West End of the Church' was indeed No. 11.

188. cf. CO 30 Nov 1681: 'Ordered that a convenient woodhouse with a wash house & oven in the chymny there to be made shall be built this yeare to the house now Dr Woodfords adjoyning to Dr Beaumont's on the north', and CO 30 June 1683 'Ordered that Dr Woodford washhouse bee fitted up . . .'

189. Mentioned in the 1649 *Survey*.

190. cf. CO 1 Dec 1682: 'that a payer of backstayres bee made into the Buttery with a Door and door-case upon the stayres at the value of 40s agreed', and TR 1682–3: 'More for his [Woodford's] woodhouse & back-stairs £2'.

191. cf. CO 29 June 1700. 'Order'd that Mr Louth have Old Materials out of the [Chapter's] Woodyard to make him a pen for sea coal: he paying for the workmanship'.

192. WB p. 32a is fixed between pages 32 and 33 with red sealing-wax. The dimensions of this leaf are the same as the other pages of the book, and the paper identical; it may therefore have been removed from the book at an early date, and kept separately. The transactions which it records have been entered again on WB p. 33, though not the first entry relating to Dr Crosse's expenses.

193. Shelving usually counted as a 'fixture', but was occasionally charged as a Wainscot Book item on the 'income' of the house, as at No. 10 in 1742 (WB p.50). Presumably Dr Alured Clarke (11th Preb. 1723–42) intended to take these shelves with him on moving house.

194. This change took place between July–November 1740, as shown by the *Insurance Memorandum* of Nov 1740, which states that 'Mr Hoadly's House (Now Mr Whishaw's) is situated on the West Side of that part of the Close called the Mount, and joins to the North End of Mr Eyre's House'.

195. See Note 91. John Butler, Bp. of Oxford, had waived his claim to £91 1s 6d, a large proportion of the wainscot money due to him from his successor in No. 3, William Buller, and this sum was acknowledged by the Treasurer as 'a Benefaction to the Church'. As a further gesture of magnanimity, John Butler made no charge for 'Dressers & Locks', which he left in No. 3 as 'standards'; and, as shown here, William Buller followed his generous example on moving from No. 11 to No. 3.

196. George Pelham was enthroned Bp. of Bristol in 1803.

197. By the beginning of the 19th century the house was in great need of repair. Work done in 1808 cost £102 (TR 1807–8) but this did not arrest the general deterioration that led to the eventual demolition of No. 11. In 1817 Charles Augustus North was excused from residence by Bishop Brownlow North, on the grounds that the house was 'insufficient for the accommodation of your family and Establishment and unfit for your Residence therein' (CA 25 Nov 1817).

198. See Ground Plan (Fig. 20). This room is now used as a drawing-room. Its wall area (approx. 75 square yards) is somewhat less than the 90 square yards arrived at by the 17th-century measurer. None of the 17th-century work has survived.

199. The perimeter of the 'Dining Room' measures 74 ft. If this entry relates to that room, a double run of cornice must be accounted for here.

200. A small 'withdrawing room' leading off the 'Dining Room' (see Fig. 20). No original fittings have survived.

201. This cupboard was probably contrived in the space 1.64 m wide by 1.16 m deep to the left of the chimney-breast.

202. The perimeter of this room, excluding the alcove formerly occupied by the cupboard, measures 41 ft 10 ins, which agrees closely with the figure quoted here.

203. See Fig. 20. Like the other ground-floor rooms in this house, the 'Hall' (now the dining-room) has been subjected to considerable alterations, and no trace of 17th-century work survives.

204. cf. the 'double doors' installed in the Deanery at roughly the same period (WB p.9–11). They were subsequently replaced there (probably *c.*1730), and in No. 12 at unknown date.

205. The original of this bill, headed 'For Worke Done att Doctor Dorills by Nickholas More paynter Stainer in the yeer 65' survives in the Cathedral Archives (MS, WCL). The text is similar, differing only in spelling and the use of numerals. However, it concludes 'Mesured att 337 yards of worke, but for the prises I leave to Mr Mure [More] & your selfe, by mee, William Taylor'. Wm. Taylor, the surveyor, had been engaged by Canon Hugh Halswell in 1664 to oversee the rebuilding of No. 4 (see p.52). At this date, it was common practice for work such as panelling and painting to be measured by an independent surveyor. In the 18th century the trade of 'measurer' became a profession in its own right.

206. The doorway from the passage to the service stairs appears to be original.

207. This is a puzzling reference. The frontispiece mentioned here is apparently an internal feature.

208. Possibly the 'hall' was panelled only up to chair-rail level.

209. The doorways leading from the main stairs to the four first-floor rooms.

210. In January 1667 Benjamin Whitear was admitted a Lay Vicar of the Cathedral in place of Wm. Fletcher, Clerk of Works and Lay Vicar, who had just died (CA 15 Jan 1666/7).

211. This is possibly the small first-floor room at the front of the house, above the 'little parlour', which has surviving 18th-century panelling up to chair-rail height (1.02 m from floor) and a late 17th-century bolection moulded fireplace opening.

212. The 'Parlour' here is a 'Dining-Parlour', synonymous with the 'Dining Room' of earlier entries, and is not to be confused with the 'Little Parlour' mentioned 2 lines later. The 'cross-beam' in the first-floor bedroom mentioned here projects several inches below the ceiling line, but the mouldings itemised have disappeared.

213. cf. the earlier entries on this page of the Wainscot Book relating to the cost of these items.

214. The entries relating to this period of the house's history are unusually disordered. Page 15 precedes p.14 chronologically, and within p.14 three sections are out of sequence in the MS and have been put in their correct order here. The order of these sections in the MS is as follows:

1) 'The Charges of Dr Charles Woodrofe . . . 23rd June 1715 Allowed *etc.*'
2) 'An Agreement made by Dr Layfield . . . *Anno Domini* 1711' [plus signatures].
3) 'More Dr Sayer's house . . . 5th October 1711 Examined *etc.*'

215. The present panelling is of the simplest kind, but could possibly have been installed at this period.

216. The calculation is as follows: £42 16s 8½d + £4 13s 9d = £47 10s 5½d, less 25% (£11 17 7½d) = £35 12s 10d.

217. It appears that Mrs Dorothy Sayer (d. 7 Oct 1728) was to continue to live in the house as the nominal tenant of Charles Layfield, whose prebendal residence it was, but as the actual tenant of Charles Woodroffe, who perhaps hoped by this arrangement to accede to No. 12 in due course.

218. This entry implies, however, that Mrs Sayer did not remain in the house for as long as expected; Layfield became the actual occupant after all ('taking the house'), and paid the wainscot money (£35 12s 9¾d) which had already been entered in the book. Woodroffe paid Layfield's executors three quarters of this sum, according to usual practice.

219. Unidentified. Some panelling of early 18th-century type has survived in a first-floor room at the rear of the house, now used as a bathroom.

220. Ralph Brideoake, M.A., Archdeacon of Winchester. Installed 1 Dec 1702. D. 25 Mar 1743.

221. This change of occupant is recorded in the *Insurance Memorandum* of Nov 1740 which states that 'Mr Sturges House (Now Mr Bournes) is Scituated upon an Eminence at the West End of the Church with a Garden behind it bounded on the North by the Great Church Yard'.

222. Margaret Sturges, daughter of Canon Wm. Lowth Sr. The *Repair Book I* (MS, WCL) shows that she continued to occupy No.12 until at least 1745. She died on 31 Dec 1785.

223. None of these standards, almost all located in the service basement, survives. The basement of the house has been completely changed in recent years by its conversion into a library.

224. In the building more or less on the site of the medieval Charnel House, to the west of No. 12.

225. In 12a?

226. In 12a?

227. There are few references to paper hangings in the Wainscot Book. In No. 7, hessian was stretched across the panels of the 18th-century wainscoting and papered (see Note 145); this was a simple way of modernising a wainscoted room in accordance with prevailing fashions. Plain plaster walls could, however, be papered direct.

228. The rear access to No. 11 was reorganised during the tenure of William Buller (12th Preb. 1763–92). Before the Commonwealth a passage had led to this house from the Churchyard, passing behind the adjoining house to the north; and this right-of-way was maintained after No. 12 was built, as shown in a *Memorandum* in CO 1 July 1712. The right-of-way seemed threatened in 1764 when Dr Pyle agreed to sign a declaration in Chapter that 'two rowes of Elms planted by me on each side of the green Yard leading to Mr Bullers back gates were not set with design to prevent the carriage of Fewel by that way he as proprietor of that House has a right . . . the said trees being ornamental'. The following year the old passage was closed and a new door made at Dr Pyle's expense 'from the little Close or Mount into Dr Pyle's premises (at the North East corner of Mr Bullers house) for the Conveyance of Coals and other Fewel to Mr Bullers House' (CA 24 June 1765).

229. The Chapter Clerk's verification of the amount payable occurs as a sum in the MS at this point:

£49:10: 0
16: 6:11¾ one fourth part deducted.
_____
£65: 7: 9¾

Glossary

Architrave. As used in WB generally refers to mouldings surrounding a doorway or window. In one or two instances it may be used in the primary sense of the lowest division of an entablature, in this case lying below the frieze at the head of the panelling.

Bar. The 'Iron bar in the Chimney' referred to in some lists of 'standards' is shown in one Inventory to have served to support pot-hooks.

Benefaction. A grant, gift, bounty or endowment.

Chimney-piece. The ornamental structure of wood, stone or marble, often with mouldings or carvings, over and around a fireplace.

Cock-loft. A small, upper loft under the very ridge of the roof. The term seems to denote something smaller than a 'Garret'.

Cooler. A large cask or tub used in brewing to cool the liquid called 'wort'.

Cornish. Mod. 'Cornice'. An ornamental moulding running round the wall of a room immediately below the ceiling. The true classical examples of panelling may be surmounted by a full entablature consisting of architrave, frieze and cornice.

Deal. A 'deal' was a sawn board of fir up to $3\frac{1}{4}$ ins thick, 7 to 11 ins wide and 8 to 20ft in length. As used by joiners, the term seems to denote a board up to $1\frac{1}{4}$ ins thick. 'Slit deal' was half that thickness.

Dresser. 1) A sideboard on which food is dressed or from which it is served. 2) A kind of kitchen sideboard surmounted by shelves for plates. The term Dresser Board may refer to the lower part only.

Fender. A metal frame in front of a fire to stop coals from rolling out into the room.

Frontispiece. In the context of the WB, this seems to refer to an internal feature, possibly a pediment over a doorway. The term can also refer to a sculpted panel.

Furnace. A 'copper' or 'oven lead'. In connection with brewing, the term denotes a large boiler fixed in brickwork in which the wort is boiled with hops before being transferred to the 'Cooler'.

Furring. A lining of battens fixed to a brick wall (which may have been plastered) to which panelling is affixed. The idea was to stop the dampness of the wall from affecting the panelling, and to obtain a flatter surface.

Garret. A room on the uppermost storey of a house, wholly or partially within the roof-space. Larger than a 'Cock-loft' and used for domestic accommodation.

Gimmer. A type of jointed hinge for a cupboard or desk door. The distinction made in the WB between 'Gimmers' and 'Joints' suggests that the latter term was used for larger door-hinges of the 'H' or 'L' type (see Fig. 7). Other 16th and 17th century uses of the term at Winchester show that it referred to hinges used to join movable flaps and lids of doors or furniture. 'Wing-hinge' is perhaps an equivalent term.

Hanging. A piece of drapery with which the walls are hung. Later extended to 'paper hangings'. One still refers to 'paper-hanging' in connection with wallpaper.

Income. See Notes to Text 43, 47, 165. An item was referred to as being put on the 'Income' of a house when it was entered as an item in the Wainscot Book. cf. the 'Income Book of St George's Windsor' discussed on p. xxi.

Inrichment. (Enrichment) The carved decoration of a moulding.

Irish stitch. The term refers to a pattern rather than a stitch: it is a flame-like pattern, also called *Point d'Hongrie*, woven in wool and 'mainly intended for a middle-class clientele that could not afford real tapestries' (P. Thornton, *17th-century Interior Decoration in England, France and Holland*, London 1971, pp. 108, 127).

Joint. A door-hinge. Two types are found: L-joints and H-joints (see Fig. 7). They are distinct from the smaller 'Wing', 'Butterfly' or 'Flap' hinge known in the WB as a 'Gimmer'.

Laying. To 'lay on' paint is to apply it. Water-colorists speak of 'laying a wash'.

Lead. An 'oven-lead' is a 'Copper': 19th-century 'Coppers' tended to be made of galvanised iron!

Mashing tub. The container in which ground malt, 'grist', is mixed with hot water, a process known as 'mashing'. The malt is stirred with a 'mashing oar' (see **Oare**).

Meash Fat. A mashing or 'meshing' vat: apparently synonymous with a '**Mashing tub**' q.v.

Mentletree (Mod. Mantel-tree). 1) A beam across the opening of a fireplace serving as a lintel to support the overlying masonry. 2) An ornamental structure of wood, marble etc. over or around a fireplace.

Oare. A paddle used to stir the malt during the '**Mashing**' process (see **Mashing Tub**).

Oven lead. A 'Copper—see **Furnace, Lead**.

Press. A large, usually shelved cupboard for holding clothes etc. The term often applies to one placed in a recess in a wall.

Quarter. Term usually used in plural. A piece of timber approx. 4 ins × 2 ins, used as a stud in partitions and other framing. According to Moxon (in his *Mechanick Exercises*) 'Single Quarters are two inches thick and four Inches broad'.

Sea coale. Mineral coal, as opposed to 'coales', i.e. charcoal. The term may imply 'coal brought by sea', though the early use of the term '*carbo maris*' in Northumberland documents suggests coal found washed out of seams by marine erosion.

Shut. A shutter. The variant '**Shuttings**' occurs in the WB.

Slab. A flat piece of stone or marble set in the floor in front of a fireplace.

Spring-bolt. A kind of bolt, distinct from a 'plate' or 'round' bolt, used to fasten a door or window.

Spring-lock. A form of lock in which a spring renders the bolt self-locking except when secured by a catch.

Stallder. A frame or 'horse' on which barrels are placed in a cellar.

Stand. See **Stallder**.

Standard. In the WB: an item of furniture or equipment deemed to form part of the 'fixtures' of a house.

Staple. In its simplest form, a U-shaped iron fitting, hammered into a wall etc. to serve as a hold for a hook, bolt etc. The term refers by extension to the box or case into which a bolt is shot.

Stuff. Building materials, especially timber. Moxon (*Mechanick Exercises*) states: 'The Wood that Joyners work upon they call in general Stuff'.

Tack. A kind of shelf, made of crossed bars of wood suspended from the ceiling on which to put bacon etc. A shelf, mantelpiece or bacon-rack.

Task-work. Work done at the rate of so much per task or unit done, i.e. 'Piece-work'.

Tenderhook. (Tenter-hook). By extension of the original meaning, a hook on which anything (meat in the WB) is hung.

Trussell. A stand for a barrel. A dialect form of 'trestle'.

Tun. The large vat in which beer is worked before it is 'tunned' or cleansed.

Tunnel. A funnel.

Vat. Here apparently some form of ladle. A vat is usually 'a shallow vessel'.

Wainscot. The term, thought to be derived from an Old High German root, refers not only to the varieties of panelling found in the post-medieval period, but also to a particular type of wood, generally oak, used in its formation.

Appendix A

Tables Showing Occupants of Close Houses

After the dissolution of St Swithun's Priory in 1539, the Chapter of Winchester Cathedral was refounded as a Dean and twelve Canons or 'Prebendaries'. The Statutes of Henry VIII permitted each Canon to absent himself from the Close for up to 80 days *per annum*, but he was expected to be normally resident in the Close. This rule was relaxed somewhat by the revised, Caroline Statutes of 1638, which demanded at least 90 days residence *per annum*, of which 21 days were to be continuous; and the year was to be so divided that at least a quarter of the Canons were always resident in the Close. From the New Foundation, therefore, each Canon was provided with a house in the Close, and, as we have seen, until 1670 each newly-elected Canon was obliged by Statute to move into the house previously held by his predecessor in the Prebend. Thereafter a more flexible situation operated.

The following lists show the names of Canons who were the official occupiers of the twelve 'prebend-houses' of the Cathedral Close. It is clear from various documentary sources that some Canons spent the minimum time required by Statute, and the names of some of the tenants who occupied the houses in their stead are occasionally recorded. Usually, though, only the name of the official, prebendal occupant is known.

The dates given are based on the assumption that any change of occupant took place at the earliest possible occasion, following the death or retirement of a Canon. In practice, the chain of house-moving that is often shown to have occurred as a result of a house becoming vacant usually took some time to complete, but the exact dates of changes are not usually recorded.

Some entries, marked with a question mark, are conjectural and arrived at by a process of elimination. The names of Canons appearing in the Wainscot Book as occupants of particular houses are printed in bold type. Where a Canon's name appears for the first time, the date given is that of his Installation or Collation. The source for biographical dates is J. E. Horne, ed., *Le Neve's Fasti Ecclesiae Anglicanae, 1541–1857*, Vol. III, London, 1974.

156

The Deanery

Aug	1660	**Alexander Hyde** [WB pp.1,9]	Inst. 8 Aug 1660	Bp. of Salisbury 1665
Feb	1666	**William Clarke** [WB pp.9–11,13]	Inst. 1 Feb 1666	D. by 22 Sept 1679
Oct	1679	**Richard Meggott** [WB p.13]	Inst. 9 Oct 1679	D. by 10 Dec 1692
Jan	1693	**John Wickart** [WB pp.13,28]	Inst. 14 Jan 1693	D. 29 Jan 1722
Feb	1722	**William Trimnell** [WB pp.28,41]	Inst. 16 Feb 1722	D. 15 Apr 1729
May	1729	**Charles Naylor** [WB pp.26,41,57]	Inst. 7 May 1729	D. 28 June 1739
Aug	1739	**Zachary Pearce** [WB pp.57–8]	Inst. 4 Aug 1739	Bp. of Bangor 1748
Mar	1748	**Thomas Cheyney** [WB pp.58,68–9]	Inst. 25 Mar 1748	D. 27 Jan 1760
June	1760	Jonathan Shipley	Inst. 14 June 1760	Bp. of Llandaff Feb 1769
Oct	1769	Newton Ogle	Inst. 21 Oct 1769	D. 6 Jan 1804
Feb	1804	Robert Holmes	Inst. 22 Feb 1804	D. 12 Nov 1805
Dec	1805	Thomas Rennell	Inst. Dec 1805	D. 31 Mar 1840

No. 1, The Close. 'The New House behind the Cloister'

Aug	1660	Joseph Gulston	Inst. 8 Aug 1660	D. 10 Apr 1669 (Dean of Chichester 1663)
Apr	1669	Robert Sharrock	From No. 11	D. 11 July 1684
July	1684	Samuel Palmer	Inst. 14 July 1684	To No. 5, July 1691 [WB p.18]
Aug	1691	Baptista Levinz, Bp. of Man	Inst. 5 July 1691	D. 31 Jan 1693
Feb	1693	?George Fulham	Inst. 5 Feb 1693	To No. 12, Aug 1694 [WB p.15]
Aug	1694	John Warner	Inst. 13 Aug 1694	D. 4 Oct 1704
Oct	1704	?Edward Waple	From No. 5 [WB p.19]	D. 8 June 1712
June	1712	Abraham Markland	From No. 7 [WB p.12]	To No. 3, June 1726 [WB p.20]
June	1726	Joseph Soley	From ?No. 2	To No. 10 by Jan 1727 [WB p.24]
by Jan	1727	**Benjamin Woodroffe** [WB pp.29–30]	Inst. 16 Sept 1726	D. 5 Aug 1770
Aug	1770	**Philip Walton** [WB p.30]	From No. 5	D. before 20 Dec 1770 [WB p.30]
Dec	1770	**William Lowth Jr.** [WB p.30]	From No. 2	D. 30 Apr 1795
Apr	1795	**Robert Hare** [WB p.30]	From No. 11 [WB p.76]	D. 14 Mar 1797
Mar	1797	**Thomas Rennell Jr.** [WB p.30]	From No. 12 [WB p.63]	Resig. 25 May 1798

No. 1, The Close—*continued*

May 1798	**Matthew Woodford** [WB p.30]	From No. 5 [WB p.74]	D. 30 Sept 1807
Oct 1807	**Edmund Poulter** [WB p.30]	From No. 3 [WB p.80]	D. 8 Jan 1832
Jan 1832	William Harrison	From No. 11	D. 1 Sept 1846
1846	?empty		

No. 2, The Close. 'The House North of the Dean's Garden'

1660	Sebastian Smith		Resig. by 6 July 1661
July 1661	Thomas Gumble	Inst. 6 July 1661	D. 9 Sept 1676
Sept 1676	Thomas Ken	From No. 11	Bp. of Bath & Wells, 1685
Mar 1685	Samuel Woodford	From No. 11	To No. 8, Sept 1689 [WB p.6]
Sept 1689	Charles Layfield	From ?No. 11	To No. 9 by June 1710 [WB p.23]
June 1710	?Mainwaring Hammond	Inst. 17 June 1710	To No. 8, Oct 1712
Nov 1712	?Thomas Spratt	Inst. 18 Nov 1712	To No. 7, ?1716 [WB p.27]
Dec 1716	?John Cobb	Inst. 12 Dec 1716	To No. 3, May 1723 [WB p.20]
May 1723	Alured Clarke	Inst. 18 May 1723	To No. 11 ?Nov 1734 [WB pp.32a,33]
Sept 1726	?Benjamin Woodroffe	Inst. 16 Sept 1626	To No. 1 by Jan 1627
Mar 1727	?Charles Naylor	Inst. 17 Mar 1727	To No. 6, June 1728
by Nov 1728	Thomas Hayley	Inst. 7 Sept 1728	To No. 6, May 1729 [WB p.37]
May 1729	**Christopher Eyre** [WB p.39]	Inst. 16 May 1729	To No. 10, ?Nov 1731 [WB p.49]
Nov 1731	**Samuel Noyes** [WB p.39]	Inst. 25 Nov 1731	To No. 5, Jun-Nov 1732 [WB p.43]
June 1732	**Robert Bourne** [WB pp.39,51]	Inst. 22 June 1732	To No. 8, Sept-Dec 1733 [WB p.31]
by Dec 1733	**Henry Stephens** [WB pp.39,51]	Inst. 8 Sept 1733	D. 13 Apr 1739
June 1739	**Thomas Cheyney** [WB p.51]	Inst. 21 Apr 1739	To No. 9 Aug-Dec 1739 [WB p.47]
Nov 1739	**Thomas Whishaw** [WB p.51]	Inst. 10 Apr 1740	To No. 5, ?Apr 1740
July 1740	**Peter Maurice** [WB p.51]	Inst. 24 Oct 1740	To No. 5 Oct 1740
Oct 1740	**Arthur Ashley Sykes** [WB pp.51-2]	Inst. 3 Apr 1749	To No. 12, Jan 1749 [WB p.61]
by Dec 1749	**Robert Eden** [WB p.52]		D. 11 July 1759
Aug 1759	**William Lowth Jr.** [WB p.52]	Inst. 2 Aug 1759	To No. 1, Aug 1770 [WB p.30]

No. 2, The Close—*continued*

by Nov	1771	Samuel Nott [WB pp.52,77]	From No. 6 [WB p.73]	D. 27 May 1793
by Aug	1793	John Garnett [WB pp.77–8]	From No. 10 [WB p.72]	To No. 8, Mar 1800 [WB p.79]
Mar	1800	Sir William Heathcote [WB p.78]	From No. 10 [WB p.72v]	D. 29 Mar 1802
Mar	1802	William Garnier [WB p.78]	From No. 10 [WB p.72v]	To No. 3, Sept 1807 [WB p.80]
by Dec	1807	Hon. Thomas de Grey [WB p.78]	Inst. 14 July 1807	To No. 10, Apr 1817
Apr	1817	Hon. Augustus Legge [WB p.78]	Inst. 26 Apr 1817	D. 21 Aug 1828
Sept	1828	Edward James	Inst. 20 Sept 1828	D. 6 Apr 1854
Apr	1855	house vacant		
	1856	house demolished		

No. 3, The Close. 'The House next the Dean's Stable'

Dec	1660	John Woodman (Commonwealth inhabitant)		
Sept	1662	assigned to William Hawkins	Inst. 6 Sept 1662	To No. 7, Sept 1664
Sept	1664	William Burt	Inst. 22 Sept 1664	D. 3 July 1679
July	1679	?Seth Ward	From No. 11	To No. 5, Nov 1680 [WB p.17]
Nov	1680	?Samuel Woodford	Inst. 8 Nov 1680	To No. 11, Nov 1681
Nov	1681	?William Harrison	Inst. 3 Nov 1681	To No. 12, Mar 1684 [WB p.15]
Apr	1684	John Nicholas [WB p.16]	Inst. 2 Apr 1684	D. 27 Feb 1712
Feb	1712	*Thomas Cheyney [WB p.20]	From No. 8 [WB p.6]	Left house by June 1712 *Non-prebendal tenant
June	1712	Thomas Newey [WB p.20]	Inst. 23 June 1712	D. 6 May 1723
May	1723	John Cobb [WB p.20]	From ?No. 2	D. 25 Nov 1724
Nov	1724	Anthony Alsop [WB p.20]	From No. 6 [WB p.21]	D. 10 June 1726
June	1726	Abraham Markland [WB p.20]	From No. 1	D. 29 July 1728
July	1728	Charles Naylor [WB pp.20,35]	From No. 6 [WB p.21]	Dean of Winchester, May 1729
May	1729	John Morgan [WB pp.35–6]	From No. 6 [WB p.37]	D. 25 May 1760
June	1726	John Butler [WB p.36]	Inst. 18 June 1760	To No. 6 (as Bp. of Oxford), June 1777 [WB p.73]
June	1777	William Buller [WB p.36,80]	From No. 11 [WB p.56]	Bp. of Exeter, 1792
	1792	Edmund Poulter [WB p.80]	From No. 10 [WB p.72]	To No.1, Sept 1807 [WB p.30]

No. 3, The Close—*continued*

Sept	1807	**William Garnier** [WB p.80]	From No. 2 [WB p.78]	Res. by 2 Sept 1831
Sept	1831	Thomas de Grey (Lord Walsingham)	From No. 10	Res. by 19 July 1834
	1834	Charles Hoare	From No. 7	D. 15 Jan 1865 (Prebend suspended)

No. 4, The Close. 'The House over against the South Door of the Deanery'

	1660	Hugh Halswell (occupied house before Commonwealth)		D. by 13 Jan 1673
Jan	1673	Thomas Sutton	Inst. 15 Jan 1673	D. by 4 Nov 1696
Nov	1696	Welbore Ellis	Inst. 7 Nov 1696	To No. 8, Jan 1701 [WB p.6]
Jan	1701	**Thomas Sayer** [WB p.19]	Inst. 13 Nov 1700	To No. 12, Nov 1702 [WB p.15]
Nov	1702	**William Delanne** [WB p.19]	From ?No. 10	To No. 9, June 1710 [WB p.23]
June	1710	**Thomas Rivers** [WB pp.19,25,46]	From ?No. 10	D. 8 Sept 1731
Sept	1731	**Alured Clarke** [WB pp.45–6]	From No. 11 [WB p.33]	D. 31 May 1742
June	1742	**John Hoadley** [WB pp.46,71]	From No. 9 [WB p.48]	Res. 12 June 1760
June	1760	**John Sturges** Jr. [WB pp.46,71,75]	From No. 6 [WB p.38]	D. 2 Oct 1807
Oct	1807	**Francis North** [WB p.75]	From No. 11 [WB p.76]	Res. by 5 Dec 1827
Dec	1827	George Pretyman	From No. 8	D. 23 June 1859 (Prebend suspended)

No. 5, The Close. 'The First House on the Left Hand in Dome Alley'

	1663	Myrth Waferer (House built by 1663–4)		D. 5 Nov 1680
Nov	1680	**Seth Ward** [WB p.17]	From No. 11	Res. by 3 Nov 1681
Nov	1681	**Abraham Markland** [WB 17–8]	From No. 11	To No. 7, July 1691
July	1691	**Samuel Palmer** [WB p.18]	From No. 1	D. 30 Oct 1701
Nov	1701	**Edward Waple** [WB pp.18–9]	From ?No. 10	To No. 1, Oct 1704
Oct	1704	**William Lowth** Sr. [WB pp.19,43]	From No. 11 [WB p.22]	D. 16 May 1732
May	1732	**Samuel Noyes** [WB p.43]	From No. 2 [WB p.39]	D. 8 Apr 1740
by July	1740	**Thomas Whishaw** [WB p.43]	From No. 2 [WB p.51]	To No. 11, Oct 1740 [WB p.55]

No. 5, The Close—*continued*

Oct	1740	**Peter Maurice** [WB p.43]	From No. 2 [WB p.51]	D. 2 Apr 1750
Apr	1750	**Samuel Rolleston** [WB pp.43-4]	From No. 10 [WB p.50]	Res. by 3 July 1756
July	1756	**Edmund Pyle** [WB p.44]	Inst. 23 June 1756	To No. 12, Nov 1756
Nov	1756	**Philip Walton** [WB p.44]	From No. 6 [WB p.38]	To No. 1, Aug 1770 [WB p.30]
Aug	1770	**Robert Ashe** [WB pp.44,74]	From No. 6 [WB p.38]	D. 13 June 1780
June	1780	**Matthew Woodford** [WB p.74]	Inst. 23 June 1780	To No. 1, May 1798 [WB p.30]
May	1798	**Lascelles Iremonger** [WB p.74]	From No. 10 [WB p.72v]	D. 6 Feb 1830
Feb	1830	**William Dealtry**	Inst. 27 Feb 1830	D. 15 Oct 1847 (Prebend suspended)

No. 6, The Close. 'The Second House on the Left in Dome Alley'

by	1662	**Henry Bradshaw** [WB pp.3,4]	Inst. 27 Sept 1660	D. 13 April 1690
Apr	1690	**Francis Morley** [WB p.4]	From No. 10	D. 1 Oct 1696
Oct	1696	**Samuel Mews** [WB p.4]	From ?No. 11	D. 9 June 1706
June	1706	**Charles Woodroffe** [WB p.21]	Coll. 10 June 1706	To No. 12 by May 1715 [WB p.14]
June	1715	**Anthony Alsop** [WB p.21]	Inst. 25 May 1715	To No. 3, Nov 1724 [WB p.20]
Nov	1724	**Richard Crosse** [WB p.21]	From No. 11 [WB pp.32a,33]	To No. 9, June 1728 [WB p.23]
June	1728	**Charles Naylor** [WB p.21]	From ?No. 2	To No. 3, July 1728 [WB pp.20,35]
July	1728	**John Morgan** [WB pp.21,37]	Inst. 31 May 1728	To No. 3, May 1729 [WB p.35]
May	1729	**Thomas Hayley** [WB p.37]	From ?No. 2	To No. 9, June 1732 [WB p.47]
Aug	1732	**Thomas Inett** [WB p.37]	Inst. 3 Aug 1732	To No. 12, Feb 1745 [WB p.61]
Feb	1745	**Jonathan Shipley** [WB pp.37-8]	From No. 10 [WB p.50]	To No. 7, May 1756 [WB p.65]
July	1756	**Philip Walton** [WB p.38]	Inst. 23 July 1756	To No. 5, Nov 1756 [WB p.44]
Dec	1756	**Francis Ayscough** [WB p.38]	Inst. 8 Dec 1756	To No. 11, Oct 1757 [WB p.56]
Nov	1757	**Thomas Balguy** [WB p.38]	Inst. 4 Nov 1757	To No. 9, Oct 1759 [WB p.48]
Nov	1759	**John Sturges Jr.** [WB p.38]	Inst. 27 Nov 1759	To No. 4, June 1760 [WB p.46]
June	1760	**Robert Ashe** [WB p.38]	Inst. 14 June 1760	To No. 5, Aug 1770 [WB p.44]
Aug	1770	**John Mulso** [WB pp.38,73]	Inst. 25 Aug 1770	To No. 10, Oct 1770 [WB p.72]

No. 6, The Close—*continued*

Dec	1770	**Samuel Nott** [WB p.73]	Inst. 28 Dec 1770	To No. 2 by March 1771 [WB p.52]
Apr	1771	**Thomas Rennell Sr.** [WB p.73]	Inst. 20 Apr 1771	To No. 12, Dec 1776 [WB p.63]
Jan	1777	**Robert Hare** [WB p.73]	Inst. 24 Jan 1777	To No. 11, June 1777 [WB p.56]
June	1777	**John Butler** (Bp. of Oxford) [WB p.73]	From No. 3 [WB p.36]	Trans. Bp. of Hereford 1788
Apr	1788	Joseph Warton	Inst. 25 Apr 1788	To No. 8, July 1790 [WB p.79]
Sept	1790	Nicholas Vere	Inst. 4 Sept 1790	D. 18 Jan 1809
Feb	1810	George Nott	Coll. 5 Feb 1810	D. 25 Oct 1841 (Prebend suspended)

No. 7, The Close. 'The Second House on the Right in Dome Alley'

by	1662	**Nicholas Preston** [WB p.12]	From No. 3	D. by 22 Sept 1664
Sept	1664	**William Hawkins** [WB p.12]	From No. 5 [WB p.18]	D. 17 July 1691
July	1691	**Abraham Markland** [WB p.12]	From No. 11	To No. 1, June 1712
June	1712	**Richard West** [WB p.12]	From No. 11	D. 2 Dec 1716
Dec	1716	**Thomas Spratt** [WB p.27]	From ?No. 2	D. 10 May 1720
May	1720	**John Cooke** [WB pp.27,53–4]	From ?No. 11	D. 2 July 1744
July	1744	**Thomas Cheyney** [WB p.54]	From No. 8 [WB p.59]	Inst. Dean of Winchester 25 Mar 1748
Mar	1748	**Thomas Whishaw** [WB pp.54,65]	From No. 9 [WB p.48]	D. 7 May 1756
May	1756	**Jonathan Shipley** [WB p.65]	From No. 6 [WB p.38]	Inst. Dean of Winchester 14 June 1760
June	1760	**Thomas Pyle** [WB p.65]	Inst. 14 June 1760	D. 3 July 1807
Oct	1807	**James Hook** [WB p.65]	Inst. 17–18 Oct 1807	To No. 8, Dec 1817
Jan	1818	**Frederick Iremonger** [WB p.65]	Inst. 9 Jan 1818	D. 11 May 1820
May	1820	**Charles North** [WB p.65]	From No. 11	D. 13 Aug 1825

No. 8, The Close. 'First House on the Right Hand in Dome Alley'

Feb	1662	William Clarke	Inst. 10 Sept 1660	Inst. Dean of Winchester 1 Feb 1666
	1666	**William Payne** [WB pp.5–6]	Inst. 3 Feb 1666	D. 26 Sept 1689
Sept	1689	**Samuel Woodford** [WB p.6]	From No. 2	D. by 13 Jan 1701

No. 8, The Close—*continued*

Jan 1701	Welbore Ellis [WB p.6]	From No. 4	Bp. of Kildare 1705 but held Preb. until Aug 1706
Aug 1706	?Alexander Forbes	From ?No. 11	D. by 16 Oct 1712
Oct 1712	Philip Barton [WB p.31]	From ?No. 2	D. June 1731
June 1731	Mainwaring Hammond [WB pp.6,31]	Inst. 24 June 1731	Res. by 7 Sept 1733
Sept 1733	Robert Bourne [WB pp.31,59]	From No. 2 [WB p.39]	To No.12, Oct 1740 [WB p.26]
Oct 1740	Thomas Cheyney [WB p.59]	From No. 9 [WB p.47]	To No. 7, July 1744 [WB p.54]
July 1744	Samuel Rolleston [WB p.59]	Inst. 13 July 1744	To No. 10, Feb 1745 [WB p.50]
Mar 1766	Sir Peter Rivers Gay [WB pp.60,79]	Inst. 25 Mar 1766	D. 20 July 1790
July 1790	Joseph Warton [WB p.79]	From No. 6	D. 23 Feb 1800
Feb 1800	John Garnett [WB p.79]	From No. 2 [WB p.78]	Res. by 5 Feb 1810 becoming Dean of Exeter
Feb 1810	Henry Jenkin	Coll. 24 Feb 1809	D. 21 Dec 1817
Dec 1817	James Hook	From No. 7 [WB p.65]	Res. 17 Aug 1825
Sept 1825	George Pretyman	Inst. 3 Sept 1825	To No. 4, Dec 1827
Dec 1827	Charles Richards	Inst. 26 Dec 1827	D. 20 Jan 1833
Feb 1833	David Williams	Inst. 9 Feb 1833	To No. 9, Mar 1834 [WB p.81]
Mar 1834	Hon. Gerard Noel	Inst. 15 Mar 1834	D. 24 Feb 1851
Feb 1851	Philip Jacob	From No. 7	D. 20 Dec 1884

No. 9, The Close. 'The House over against the West Side of the Deanery'

1663	William Lewis		Res. by 5 Oct 1664
Oct 1664	Henry Beeston	Inst. 5 Oct 1664	Res. by 4 Jan 1696
Jan 1696	?William Harris	Inst. 8 Jan 1696	D. 9 Nov 1700
Jan 1701	?Robert Eyre	Inst. 15 Jan 1701	To No. 10 by June 1710
by June 1710	Charles Layfield [WB p.23]	From No. 2	To No. 12, June 1710 [WB p.14]
June 1710	William Delanne [WB p.23]	From No. 4 [WB p.19]	D. 23 May 1728
May 1728	Richard Crosse [WB pp.23,47]	From No. 6 [WB p.21]	D. by 1 July 1732
July 1732	Thomas Hayley [WB p.47]	From No. 6 [WB p.37]	D. 12 Aug 1739
Aug 1739	Thomas Cheyney [WB p.47]	From No. 2 [WB p.51]	To No.8, Oct 1740 [WB p.59]

No. 9, The Close—*continued*

Oct	1740	John Hoadley [WB pp.47–8]	From No. 11 [WB p.55]	To No. 4, June 1742 [WB p.46]
May	1742	Thomas Whishaw [WB p.48]	From No. 11 [WB p.55]	To No. 7, Mar 1748 [WB p.54]
Mar	1748	Richard Exton [WB p.48]	Inst. 26 Mar 1748	D. 22 Sept 1759
Sept	1759	Thomas Balguy [WB p.48]	From No. 6 [WB p.38]	D. 19 Jan 1795
Jan	1795	Robert Barnard [WB pp.48,81]	From No. 10 [WB p.72]	D. 25 Feb 1834
Feb	1834	David Williams [WB p.81]	From No. 8	D. 22 Mar 1860

No. 10, The Close. 'The House at the South-West Corner of the Mount'

	1660	Edward Stanley	House survived Commonwealth	D. 26 Aug 1662
Sept	1662	Richard Hyde	Inst. 6 Sept 1662	D. by 22 Sept 1666
Sept	1666	George Beaumont	Inst. 29 Sept 1666	Res. by 4 Apr 1684
Apr	1684	Francis Morley	Inst. 5 Apr 1684	To No. 6, Apr 1690 [WB p.4]
Apr	1690	?Edward Waple	Inst. 29 Apr 1690	To No. 5, Nov 1701 [WB p.18]
Nov	1701	?William Delanne	Inst. 4 Nov 1701	To No. 4, Oct 1704 [WB p.19]
Oct	1704	?Thomas Rivers	From ?No. 11	To No. 4, June 1710 [WB p.19]
June	1710	Robert Eyre [WB p.24]	From ?No. 9	D. 15 Oct 1722
Oct	1722	John Sturges Sr. [WB p.24]	From ?No. 11	To No. 12 by Jan 1727 [WB p.26]
by Jan	1727	Joseph Soley [WB pp.24,49]	From No. 1	To No. 11, Sept 1731 [WB p.33]
Nov	1731	Christopher Eyre [WB pp.49–50]	From No. 2 [WB p.39]	D. 9 May 1743
May	1743	Jonathan Shipley [WB p.50]	Inst. 27 May 1743	To No. 6, Feb 1745 [WB p.37]
Feb	1745	Samuel Rolleston [WB p.50]	From No. 8 [WB p.59]	To No. 5, Apr 1750 [WB p.43]
Apr	1750	Nicholas Lechmere [WB pp.50,72]	Inst. 26 Apr 1750	D. 15 Oct 1770
Oct	1770	John Mulso [WB p.72]	From No. 6 [WB p.73]	D. 21 Sept 1791
Nov	1791	Edmund Poulter [WB p.72]	Inst. 9 Nov 1791	To No. 3, 1792 [WB p.80]
Jan	1793	John Garnett [WB p.72]	Inst. 15 Jan 1793	To No. 2 by Aug 1793 [WB p.77]
Aug	1793	Robert Barnard [WB p.72]	Coll. 14 Aug 1793	To No. 9, Jan 1795 [WB p.76]
Feb	1795	George Turner [WB p.72]	Inst. 14 Feb 1795	To No. 11, Apr 1795 [WB p.76]
July	1795	Hon. Edward Legge [WB p.72–72a]	Inst. 18 July 1795	Res. 13 Mar 1797

No. 10, The Close—*continued*

May	1797	**Lascelles Iremonger** [WB p.72a]	Inst. 10 May 1797	To No. 11, Nov 1797 [WB p.76]
Nov	1797	**Hon. George Pelham** [WB p.72a]	Inst. 18 Nov 1797	To No. 11, May 1798 [WB p.76]
May	1798	**Sir William Heathcote** [WB p.72a]	Coll. 26 May 1798	To No. 2, Mar 1800 [WB p.78]
Mar	1800	**William Garnier** [WB p.72a]	Inst. 7 Mar 1800	To No. 2, Mar 1802 [WB p.78]
Apr	1802	Francis North	Inst. 9 Apr 1802	To No. 11 1803 [WB p.76]
Apr	1803	John Hawtrey	Inst. 14 Apr 1803	D. 8 Apr 1817
Apr	1817	Hon. Thomas de Grey	From No. 2 [WB p.78]	To No. 3, Sept 1831
Sept	1831	Thomas Garnier	Inst. 3 Sept 1831	Inst. Dean of Winchester 18 Apr 1840
Aug	1840	Samuel Wilberforce	Coll. 13 Aug 1840	To No. 12, Dec 1844

No. 11, The Close. 'The Middle House on the West Side of The Mount'

	1660	William Clarke	Inst. 10 Sept 1660	To No. 8, 1662
	1662	Walter Darell (CA 1 Dec 1662)	Inst. 5 Nov 1661	To No. 12 (completed by 1665)
Dec	1663	John Ryves (CA 22 Sept 1663)	Inst. 8 Dec 1660	D. by 2 Sept 1665
Sept	1665	Robert Sharrock	Inst. 3 Sept 1665	To No. 1, Apr 1669 (on exchanging Prebend)
Apr	1669	Thomas Ken	Inst. 12 Apr 1669	To No. 2, Sept 1676
Sept	1676	?Seth Ward	Inst. 15 Sept 1676	To ?No. 3, July 1679
July	1679	Abraham Markland	Inst. 4 July 1679	To No. 5, Nov 1681 [WB p.17]
Nov	1681	Samuel Woodford	From ?No. 3	To No. 2, March 1685
Mar	1685	Giles Thornborough	Inst. 6 Mar 1685	D. Dec 1687
Dec	1687	Charles Layfield	Inst. 23 Dec 1687	To No. 2, Sept 1689
Oct	1689	?Samuel Mews	Inst. 5 Oct 1689	To No. 6, Oct 1696 [WB p.4]
Oct	1696	**William Lowth Sr.** [WB p.22]	Inst. 8 Oct 1696	To No. 5, Oct 1704 [WB p.19]
Oct	1704	?Alexander Forbes	Inst. 7 Oct 1704	To ?No. 8, Aug 1706
Aug	1706	Richard West	Inst. 1 Aug 1706	To No. 7, June 1712 [WB p.12]
Nov	1712	?John Cooke	Inst. 17 Nov 1712	To No. 7, May 1720 [WB p.27]
May	1720	?Charles Trelawney	Inst. 13 May 1720	D. 24 Aug 1721
Sept	1721	?John Sturges Sr.	Inst. 15 Sept 1721	To No. 10, Oct 1722 [WB p.24]

No. 11, The Close—*continued*

Oct	1722	**Richard Crosse** [WB p.32a]	Inst. 31 Oct 1722	To No. 6, Dec 1724 [WB p.21]
Nov	1724	**Alured Clarke** [WB pp.32a, 33]	From ?No. 2	To No. 4, Sept 1731 [WB p.45]
Sept	1731	**Joseph Soley** [WB pp.33, 55]	From No. 10 [WB p.49]	D. 25 Nov 1737
Dec	1737	**John Hoadley** [WB p.55]	Inst. 5 Dec 1737	To No. 9, Oct 1740 [WB p.47]
Oct	1740	**Thomas Whishaw** [WB p.55]	From No. 5 [WB p.43]	To No. 9, May 1742 [WB p.48]
June	1742	**Richard Nash** [WB pp.55-6]	Inst. 24 June 1742	D. 18 Oct 1757
Oct	1757	**Francis Ayscough** [WB p.56]	From No. 6 [WB p.38]	D. 15 Aug 1763
Sept	1763	**William Buller** [WB p.65]	Inst. 1 Sept 1763	To No. 3, June 1777 [WB p.36]
June	1777	**Robert Hare** [WB pp.56, 76]	From No. 6 [WB p. 73]	To No. 1, Apr 1795 [WB p.30]
Apr	1795	**George Turner** [WB p.76]	From No. 10 [WB p.72]	D. 30 Oct 1797
Nov	1797	**Lascelles Iremonger** [WB p.76]	From No. 9 [WB p.72a]	To No. 5, May 1798 [WB p.74]
May	1798	**Hon. George Pelham** [WB p.76]	From No. 10 [WB p.72a]	Bp. of Bristol 1803
	1803	**Francis North** [WB p.76]	From No. 10	To No. 4, Oct 1807 [WB p.75]
Oct	1807	**Edward Salter** [WB pp.76, 82]	Inst. 17 Oct 1807	D. 25 May 1812
June	1812	**Charles North** [WB p.82]	Inst. 11 June 1812	To No. 7, May 1820 [WB p.65]
May	1820	William Harrison	Inst. 16 May 1820	To No. 1, Jan 1832
Feb	1832	William Wilson	Inst. 4 Feb 1832	To No. 6, Oct 1741
Nov	1841	Scheme for demolition of house proposed at Chapter.		
Mar	1842	Seal set to Scheme.		
June	1845	Seal set to scheme to demolish portion at first intended to remain.		

No. 12, The Close. 'The House at the North-West Corner of the Mount'

Dec	1663	**Walter Darell** [WB pp.7-8, 15]	From No. 11	D. 29 Mar 1684
Mar	1684	**William Harrison Sr.** [WB p.15]	From ?No. 3	D. 7 Aug 1694
Aug	1694	**George Fulham** [WB p.15]	From ?No. 4	D. by 26 Nov 1702
Nov	1702	**Thomas Sayer** [WB pp.15, 14]	From ?No. 4	D. 3 June 1710
June	1710	**Charles Layfield** [WB pp.14, 26]	From No. 9 [WB p.23]	D. by 21 May 1715
by May	1715	**Charles Woodroffe** [WB pp.14, 26]	From No. 6 [WB p.21]	D. 13 Feb 1727

No. 12, The Close—*continued*

by Jan	1727	John Sturges Sr. [WB p.26]	From No. 10 [WB p.24]	D. 11 Oct 1740
Oct	1740	Robert Bourne [WB pp.26, 61]	From No. 8 [WB p.59]	D. 5 Feb 1745
Feb	1745	Thomas Inett [WB p.61]	From No. 6 [WB p.37]	D. 4 Jan 1749
Jan	1749	Arthur Ashley Sykes [WB p.61]	From No. 2 [WB p.52]	D. 23 Nov 1756
Nov	1756	Edmund Pyle [WB pp. 61-3]	From No. 5 [WB p.44]	D. 14 Dec 1776
Dec	1776	Thomas Rennell Sr. [WB p.63]	From No. 6 [WB p.73]	Res. by 25 Jan 1779
Jan	1779	Thomas Rennell Jr. [WB p.63]	Coll. 25 Jan 1779	To No. 1, Mar 1797 [WB p.30]
Mar	1797	Philip Williams [WB p.63]	Inst. 25 Mar 1797	D. 27 Dec 1830
Jan	1831	William Vaux [WB p.63]	Inst. 15 Jan 1831	D. 30 Dec 1844
Dec	1844	Samuel Wilberforce	From No. 10	Res. by 10 June 1845
June	1845	Thomas Woodroffe	Inst. 21 June 1845	D. 14 May 1878

Appendix B

Workmen Mentioned in the Wainscot Book

Barefoot, William. *Painter.* Work at No. 4, 1712 [WB pp. 19, 25]. Held two shops in Winchester, called 'The Shambles', by lease from City of Winchester (as appears in his Will). Described as 'of the City of Winton, Painter', he died by Oct 1716 (HRO A Wills 1716). Asked to be buried in Churchyard.

Baskerville, John. *Virger, Porter* and, later, *Clerk of Works.* References to his 'Account Book', presumably similar document to *Account Book of Wm. Fletcher,* MS, WCL, [WB pp. 9–11]. Admitted Virger and Janitor (Porter), 25 Nov 1666. Clerk of Works from *c.*1675. Numerous refs. in TRs and CA to felling of timber brought to Close for building projects. Lived in No. 11 in 1681 (see p. 110). Died 1694.

Bates, Nicholas. *Joiner.* Wainscoting at No. 8, 1666 [WB p. 5]; Deanery, *c.*1763 [WB p. 9]. Described as a 'Country' (i.e. non-London) joiner'. Possibly related to Wm. Bates, Carpenter, active in Close 1662–5.

Biden, John. *Carpenter.* Work at No. 8, 1779 [WB p. 79]; Deanery, 1786 [WB p. 68]. Payments for 'working on Church' (TR 1780–1); 'stalling Lockburn' (TR 1782–3). Probably identical to 'Biden', Carpenter, employed at Castle Hall, 1774 (QO18, 159). A 'John Byden', Carpenter, was employed at Castle Hall, 1749 (QM6, 388), which seems rather early. Possibly son of Joseph Byden, Carpenter, employed at Castle Hall, 1732–40 (QO12, 15; QM6, 49; QO13, 360).

References peculiar to this section:

HC: *Hampshire Chronicle.*
WCM: *Winchester College Muniments.* I acknowledge the generous help of Dr Roger Custance and Mr Paul Yeats-Edwards.
QM: Minute Books, Hampshire Quarter Sessions (HRO).
QO: Order Books, Hampshire Quarter Sessions (HRO).
QT: Account Books, Hampshire Quarter Sessions (HRO).

Some data from the Quarter Session records derived from 'Extracts from official records illustrating the County's care of the Great Hall, Winchester Castle, from C17th to C20th', prepared by C.R. Davy, Miss E. Templar Stokes and Miss P. Butler, of HRO, here gratefully acknowledged. I also acknowledge the generous help of Dr Beatrice Clayre, of the Winchester Research Unit, for numerous additional references, and Winchester Research Unit for the HC references.

Broadway, Thomas. *Painter.* Work at No. 7, 1726 [WB p. 27]; No. 12, 1727 [WB p. 26]; No. 9, 1729 [WB p. 23]. Work at Win. Coll., 1727-57 (WCM 32935-8). 'Master of Wm. Cave, Sr.', as appears in WCM 32938. Probably died 1757-8: invoice signed 'Ann Broadway' for painting at Castle Hall in 1758 (QT9, 1758). Succeeded by Wm. Cave, Sr., at Win. Coll. (WCM 32938-9). An extensive Winchester family: Thos. Broadway, Carrier attested 1715 (mortgage, HRO 47M. 48/48), died before Oct 1733 (HRO A Wills 1733), may be related; as may be a second 'Thomas Broadway', Husbandman, of St Bartholomew Hyde, d. before Dec 1736 (HRO B Wills 1736). A 'John Broadway', Cordwainer, witnessed will of Wm. Barefoot (q.v.) in 1703. Two members of the Broadway family were Choristers at Cath. in 17th century.

Butler, Edward. *Joiner/Carpenter.* Work at No. 4, 1712 [WB pp. 19, 25]; No. 3, 1712-23 (undated) [WB p. 20]. *Clerk of Works* 1710 (temporary appointment only?) in place of Wm. Prior, infirm (CA 8 Dec 1710). Licence to alienate lease of tenement near Seagrim Mills held from Win. Coll. granted Nov 1720 (described as 'of the Soke, *Carpenter*') (HRO 41M 67/6).

Cave, William Sr. *Painter.* Work at No. 2, 1772 [WB p. 77]; No. 8, 1788 [WB p. 79]. Apprentice of Thomas Broadway (q.v.). Extensive work at Win. Coll. 1757-1802 (WCM 32938-63), in conjunction with son, Wm. Cave Jr. from 1764. Work by 'William Cave' at Castle Hall, 1783 (QM10, 399); 1808 (QO27, 135); 1811 (QO28, 132). Father of James Cave, artist. Died Nov 1813 (obit., HC 29 Nov 1813) (HRO B Wills 1815). See also B. Carpenter Turner, *Winchester,* Southampton, 1980, p. 81.

Cole, Robert. *Joiner.* Work at Deanery, 1681 [WB p. 13]; No. 7, 1685 [WB p. 12]; No. 5, 1693 [WB p. 18]; No. 12, 1705 [WB p. 14]. Possibly related to Wm., Jas. & Robt. Cole (*Account Book of Wm. Fletcher,* MS, WCL). His partner in 1685 named as Thos. Deverell (q.v.); perhaps the same as his anonymous 'partner' in 1693 [WB p. 18]?

Colpes or Coppes, Thomas. *?Joiner.* Witnessed two wainscot bills for work at No. 6, 1662 [WB p. 3].

Cropp, ?. *Brazier.* Sold a 'copper' to Wm. Payne for No. 8, 1666 [WB p.5]. A 'Thomas Cropp' surveyed Castle Hall, 1695 (QO3, 135).

Dalley, Thomas. *Joiner.* Installed 'oak wainscot' at No. 8, 1666 [WB p. 5]. Removed wainscot at No. 2, 1673 (TR 1674-5 p. 14). Died Jan 1718/9, described as 'of Par. St Mary Calendar . . . joiner' (HRO A Wills 1718).

Deverell, Thomas. *Joiner.* Work at No. 7, 1685, as partner of Robt. Cole (q.v.) [WB p. 12]; possibly also No. 5, 1693 (ref. to Cole's 'partner')[WB p. 18].

Earle, John. *Carpenter.* Wainscot & shutters at No. 7, 1726 [WB p. 27]. ?Work at Kingsclere for Win. Coll., 1756 (WCM 34514).

Fawker, Thomas. *Joiner.* Wainscot at No. 6, 1662 [WB p. 3].

Fletcher, William. *Clerk of Works.* Witnessed bill for wainscot work at No. 6, 1662 [WB p. 3]. Lay Clerk, 1635 (CA 4 Dec 1635). Supplied building materials to D & C (TR 1636-7 p. 5 *et passim*, TR 1639-40 p. 5 *et passim*). As 'Grocer & Lay Vicar' leased tenement near Kingsgate Arch, 1639 (LB XII p. 127). Appointed sub-sacrist, 1642 (LB XII p. 147). Appointed Clerk of Works, 1660 (CA 24 Nov 1660). His *Accounts Book* is a valuable record of building operations in early 1660s (see p. 62-3). Lease of tenement near Segrims Mills, June 1663 (LB XV p. 125), described as Wm. F. 'of the Close, Gent'. Died between 25 Nov 1666 and 15 Jan 1666/7. Replaced as Clk. of Works by Giles Lamphire (CO 4 July 1668), and as Lay Vicar by Benjamin Whitear.

Goodsall or Goodsale, Walter. *Joiner.* Wainscot work at No. 12, 1727 [WB p. 26]; Joiner's work at No. 9, 1729 [WB p. 23]. Died at his house in 'Barastiching Lane' (Modern Canon Street), March 1764, leaving tools to his wife (HRO A Wills 1764).

Hayes, John, and his sons, **Edward & George.** *Carpenters/Builders.* Work at No. 8, 1781 & 1788 [WB p. 79]; No. 5, 1783 [WB p. 74]; No. 12, 1786 [WB p. 63]; No. 3, 1788 [WB p. 80]; No. 2, 1791 [WB p. 77]; No. 4, 1793 & 1795 [WB p. 75]; No. 1, 1795 [WB p. 30]; No. 9, 1796 [WB p. 81]; No. 11, 1797 & 1798 [WB p. 76]. Other works for D & C included work on roof of Chapter Room (now WCL Exhibition Room) (estimate dated 24 May 1797, MS, WCL); 'Stalling River & Repairing Bridge in Dean's Garden' (TR 1798-9). Considerable amount of carpentry work for Win. Coll. (WCM 32547-93). Work at Castle Hall, 1783 (QM10,?); 1791 (QO22, 41); 1799 (QO25, 50) (making chairs) and QT10, 1799. Possibly descended from 'John Hayes' who brought loads of timber from Horsebridge for D & C in 1633-4 (TR 1633-4). 'William Hayes', Cabinetmaker of City of Winch. died by 1778 (HRO Admon 1778). John Hayes Sr., Carpenter, died 1792 (obit., HC 24 Sept 1792), and the business was taken over by his sons, first Edward, then George. Edward Hayes was described in an Indenture of 1793 as 'Edwd. Hayes of City of Winton, Builder, Gent' (HRO 11M70/40). He died 1800 (obit., HC 22 Sept 1800), and was succeeded in business by his brother, George. George Hayes was described in a Marriage Settlement of 1796 (HRO 23M70/19) as 'Timber Merchant, of Par. St Michael'). Another brother, John Hayes Jr., described as 'Gent' in 1793 Indenture (see above).

Housman, Valentine. *Joiner.* Oak panelling in two rooms at No. 3, 1687 [WB p. 16]. Also thought to be responsible for panelling in Winchester College Chapel, now in New Hall: Payments to 'Howsman, fabro lignario' in Bursar's accounts for 1682-3. See J. H. Harvey, 'Winchester College', *Journal of the Archaeological Association,* Vol. XXVIII (1965) p. 126, and J. H. Harvey 'The Buildings of Winchester College', in R. Custance, ed., *Winchester College Sixth Centenary Essays,* Oxford, 1982, p. 99. Housman was 'one of the leading joiners employed [by Wren] on the London City Churches'. (Harvey, 1965, p. 126).

Inglefield, John. *Whitesmith/Locksmith.* Work at No. 4, 1795 [WB p. 75]; No. 9, 1796 (described as 'Plumber') [WB p. 81]. Further work at Cathedral, TR 1780-81; 1800-1 (repairing Iron rails at West Door). Locksmith's work at Win. Coll. 1782-96 and, with his son, 1792-1812

(WCM Add./44, WCM 32774-806). Work at Castle Hall, 1789-90 (QO21: 145v, 158v, 176v, 196v, 207v, 218). John Inglefield 'of Par. St Michael . . . Whitesmith' died 1812 (obit., HC 1 June 1812), (HRO A Wills 1812), leaving house in Canon Street to daughter & niece. His son took over business, working at Cath. & Win. Coll. in conjunction with Mr Stripp. Another son, John Inglefield Jr., died 1810 (obit., HC 14 May 1810). See also HC 4 June 1810.

Lucas, family. *Masons, Bricklayers and Builders.* Work at No. 12, 1786 [WB p. 63]; No. 11, 1793 [WB p. 76]; No. 4, 1795 [WB p. 75]; No. 9, 1796 [WB p. 81]. Many references between 1770-1819 when 'Messrs Lucas' were employed as official masons to the D & C. Details known of the following members of this extensive Winchester family:
1. William Lucas, Bricklayer to D & C 1662 (*Account Book of Wm. Fletcher,* MS, WCL). Died by 1684 (HRO B Wills, 1684: 'Wm. Lucas Sr. of the Soke'): bequests to sons William Jr., Nicholas, Joseph.
2. William Lucas Jr. Son of (1). Work at Cath. 1661-2 (*Account Book of Wm. Fletcher,* MS, WCL).
3. John Lucas, of City of Winch., Bricklayer, died intestate 1768 (HRO Admon 1768).
4. Henry Lucas, Sr., Bricklayer, employed at Castle Hall, 1775-81 (QM9, 356; QM10: 74, 83, 165, 180, 253). Died Oct 1800 (obit., HC 27 Oct 1800).
5. John Lucas, Sr., Bricklayer, Brother of (4). Father of (6) and (7).
6. John Lucas, Jr., 'Mason' to D & C until he resigned, 1819 (CA 25 Nov 1819) and was replaced by Mr Filer. He died 1820 (obit., HC 13 Mar 1820).
7. Henry Lucas, Jr., died 1818 (obit., HC 27 April, 1818). In his will (HRO A Wills 1818) he asked to be buried near father and uncle, (5) & (4). Details of grave ('Portland Stone Tomb in one Block') on St. Giles' Hill.
Nos. (6) and (7) comprised the firm of 'Messrs Lucas': works at Win. Coll., 1805-6 (WCM 32917a-b); 1805-6 (WCM 32918); etc.
8. Henry Lucas, of E. Soke, builder, d. 1812 (obit., HC 23 Mar 1812): relationship to above uncertain.

Masters, Samuel. *Painter.* Painted deal panelling in Great Dining Room and Bedchamber of Deanery, 1673 [WB p. 11]. His wife received payment for 'priming windowes & rafters' at No. 4 in 1674 (TR 1674-5).

More, Nicholas. *Painter-Stainer.* Painting work at No. 12, 1665 [WB p. 8]. Gilding work in Queen's bedchamber at Ham House in 1673 ('Nicholas Moore').

Nicholas, George. *?Joiner.* Witnessed wainscot bill for work at No. 6, 1662 [WB p. 3].

Oke, ? *Joiner.* Deal panelling and chimney-pieces at Deanery, 1673 [WB pp. 9, 10] together with fellow 'London joiners', Whetstone and Lewis.

Pryor, William. *Joiner* (probably later *Woodward* and *Clerk of Works*). Wainscot in Deanery, 1693 [WB p. 13]. 'Infirm' in 1710 (CA 8 Dec 1710), and Robert Pescod appointed Woodward, and Edward Butler, Clerk of Works.

Spender, Francis. *Joiner.* Wainscot installed at No. 6, 1662 [WB p. 3]. Also responsible for wainscot in No. 5 (*Account Book of Wm. Fletcher*, MS, WCL, pp. 22a, 23v).

Stone, ? *Joiner/Carpenter?* Wainscot at No. 7, by Jan 1720 [WB p. 27]. Possibly ancestor of James Stone, Carpenter, employed at Castle Hall, 1765–82 (QM8, 40; QO18, 159; QM10: 87, 129, ?, 277). A 'Thomas Stone' worked on timber at Castle Hall, 1656 (QO3, 299).

Walldin or Waldin/Walden, Samuel, Sr. (and Jr.) *Mason/Paviour.* Samuel Walldin Sr., probably son of Samuel Walldin 'Husbandman' of Hyde Street, Par. St. Bartholomew, Hyde (HRO A Wills 1770). Work at No. 3, 1777 and 1778 [WB p. 80]; No. 8, 1781 [WB p. 79]; No. 5 (chimney-piece), 1783 [WB p. 74]; No. 9, 1796 [WB p. 81]; No. 11, 1798 [WB p. 76]. Numerous bills in TRs, 1780–99. Sculptor of memorial in Winch. Cath. to Sir Villiers Chernocke (d. 1779), described and illustrated in G. H. Blore, *The Monuments of Winchester Cathedral*, 1983 edn., p. 19. Active as Paviour and Stonemason at Win. Coll., 1781–1818 (WCM 32863–902), working with son from at least 1782. As 'Waldrin', repaired road from Westgate to Castle Hall, 1763 (QT9, 1763). Obit., HC 1 Oct 1804. Obit. of Samuel Walldin Jr., Stonemason, HC 27 March 1820.

Weddell or Widdell, Henry, Sr. (and Jr.). *Stonemason.* Work at No. 2, 1791 [WB p. 77]; No. 11, [WB p. 76]. Work at Win. Coll. (as 'H. Widdell'), 1788 (WCM 35386). Work at Castle Hall, 1789–90 (QO21: 176v, 196v). Died 1804 (obit., HC 30 April 1804), Will HRO A Wills 1805, described as 'Henry Weddell Sr. of City of Winchester, Mason', and business carried on by his son (HC 30 April 1804). Son, Henry Weddell Jr., working at Win. Coll., 1811 (WCM 32919), 'Carving a Parterra [*patera*] in Statuary . . .'; and 1818 (WCM 32902).

Whetstone, ? *Joiner.* Deal panelling and chimney-pieces at Deanery, 1673 [WB pp. 9, 10] together with fellow 'London Joiners', Lewis and Oke.

White, John. *Painter.* Work at No. 4, 1712 [WB p. 25].

Willis, ? *Joiner.* Work at Deanery, 1673 [WB p. 9], described as 'Country joiner'.

Willis, ? *Painter.* Work at No. 8, 1781 [WB p. 79]; No. 2, 1791 [WB p. 77]; No. 9, 1796 [WB p. 81]. A 'Willis, painter' worked at Nos. 6, 7, 8 in 1767–8 (TR 1767–8). A 'Willis, painter' on permanent Chapter building staff in 2nd quarter of 19th century, until TR 1844–5 when the last payment to him was made.

Appendix C

Table of Chapters Clerks, 1660–1814.

Harfell, John. Notary. Lay Vicar from 1637. Later Minor Canon. Leased house & shop on E. side of Kingsgate Street later leased to Wm. Fletcher (q.v.) (LB XII 120v, 127). Appointed Chapter Clerk, Registrar and Auditor to D & C, 1660 (LB XIII 4–5 Sept 1660 & CA 13 Nov 1660). Died Oct 1680 (buried 24 Oct)—ledger stone in S. Aisle of Cathedral—and succeeded by Thomas Cranley, his son-in-law. For further biographical details, see B. Carpenter Turner 'A Royalist Chapter Clerk and his Family', *Record*, 40 (1971), pp. 29–33, where it is suggested that Harfell may have been the author of the *Narrative* of 1675.

Cranley, Thomas. Successor to John Harfell (1680), having married his daughter, Barbara. Notary. Occasionally acted as Harfell's deputy. Died 1720 (buried 17 Oct).
For further details, see B. Carpenter Turner *ibid.*

Barton, Charles. Acting Chapter Clerk in 1719 (CA 22 July). Appointed Chapter Clerk and Auditor between June–November 1720. Died Dec 1736; buried 4 Dec (Burial Register fo. 12).

Pescod, William. First signature in Chapter Books 23 June 1737. Relinquished Chapter Clerkship to John Dison between 9 Mar 1757–29 June 1758. Died 18 Feb 1760 (ledger stone in Cathedral).

Dison, John. Appointed between 9 Mar 1757–29 June 1758. Died *c.* 20 June 1770 (buried 24 June; ledger stone in Cathedral). Successor appointed CA 23 June 1770.

Yalden, William Jr. Son of Chapter Steward of same name. Appointed Chapter Clerk in 1770, aged 18, for term of three years in place of 'Mr Dison, deceased' (CA 23 June 1770). Appointment apparently made permanent subsequently. Last signature in Chapter Books appears 18 Sept 1783.

Burt, B. Deputy Chapter Clerk: signatures in WB from Dec 1770 to Nov 1774.

Ridding, John. Exact date of appointment uncertain. Change of hand in Chapter Minute Book suggests appointed *c.* Nov Chapter 1785. Died late in 1813; Chapter Clerkship vacant by Jan 1814 and eventually filled by James Lampard after considerable argument in Chapter.

173

Index of Persons and Places

Numerals in brackets, e.g. (n.4) refer to footnotes on the pages cited. Numerals in italics refer to the Notes on the Text, pp. 130–55. Dates of Bishops, Deans and Prebendaries are taken from Joyce M. Horne, ed., *Le Neve's Fasti Ecclesiae Anglicanae 1541–1857,* Vol. III, London 1974.

Index of Subjects

Numerals in italics refer to the Notes on the Text, pp. 130-55.